# ETHICS AND THE MORAL LIFE

# ETHICS AND THE MORAL LIFE

BY

BERNARD MAYO

LONDON
MACMILLAN & CO LTD
NEW YORK · ST MARTIN'S PRESS
1958

MACMILLAN AND COMPANY LIMITED
*London Bombay Calcutta Madras Melbourne*

THE MACMILLAN COMPANY OF CANADA LIMITED
*Toronto*

ST MARTIN'S PRESS INC
*New York*

PRINTED IN GREAT BRITAIN

# CONTENTS

## PART ONE: MORAL DISCOURSE

CHAPTER PAGE

## PART THREE: TOWARDS A NEW HUMANISM

# *PART I*

# MORAL DISCOURSE

*In spite of pretensions to absolute truth, the results of philosophy are always tested by the effects, and by the judgments of other philosophers. There is always an appeal to a circle of people. The same is true of values in art, in morals. A man cannot stand alone on absolute ground, but always appeals to his fellows.*

T. E. HULME

CHAPTER I

# AIMS AND METHOD IN MORAL PHILOSOPHY

## 1. *Foreword*

Books on moral philosophy, I shall argue, are not written in order to help people to live better lives. What are they for, then? They are written by people who are trying to get clear to themselves, and to make clear to others, what morality is. But this is, on the face of it, paradoxical. For in a sense we all know what morality is. Morality, more than anything else in human life, is something we just cannot get away from. We are not all scientists, few of us are artists, many of us have no religion. But all of us have to deal, at one time and another, with the problem of moral decision. We have to be able to answer questions of the form 'What ought I to do?' And if moral philosophy does not claim to answer questions of that sort, what does it claim to tell us?

It is a peculiarity of philosophy that this very question — what does it tell us? — is itself obscure. Let us make a few distinctions. The *moralist* claims to tell us what we ought to do; that is, to answer questions of the form 'What ought I to do?'; and his task is complete when he has given answers to all questions of that sort which people have actually raised or are likely to raise. The practitioner of *descriptive* ethics claims to tell us what people's moral views are; that is, to answer questions of the form 'What do people in society S think about suicide?'; and his task is complete when he has given a list of all the moral principles which are held at a particular time in a particular community, in so far as they can be formulated. But the practitioner of *philosophical* ethics — the moral philosopher — has a different task from either of these; and his task is never complete. A book of philosophy has no beginning and no end; the writer cannot say in the first chapter what he is going to tell us, nor in the last chapter what he has achieved. Philosophy has no destinations.

These remarks about philosophy are themselves philosophical remarks and, accordingly, open to dispute. Many philosophers, probably most, have thought, on the contrary, that philosophy can tell us truths about the world, including moral truths; and they would think it a barren subject (as some do today) if these claims could be shown to be illegitimate. We must, then, to some extent explain and justify a point that is cardinal to the conception of philosophy implicit in this book, namely that philosophy has no destinations.

2. *Philosophy as the Study of 'Meta-Questions'*

Philosophy is travel, but not arrival; search, but not discovery; enquiry, but not knowledge. In particular, moral philosophy is not moral knowledge. Yet when Plato adapted to purposes of his own the Socratic maxim that Virtue is Knowledge, he went on to claim (as Socrates did not) that the moral philosopher is the man who knows, and that other people ought to resort to him for guidance — especially on moral and political matters; and that training in moral philosophy is an essential qualification for the arts of government. And ever since, there have been moral philosophers who have claimed, or others who have claimed on their behalf, that they have acquired by their philosophical technique an insight into the nature of goodness or of the good life, which is denied or only partly vouchsafed to the ordinary man. Now it is an understandable view (though a false one) that any philosopher who investigates problems arising in the field of morality should be thought of as seeking to acquire knowledge — moral knowledge; and that anyone whose enquiries are regarded as successful should be looked on as more knowledgeable than the ordinary man. This tendency will be powerfully reinforced if, as is often the case, people in general are perplexed about moral problems and are looking for moral guidance. To whom else should they turn, if not to one who has made a special study in that very field?

Not all philosophical disciplines touch our everyday lives as intimately as moral philosophy does; and it may be easier to resist the temptation of casting the moral philosopher in the role of a supremely qualified adviser, if we consider him side by side with philosophers who concern themselves with other topics. Take, for instance, philosophy of mathematics or philosophy of science. No one (or hardly anyone) ever suggests that by studying these, or by consulting experts in them, we might become better geologists or more efficient calculators. If one were to ask the question 'What sort of knowledge should we expect to acquire by studying the philosophy of mathematics?' the answer would not, of course, be 'mathematical knowledge', because we get that by studying mathematics and not philosophy. All that could be said, speaking in terms of 'knowledge', would be 'knowledge of the philosophy of mathematics', but that could only mean what is written in books of mathematical philosophy, such as Frege's *Foundations of Arithmetic*. But if one drops the word 'knowledge', and asks simply what one 'gets out of' the philosophy of mathematics, the answer is that one gets discussions of certain problems or puzzles. But they are not mathematical problems or puzzles. The problem of finding a number which is divisible by three given numbers and is the lowest number so divisible, is a mathematical problem; and so is the problem of proving that two lines drawn from a point on the circumference of a circle to opposite ends of its diameter will enclose a right angle. But the problem of saying just what sort of thing a number is, is a philosophical problem; and so is the problem of explaining what are the circles which geometry treats of, but which cannot be identified with the circular diagrams we draw on blackboards. The relation between these two different kinds of problem must be made clear, if we are to have a satisfactory definition of 'philosophy'; and I shall return to it shortly. In the meantime we need a name for it; and I shall adopt a useful current jargon and say that, while a mathematician is concerned with mathematical problems, a mathematical philosopher is concerned with *meta*-mathematical problems. And so for other branches of philosophy.

If we now turn to moral philosophy, treating it as a typical case, we may find it easier to say that one cannot expect moral philosophy to yield moral insight, any more than one can expect geological insight to accrue from philosophy of science; that moral philosophy is not knowledge, but is a discussion of problems and puzzles — yet not a discussion of *moral* problems. For example: whether a conscientious objector to military service has nevertheless a duty to defend his country, is a familiar type of moral problem. But the problems of explaining what conscience is, or what precisely is meant by 'duty', are philosophical problems; not moral ones, but meta-moral ones.

### 3. *Two Kinds of Philosophy*

Some find this result unpalatable. To others it is a commonplace. The difference between them corresponds to a difference between two views of the function of philosophy, which I shall call, for the sake of simplicity rather than historical accuracy, the Platonic and the Socratic. According to Platonism, philosophy is knowledge, the philosopher is an expert and the moral philosopher is a moral (and political) expert, qualified and indeed obliged to provide the practical guidance that the public demands or needs.

Further, philosophy is (potentially at least) complete and final. It may in practice comprise several lines of enquiry — logic, ethics, and so on, distinguished according to convenience for research — but all these departments are supposed to be correlated and, in the end, unified. A favourite way of summarising these features of Platonism is to say that each branch of philosophy has as its special study the nature of a certain very general concept: Ethics studies the Good, Logic is concerned with Truth, Aesthetics with Beauty, and so on. According to Plato, these ultimates are the Forms or Ideas; according to modern Platonists they are the Values. Because the Values relate to all human activities, philosophy is potentially complete; because they are themselves related in the single concept of Value, philosophy is potentially unified; because they are eternal and unchanging, philosophy is potentially final.

According to Socrates, philosophy is not knowledge, and the

moral philosopher is no expert; Socrates carefully refrains from offering the sort of practical advice that Plato presses on us. Philosophy is not knowledge, but enquiry. It is a process of asking questions and trying to answer them. Indeed the Greek word 'philosophy' was originally coined to mark the very distinction we are here concerned with — between philosophy proper and expertness or 'wisdom'. Literally it means the practice of one who *seeks* wisdom, as distinguished from the expert who *has* it. This was at least a partial recognition of the true function of philosophy. But it was not enough, since it did not provide a means of distinguishing philosophical enquiry from other kinds of enquiry. One main distinction is roughly this. Ordinary enquiries are connected with the process we call learning. Learning involves teaching (the possibility of self-teaching does not introduce any significant qualification) and both involve the acquisition and transmission of expertness in some field or other. Ordinary, non-philosophical questions are ones which we learn to answer either by consulting an expert, or by acquiring the appropriate technique for answering them in the way in which he would answer them. What distinguishes philosophical questions from ordinary ones is that there are no experts to consult and no recognised or appropriate procedures for settling them in the absence of an expert. Historical enquiry is not philosophy because any historical question can be settled either by consulting an historian, or, if no historian knows the answer, by practising the recognised methods of historical enquiry. Similarly a mathematical problem is one which can be solved either by consulting a mathematician or by doing the appropriate mathematics ourselves.

Now there are moral questions which we might very well be content to deal with in the same way. Indeed morality is something which has to be learned, and those who are responsible for the moral education of the young do in fact assume the capacity of moral experts. Nor is this procedure confined to children. If one asks such a question as 'Why should I obey laws enacted by corrupt rulers?' one might, as Plato showed, either be content to accept the 'expert' verdict of custom and tradition: 'Because it is the law'; or one might reject this and consult another expert, the Sophist who says 'Don't obey the law but watch that you don't get caught'. But if I persist in asking 'But what is it *really* right for me to do?' I have rejected both the advice of custom and the advice of self-interest, and I am left with a seemingly intractable problem revolving round the concepts 'really right', 'just', and 'ought'.

Socrates happened to be specially interested in just these concepts, and in the 'meta-moral' problems to which they give rise. The philosophical tradition which he and Plato inaugurated has never cut itself loose from its origin in moral philosophy; but there was no antecedent necessity for philosophy to be concerned with moral problems. 'Socratic' philosophy is enquiry into certain sorts of intellectual perplexity wherever they may happen to arise. And intellectual perplexities may arise in any field whatever: in morals and mathematics, in history and art, in science and religion. What makes philosophical problems out of such perplexities is not the presence or emergence of features or aspects of a subject, world or universe standing behind or above the researches of scientists or theologians. Philosophy has no subject-matter and is concerned with no single theme, however general. It might almost be said that philosophy has only a negative unity: namely, that it is concerned with problems which are *not* decidable in terms of the particular theory, discipline or technique out of which they arise, nor of any other. It is just a study of 'meta-' problems. After all it would be difficult to find any common features, except this negative one, in such an assortment of philosophical questions as the following:

Can light be both corpuscular and undulatory?
Will the future resemble the past?
Could all my waking life be really a dream?
Why ought a man to do his duty?
Can God's existence be demonstrated?

### 4. *Philosophy as Synopsis*

Nevertheless the idea of a system, which would give a positive unity to a philosophy, is not an idle hankering. Besides the critical, puzzle-mongering aspect of philosophy, there is a synoptic and constructive aspect as well. The philosopher is not content merely to investigate questions that puzzle the experts, each on its own merits. He wants to find connections between them; to generalise; to establish relations between different fields of enquiry (such as history and psychology) and, more important, between the larger areas of human activity such as art, morality, religion and science. (I shall refer to this, later, as the mapping of bridges and barriers.) Further, this is not merely a legitimate ideal. It may be a necessary part of the task. Generalising the methods which have been found to work in one field may suggest ways of going to work in quite different fields. For example, if the philosopher is puzzled about the meaning of the word 'wrong', where something is said to be morally wrong — and this is a 'meta-moral' problem — he may find it illuminating to formulate the corresponding meta-mathematical question, 'What is it for someone to get the solution of an equation wrong?' or even the meta-aesthetic question, 'What is it for an artist to get his colours wrong?' On the other hand, such generalisations can also be dangerous. A prominent example is the mistake of the positivists, who assumed that the methods found to work in the analysis of scientific propositions could also be applied to the analysis of morals and religion.[1]

This synoptic function of philosophy is important for several reasons. In the first place, it gives a partial justification to the traditional conception of the philosopher's task, which has come in for a good deal of severe criticism lately. Secondly, it has a certain appeal to those who are disturbed by the increasing specialisation and departmentalisation of knowledge. Thirdly, it suggests for philosophy the role of mediator in the intellectual dilemmas which we are so familiar with: Science versus Religion, Psychology versus Free Will, and Matter versus Mind.

## 5. *The Three-Tier Model*

Some of the things I have been saying about the function of philosophy can be brought out by means of a simple model.

[1] P. 90.

(Like all models, it represents only certain features of the original and can be misleading if interpreted as a complete account of the matter.) According to this model, we are to think of people engaged in activities on three different levels. As we should expect, the philosopher is at the top; this corresponds to such truth as there is in the popular view of the philosopher standing aside from the bustle of everyday activity in order to analyse or systematise. On the lowest level are people who are simply acting: these we shall call the actors. On the second level are people who criticise, evaluate or comment on the actors: these are the critics. (The theatrical simile is not intended, though it will do no harm.) Where the model over-simplifies, of course, is in suggesting that action and criticism are always separate. On the contrary, all action to which we apply epithets such as 'considered', 'reflective' or 'self-critical', is action combined with criticism; and this is opposed to habitual, instinctive or automatic behaviour.[1] On the other hand, criticism at least can be divorced from action; it is possible to do nothing oneself but merely to criticise what others do. And even in the case of self-critical activity, it is convenient for purposes of exposition to consider the action and the criticism separately. For instance, a mathematical examiner criticises the performance of a candidate by applying certain mathematical principles to the work before him; when he himself is engaged in calculation, he writes down numbers in accordance with those same principles. Similarly, from the point of view of logic it is immaterial whether a speaker employs an argument whose validity is appraised by himself, or by someone else; but it is convenient to regard the arguing, and the appraisal of the validity of the arguing, as two distinct activities, and my distinction between actors and critics is meant to bring this out. We can express the differences between the three kinds of activity by saying that the actors are

[1] This must not be taken to imply the view (sufficiently castigated by G. Ryle in *The Concept of Mind*) that intelligent action, or even reflective action, differs from behaviour in the presence of a separate act of mind, causally related to an act of body. All that is meant is that in self-critical activity, as opposed to other kinds, the agent is in a position to explain to himself and to others, at the time, what he is doing and why, as opposed to not being able to explain these things, or being able to explain them only *ex post facto*.

merely acting, they are not thinking what they are doing; the critics are not doing anything, but are thinking about what is done; in particular, they are making comments or criticisms in the light of criteria or principles. Finally the philosophers are neither doing, nor thinking about what is done; they are thinking about the criteria or principles of the critics, about the concepts used in their thinking. While critical thinking is once removed from practice, philosophical thinking is twice removed.

## 6. *Ethics and the Three-Tier Model*

In order to apply this model to the special case of moral philosophy, we must notice a distinction which has received a good deal of emphasis in ethics and which fits neatly into the three-level scheme. It is the distinction between moral choice and moral judgment; between what happens when somebody faced with an actual moral problem acts decisively in one way or another, and what happens when somebody who is not himself faced with a first-hand moral problem makes an ethically relevant comment on someone else's action. A characteristic expression in the first situation is 'I ought to do X': a characteristic expression in the second case is 'He was right to do X'. In other words, the contingencies of the moral life seem to call for two different kinds of activity, the activity of the moral agent, who makes decisions, and the activity of the moral spectator or judge, who issues moral verdicts or appraisals. Here too, of course, the distinction is in practice artificial, and the two roles are often combined. Indeed, as we shall see, it is a fundamental point in the philosophy of ethics that they must be capable of being combined. These, then are what correspond in ethics to the actors and the critics. And here again criticism implies criteria; accordingly we have the moral philosopher, who is neither doing what ought to be done nor saying what ought to be done, but examining criteria, the principles of moral judgment, the standards, which the moral critics apply in their assessment of moral actions.

The three-tier model enables us to state fairly precisely the relation between moral philosophy and practical life. In the first place, any tendency to blur the distinctions between the three levels will obscure this relation and make it difficult to grasp the function of moral philosophy. This is especially true if we blur the distinction between the two upper levels; for this is to confuse the function of the philosopher with the function of the moralist. This happens whenever a philosopher is expected or induced to make criticisms or recommendations, to moralise or to preach. It is not wrong for the moral philosopher to moralise; it is only wrong to think that it is the business of moral philosophy to moralise. Philosophers are not specially gifted or exalted preachers, any more than they are specially skilled mathematicians. The business of moral philosophy is not to enunciate moral principles, but to study them.

But can we, after all, really accept this conclusion? Must we admit that the philosopher has no contribution to make, in his official capacity, to the solution of practical problems of living? Should he turn a deaf ear to those who seek his advice? Can we so lightly dismiss the contrary evidence, the example of the great philosophers of the past? For it is certainly true that our conclusions are contradicted by the practice of most philosophers whose names are remembered; and not only by Platonists and rationalists. For we find that many of their opponents — empiricists and analysts — are almost equally prone to mix moral philosophy and moral preaching. Locke, for instance, champions the right to private property; Mill defends the claims of justice and the superiority of refined pleasures over sensual ones, from the standpoint of moral philosophy; Butler uses his philosophy to uphold the Christian moral code. Even G. E. Moore holds that Casuistry (the discovery of practical rules of conduct) 'is the goal of ethical investigation.'[1] Finally, consider how even a thoroughgoing adherent of the modern analytical movement finds it hard to avoid the suggestion that ethics might after all have a practical function. Professor Nowell-Smith's admirable book on *Ethics*[2] has as its sub-title 'A study of the words and concepts that we use for answering practical questions. . .'

[1] *Principia Ethica*, p. 5.
[2] Pelican Books, 1954.

This is orthodox analytical doctrine; so too is the explicit statement (p. 83) 'The task of the moral philosopher is to map the mutual relationships of moral words, sentences and arguments.' But later comes the surprising admission (p. 319) that 'Moral philosophy is a practical science; its aim is to answer questions in the form "What shall I do?" '; and although 'no general answer can be given to this type of question' and 'the most a moral philosopher can do is to paint a picture of various types of life in the manner of Plato and ask which type you really want to lead', nevertheless it is clearly implied that the original question is reasonable, even if the only available answer is disappointingly uninformative.

These discrepancies between the practice of philosophers and our three-tier model cannot be ascribed merely to the inconsistency of most philosophers. Rather the reason is this. Just as the notion of controlled or intelligent action involves a combination of the activities on the two lower levels of our model, so there may well be a combination of the activity of the philosopher with those other activities, particularly the second-level activity, namely (in the case of moral activities) moralising. This possibility of a combination, however, does not show that it is any part of the function of philosophy to moralise, or that the moral philosopher is in any way better qualified than anyone else to give practical advice. But just as the actor (to revert to the terms of our model) is not only able to combine the role of critic, but is likely to be a better actor if he does, so perhaps the critic who combines the role of philosopher, or the philosopher who turns critic, is likely to be a better critic. This suggests that we can, after all, concede something to those who would like to feel that philosophy, especially moral philosophy, may be of some practical benefit to mankind. On the one hand there are moral problems on which it would be almost impertinent for the philosopher to advise; philosophical qualities, as John Stuart Mill once said to a lady who asked his advice as to whether she ought to leave her husband,[1] do not include 'that of being a competent adviser and director of consciences in the most

[1] *Letters of John Stuart Mill*, ed. Hugh S. Elliot, vol. II, p. 249.

difficult affairs of private life'. (The same might be said of public life too, against the philosopher-king.) If he is asked for his advice in such cases, it is almost certain that he will be approached in his capacity as an honest and sensible man (if he is one) and not in his special philosophical capacity. On the other hand there are certain moral problems which can be at least half-solved by an attention to philosophy.

One way in which this can happen has been suggested by Mr. Nowell-Smith in the passage quoted above. The moral philosopher may be better able than other men to see just what a moral argument hinges on, up to what point disputants are agreed and just where they begin to differ, what basic assumptions are needed to justify a particular moral standpoint or what policy of action or 'way of life' a person is committed to upholding if he makes a certain sort of moral judgment. Another way in which moral problems can be half-solved by philosophy is this. As we shall see,[1] a live moral problem may be any one of a number of different kinds of problem, or even a confusion of several kinds. Is it a conflict of moral principles? Is it a case of blank bewilderment where I need some principle or other? Is it a case of duty versus inclination? Or is it really one inclination against another, with no genuine moral issue involved? The classification of the problem may well be a step towards its solution, in accordance with the maxim that a well-formulated question is nearer its solution than a badly-formulated one.

The upshot of this is that, while it is not the business of the moral philosopher to preach, it is always his business to enlighten; and the enlightenment which consists in the clarification of a moral issue may well be practical guidance also. The moral philosopher is more likely than other men to penetrate the barrier of emotionally charged words in which moral discourse abounds, to see what the issues really are, and to help others to see them too.

## 7. *The Problems of Moral Philosophy*

Finally, turning from moral problems to philosophical prob-

[1] Ch. VII.

lems, can we say what the problems of moral philosophy are? We have already seen that there is no unity among philosophical problems in general except the negative feature of being undecidable in terms of the particular discipline out of which they arise, or indeed of any other discipline. The same is true of the problems of moral philosophy. There is no one problem or set of problems which it is the specific business of the moral philosopher to investigate. We may, of course, introduce a spurious unity by saying that the task of moral philosophy is an enquiry into the nature of the Good, but that is no more enlightening than saying that the task of metaphysics is an enquiry into the nature of the world. These statements may be true, but they are vacuous, since there is hardly any sort of enquiry which such a definition excludes. The only unity to be found in moral philosophy is that it is concerned with what Bishop Butler called 'speculative difficulties' about conduct; and this means that its problems are related to moral problems, but cannot be solved in the way in which moral problems themselves are solved. Anyone who is tempted to look for a single theme or subject-matter or problem-specimen in moral philosophy need only consider a short list of questions which have actually been asked in the course of the history of ethics. 'What is the meaning of "just"?' 'Can a man know what is wrong and yet do it?' 'Can any moral truths be discovered by reasoning?' 'Is an act of justice right because it is just or because it promotes the greatest happiness of the greatest number?' 'Does the word "good" stand for a characteristic, as the word "yellow" does?'

I suggest that not only have such questions nothing in common save a vague reference to 'conduct': they are also 'speculative' questions, on the solutions of which (except in the indirect ways already noted) nothing that is practical hinges.

CHAPTER II

# STANDARDS AND PRINCIPLES

## 1. *The Need for Decisions*

We can now begin to consider a selection of problems in moral philosophy. My selection will, I hope, be wide enough to cover a fair sample of topics which have been commonly discussed in moral philosophy, as well as a few which have not. It may even be wide enough to come within range of answering the time-honoured question 'What is the nature of morality?' (or 'of the Good', 'of Moral Values', etc.). In spite of the variety of questions in moral philosophy, there is one which stands behind them all. I do not mean the vacuous 'What is the nature of morality?' since it is a mere platitude to say that all moral philosophers have concerned themselves with that. There is a more specific, though still somewhat vague, question which will serve as a starting-point.

It is this. How is it that a man's recognition of a moral principle can make a difference to his conduct? How is it that a man's decision that a certain act is what he ought to do, can also decide him to do it? Given that a certain act is my duty, why should I perform it? Or given that it is wrong, why should I abstain? Why is the moral law not something which I can be content to acknowledge with awe and reverence, but something that can prompt me to act contrary to my inclinations?

There is an answer to all these questions which, though obviously true, is somewhat vacuous. It is that the function of morality is to control and guide conduct; to help us to find answers to questions about practical decisions which we want to ask and which we need to answer. These questions will be of the form 'What am I to do?' But the truism that it is the function of morality to guide conduct is uninformative, because there are very many ways in which conduct can be guided, and morality is only one of them. One might try the obvious line of saying that morality provides answers not just to questions of the form 'What am I to do?' but to questions of the form 'What *ought* I to do?' But this does not help, for two reasons: firstly, many questions even of this form are obviously not moral questions (for example, 'What train ought I to catch?') and, secondly, even if we were able to eliminate the non-moral 'ought's, we should still be left with the same problem in a new guise, namely the problem of explaining the meaning of 'ought'; indeed the problem would already have reappeared in the attempt to distinguish between the non-moral and the moral 'ought's.

So instead of attending to the form of the question it will be better to examine the different ways in which one can come to a decision on the general question 'What am I do do?' and look for something which distinguishes the moral kind of decision from the others. Suppose, for instance, that the question is about making a Yorkshire pudding; then the answer is in the cookery book and the decision is not a moral decision, but a decision to follow the instructions of Mrs. Beeton. Similarly, if the question is about designing a house, or translating *Schmerz*, or completing my income tax return. None of these, in typical cases, involves moral decisions.

But let us look again at the last example, which is specially instructive since it has potentially, so to speak, a foot in both worlds, moral and non-moral. If one asks 'How should I fill up my form?' or, more specifically, 'What figure am I to enter under the heading "Other Income"?' one kind of answer is found by consulting the printed instructions 'How to Fill up your Form', or, if these are insufficiently explicit, by consulting H.M. Inspector of Taxes. This kind of answer is, in essentials, like Mrs. Beeton's answer. But there is the possibility that I may reject this answer; not because I mistrust its accuracy or its authoritativeness, but because I am looking for a different kind of answer. For instance, I may be interested in concealing my true income with the intention of paying less than the prescribed amount of tax; and there may very well be another set of 'instructions', not printed on the form or countenanced by the Inspector of Taxes, which I may choose to consult and in accordance with which I shall decide to enter a figure different from the one I should have entered according to the official instructions.

Now suppose I am in doubt which of these two sets of 'instructions' I am to follow. Is there a third set of instructions according to which I shall be directed to follow one or other of these two? Somehow it seems there must be, because it always makes sense to ask 'What shall I do?' including 'What instructions or principles shall I follow here?' For example, a friend or confidential adviser may instruct me to observe the income tax laws, or alternatively to ignore or circumvent them to my financial advantage. And of course I can still hesitate and ask whether or not I am to follow my friend's advice. But so long as I hesitate, I am looking for an answer; I am prepared and anxious to accept some answer, to follow some instruction or advice, though not necessarily the answer or advice that is actually forthcoming. It is in regard to this hesitative frame of mind that we speak most readily of 'making a decision'. My compliance with, or infringement of, a given instruction may or may not, by itself, involve a decision. In making out my income tax return I may very well come to a decision; but when I give a hand-signal before turning my car off the main road, it is unlikely that I decide beforehand to do so. Yet both actions are required by a rule. Actions in accordance or discordance with instructions or principles, then, need not involve decisions, but a problem *whether* to act in accordance with a principle can only be solved by a decision. Morality has something to do with decision.

## 2. *Moral Guidance and Moral Control*

Now all sets of instructions, rules and laws are action-guiding devices. To say that it is the function of morality to guide action does not distinguish morality from law or even from grammar or pressure-cooking recipes. Part of what is needed is to point to the element of decision; but this is not enough. For clearly I can be in doubt whether to follow the instructions of

Mrs. Beeton or of some other expert, if they happen to disagree, and a decision between them is very unlikely to be a moral decision. The traditional role of moral philosophy offers a tempting answer: moral decisions are *ultimate* decisions, that is, decisions in accordance with principles which one cannot hesitate whether to accept or not: they are just 'there'. We shall see that there is an important truth in this answer.[1] But we must reject it as it stands, or at least set it aside, since it leaves us exactly where we were in relation to the original problem, namely, how the recognition of principles, ultimate or proximate, can or need affect our conduct. We cannot get beyond the truism that it is the function of morality to guide conduct, until we have considered in some detail what exactly is meant by 'guidance' or 'control', and what moral guidance and moral control really are.

So far I have been using the word 'guide' somewhat more readily than the word 'control' or 'regulate'. The point of this was to emphasise that moral regulation is more of the nature of guidance which we seek than of the nature of control which is imposed on us. But we can reinstate the word 'control' if we beware of the illusion that moral control would be like a pilot controlling an aircraft or a dictator controlling a country's economic system. The word 'regulate' has a special advantage over the word 'guide'. Regulation suggests something which guidance does not, namely the application of a system of rules or principles. A guide may lead us to a destination which we should have failed to reach without him, but he may not employ any rules or principles. He may just know the country 'like the back of his hand'. But moral guidance is not (to retain the geographical metaphor) showing and being shown danger-points and beauty-spots: it is showing and being shown how to find one's way about a country which is only roughly mapped though not altogether uncharted. Route-finding in such conditions, whether for oneself or for others, requires the application of principles, and not only of map-reading principles. The traveller's actions are not merely guided, but regulated. A blind

[1] Ch. IX.

man can be guided, but a blind man cannot pioneer a route. Similarly a morally untutored and untutorable man could live an outwardly exemplary life if he were in constant touch with a moral adviser whose instructions he implicitly obeyed; but he could not live a moral life. For he could not take any decisions in the light of moral principles; his actions are guided but not regulated. What it is to be regulated, as distinct from merely guided, we must next enquire.

### 3. *The Regulation of Behaviour*

What distinguishes conduct from behaviour is that it is behaviour subject to control. There are, however, many ways in which behaviour can be said to be controlled or regulated, and correspondingly different senses which these words may bear. Thus we speak not only of a man's actions being regulated by the laws of a state, but also of his breathing being regulated by the rate of oxygen consumption in his body. But this latter is also the sense in which we speak of the clock's movement being regulated by its pendulum; and however much of a man's behaviour may be regulated in this mechanical sense, it is a postulate both of common sense and of all philosophical ethics that this is not the whole story. There is such a thing as conduct which is behaviour subject to voluntary control; and actions such as breathing, which can on occasion be subjected to voluntary control but are normally automatic, do not count as conduct.

There still remain, however, many different ways in which human behaviour can be subject to human control. Behaviour can be controlled by means of training, threats, incentives, propaganda, commands, reasoned persuasion, the Law, the rules of chess, or moral principles. Of these the earlier-mentioned methods tend to be available for the control of animal behaviour too, while the later-mentioned ones tend to apply only to human behaviour. We never speak of animal conduct. Human conduct, or conduct *tout simple*, is behaviour controlled by human agency in one or more of the ways in which animal behaviour is not controlled.

The most important difference between the kind of control

which relates to conduct and the kind which results only in modified behaviour is that a person conducting himself is able to say what it is that controls his conduct. (The animal cannot say, not because he knows but has no language, but because, having no language, he cannot know. We might want to say that some people, too, cannot say. But the distinction between the 'practical man' and the 'thinker' is only relative: a man of action who literally never could formulate any maxims of conduct at all would not be a man.) In both the animal and the human being, behaviour under control is different from what it would be in the absence of control; but the human being is not only subject to control, he is also, in suitable circumstances, able to control other human beings and himself while the animal is not. An animal might be trained to perform a few rudimentary chess moves, but he would not have learnt the rules of chess, not even the rules governing the few moves he can make without error: for he would not be able to teach other animals even those moves. It is language, the monopoly of human beings, that provides the common link between controller and controlled, and what characterises human conduct is that it is controlled by methods involving the use of language.

I have emphasised the nature of control at this early stage because it seems to me to be the one firm fact about morality which can serve as a basis for theory. Any philosophy of ethics which attempts to say anything about the nature of moral values, or the definition of goodness, without first examining the way in which a morality is a regulative system, is starting off on the wrong foot. Many philosophers have gone wrong in this way; they have tried to say, for instance, what goodness is, and then faced the intractable problem of explaining how the recognition of goodness can prompt a man to act in one way rather than another. The chief and irreducible function of a moral principle is to regulate conduct; the reason why we adopt moral principles at all is that human beings need regulation; the point of making almost any ethical remark is in one way or another related to this regulative function of morality. But this regulative function is not simple, and other philosophies which have recognised its importance have tended to fall into the opposite mistake of taking a simple form of regulation, such as the command, as providing a model for all moral discourse.

### 4. *Evaluative and Imperative Language*

I think the reason why it is so easy to fall into one or the other of these opposite errors is to be found by considering the common and characteristic words which occur in the expression of our moral judgments. These include such words as 'ought', 'duty', 'good' and 'wrong'. These words are sometimes thought of as standing for specifically moral concepts, but this is a mistake, since every one of them can be used in contexts which have nothing to do with morality. This generality of usage can, however, be turned to good account, and an examination of the uses of such words in non-moral contexts throws a good deal of light on their functions in moral discourse. Now some of these words are used in ways which strongly suggest a regulative function, while others strongly suggest a descriptive or adjectival function. For instance, 'ought', 'duty' and 'may' imply a regulative context; sentences containing the first two seem to serve as instruments by which a speaker brings pressure to bear on somebody to do something, while sentences containing 'may' suggest a relaxation of pressure ('You may smoke' relaxes the pressure exerted by a No Smoking rule). Other words, however, such as 'good', 'right' and 'wrong' seem to be used descriptively.

This difference has not always been taken for what it is, namely a reflection of two different ways in which moral language is used for the purpose of regulating conduct. Instead it has been too often assumed that moral language has one sort of function, and that the sort of function it has is reflected in one set of words rather than the other. 'Good' and 'right', for instance, are adjectives, and the usual function of adjectives is to attribute qualities to things; now we attribute qualities to things when we make statements about them; moral language, from this point of view, will be regarded as the making of statements, and it will make perfectly straightforward sense to ask whether moral judgments are true or false. It is a characteristic procedure of this school to try to define some of the 'moral' words in terms of others, the regulative in terms of the descriptive: 'duty' is to mean the same as what is right or what is productive of most good.

On the other hand, the first set of words ('ought', etc.) may be taken as primary and attempts made to explain the second in terms of the first. 'This is good' may be said to mean the same as 'You ought to approve of this', or 'This is wrong' to mean 'You ought not to do it'. The first school takes the apparently descriptive function of ethical language as primary and tries unsuccessfully to hang its regulative function on a descriptive hook; the second school takes the regulative function as primary and tries to reduce moral judgments to commands or coaxings.

Both these policies are mistaken. What we must recognise is that moral language exercises its general function of controlling conduct in a variety of ways, to which no one-sided theory can do justice. However there are types of expression, corresponding to the two sets of 'moral' words given above, which between them cover most of the field. Admittedly to concentrate on these two types commits us to a two-sided theory when perhaps a many-sided one is needed, but at least it will be less distorting than the one-sided kind.

These two types of expression, or rather of expressive function, are the evaluative and the imperative types. The standard pattern for the evaluative type is 'X is good'. The standard pattern for the imperative type is 'You ought to do Y'. Neither of these can be reduced to the other, and the relations between them, though close, are not simple. I call the first type evaluative rather than descriptive because it is not at all clear that I am describing anything when I say that it is good or bad. Certainly I describe a cheese when I say that it is green; that is just what describing is; and there is complete grammatical similarity between saying that it is green and saying that it is bad. But grammatical similarity is no conclusive evidence of similarity of function. For 'good' and 'bad' might not be like 'red' and 'green' but like 'nice' and 'nasty', which are fairly clearly not descriptive. If we overhear somebody applying the epithet 'nasty', we certainly acquire no information, except that he is displeased about something; if we know to what the epithet is applied (say an ice-cream) we may indirectly acquire some information, by inference from our knowledge about what sort of qualities of ice-cream would offend normal people; but the epithet itself does not describe anything, it merely expresses the speaker's distaste. Indeed certain theorists have gone as far as to assimilate moral epithets with expressions of distaste and of certain other feelings. They will be criticised later; at present I am only concerned to justify my choice of the term 'evaluative', and for this it is enough to point out that in calling something good or bad I am performing an evaluation, an assessment or appraisal. This I am certainly not doing when I call something red or green.

One type of expression, then, I call evaluative. The second type I call imperative because words of this type occur in sentences which are addressed to people with a view to affecting their actions. Such sentences need not be in the 'imperative mood' recognised by grammar. Indeed a simple grammatical imperative, 'Do so-and-so', is never a moral utterance; commands, so far from providing the basic pattern of a moral judgment, are just one of the things that a moral judgment never is. But moral judgements involving the second type of expression do share with grammatical imperatives the important characteristic of being addressed to someone with a view to affecting action.

## 5. *Evaluations and Standards*

Now both moral evaulations and moral imperatives are complex uses of language. In order to evaluate something it is not enough to apply an evaluative epithet such as 'good'. In non-moral situations it is obvious that we evaluate all sorts of things, such as spades, cakes and whist hands; and we do so by arranging them in some order of preference depending on our purpose in dealing with the thing in question. Take spades for example. To say that this spade is better than that is, in part, to say that I would prefer it to the other for digging my garden. (If I have some purpose in mind other than digging, such as using the spade as a weapon, I may change my order of preference.) But it is not merely that *I* prefer it. For if I am evaluating the spade, as I should be doing if I use the word 'better', then I also imply that any other competent gardener would choose this spade rather than that. This implication is an important feature of moral language, though the illustration in which it occurs is a non-moral example. It is largely what distinguishes evaluations from expressions of taste and distaste. Such an expression might find a place in our example, if, for instance, I use a particular spade not because it is better than the other, but for 'sentimental reasons', even though I acknowledge that a competent and unsentimental gardener would choose the other. In such a case I am precluded from using the word 'better' to justify my choice, just because of its extra-personal implications.

To pass from 'better' to 'good'. To say that this is a good spade is to say that, if I were choosing spades, I would prefer this one to most others, and so would other people. Moral evaluations, however they differ from non-moral ones, agree in this. To say that a thing or action is good is, in part, to say that I and others would rate it more highly than others of its class; to say that a person is a good man is, in part, to say that I and others would rather have his qualities than those of most other men. The fact that 'good' carries with it a scale of preference has induced some philosophers, quite plausibly, to propose that the basic moral evaluative concept should be not 'good' but 'better'.[1]

Now just as my preferring one spade to another depends on my knowledge or belief about certain qualities of the spade relevant to the purpose in hand (such as strength and manageability) in virtue of which I am able to place the objects in order of preference, so my judging one action better (morally) than another depends on my recognition of certain characteristics of the actions. Or to put it another way, just as my preferring this spade to that necessarily implies my preferring a spade just like this one to another just like that one, so my moral preference of one action over another goes with a readiness to prefer any

[1] E.g. H. H. Price, in *Mind*, xl (1931), p. 353.

action of the first type to any action of the second type. If I commend a person's action in a particular case, then this is a moral preference only if I am prepared to commend all such cases similarly; if I am merely swayed emotionally by particularities or personalities in the case, and am not prepared to generalise my judgment, then my case is like that of the man who prefers a spade for sentimental reasons: his attitude is not correctly expressed by a locution involving an appraisal-word such as 'good'.

Finally, and generally, a particular evaluation is the application to a particular case of a standard of preference. Normally it will be a standard which I already hold, but since standards have to be created, raised or lowered, as well as merely held or maintained, room must be found for evaluation in these unusual cases. The extension is simple. Either the evaluation is the application of an existing standard, or it sets the standard for future evaluations in the same field. My appraisal of the spade is either an application of my existing standards on garden tools, or it sets a standard for future appraisals in that field. Similarly in morals. My judgment that something is morally good is either an application of an existing moral standard, or else it inaugurates a standard by which I propose to judge in future. The alternative is particularly important in moral theory, since the kind of moral philosophy which I shall be adopting insists on the derivation of moral judgments from moral standards and this is often felt to be objectionable on the ground that it leaves no room for 'moral pioneering' — for the creation and alteration of the standards themselves.[1] Evaluation, then, is always in the light of standards, whether existing already or created in the act of evaluating. Moral evaluative expressions occur characteristically in the application of moral standards.

## 6. *Imperatives and Principles*

The logic of moral imperative expressions is somewhat different. These are expressions such as 'ought' and 'duty'. Just as it is not enough, in order to perform a moral evaluation, to

[1] P. 202.

utter an evaluative epithet, so it is not enough, in order to achieve a moral imperative, to utter a grammatical imperative. To say that you ought to do X is not to say 'Do X'. In non-moral situations involving 'ought', such as 'You ought to move your queen' or 'You ought to read *Animal Farm*', there is not a command to move the white queen, or to read a certain book. But if there is no command, what is there to affect action? We could try the language of preference which worked with evaluative expressions, and say that 'You ought to move your queen' means something like 'If I were you, I (and any other competent chess-player) would prefer moving my queen to leaving it where it is', but this is highly unnatural; since there are only two possibilities (to move or not to move) there is no real scale of preference.

What is at the back of 'You ought to do X', whether in moral or non-moral cases, is not a standard, but a principle. My judgment that you ought to move your queen necessarily implies a judgment that anyone else in a similar game-situation ought to move his queen (if he wants to win); it is an application to a particular case of a general principle to the effect that (for example) important pieces should not be sacrificed without compensating gains (if victory is desired). Similarly my judgment that it is your duty, here and now, to tell the truth is an application of a principle about truth-telling (with the important exception, that there is no 'if'-clause). In general, my judgment that you ought morally to do X is an application of a moral principle.

Again, as in the case of standards, the principle need not be one which I already accept. Normally it will be; but again we must allow for moral pioneering, and add that the principle in question need not be one to which I already subscribe, it may be one which I adopt in the act of judging. For if I judge that you ought to do X, when I do not happen to subscribe to any principle about X, my judgment must itself be taken as setting up such a principle, and committing me in future to making similar judgments, should a similar situation recur. That is, if my judgment *is* a judgment. For just as an evaluative judgment, whether moral or non-moral, is not the expression of a preference which is merely personal or sentimental, so an imperative judgment involving the word 'ought', whether in its moral or its non-moral sense, is not a personal command, or the expression of a personal wish that someone would do X. Moral imperative expressions, then, are applications of moral principles, as moral evaluative expressions are applications of moral standards.

## 7. *On the Logic of Standards and Principles*

Moral evaluations and moral imperatives evidently imply the existence of moral standards and principles. It might seem that such a conclusion is a truism and could have been asserted immediately without the foregoing discussion. It is true that everyone (except a few philosophers) knows that there are moral standards and moral principles; and the purpose of our discussion was not to prove that there are such things, but to distinguish clearly between them and to say something about how each is related to moral language on the one hand and to moral conduct on the other. We may summarise these relations as follows.

(1) Moral principles are related (*a*) to moral language, by providing a source of moral imperatives in particular situations in which there is a question of doing something: the rule tells us to do X in situations of type S, and the application of this rule to a particular situation which exemplifies S yields the imperative to do X. Moral principles are related (*b*) to moral conduct, both by the derived moral imperatives which are used to affect action, and by the fact that actual conduct can be commended, or blamed, for being in accordance with, or contrary to, the principle.

(2) Moral standards are related (*a*) to moral language by providing a source of moral evaluative expressions in application to situations in which there is a question of preference; they are related (*b*) to moral conduct in a way which is rather more complicated. Briefly, the standard in accordance with which I judge that some action is good is a reflection not only of my readiness to prefer that action to others, but also of my readiness to com-

mend actions of that type to other people, in suitable circumstances. To say that it was good to pardon a prisoner means not only that I would have preferred that action to its alternatives, but also that I think others ought to have preferred it, and ought in future to prefer clemency to rigour. Thus, while 'good' does not mean 'what you ought to approve of', it does contain this, or something like it, as a component of its meaning. This is one aspect of the complex relations between evaluative and imperative functions of moral language.

For another aspect of these relations we shall next consider a most prominent pair of ethical words, 'right' and 'wrong'. Grammatically they function as adjectives, like 'good' and 'bad'; but logically they are much closer to 'ought' and 'ought not'. In other words, they are not evaluative, but imperative. To say that an action is wrong is not apply a scale of preference, since it is not to say that there are other actions which are less wrong. An action is either right or wrong or neutral: it cannot be more or less wrong, as it can be more or less evil. An action is right if it conforms to an accepted principle or rule, wrong if it violates one. Since there are no degrees of rule-breaking — a rule is either observed or it is infringed — there can be no degrees of right and wrong, and it is no accident that 'right' and 'wrong' have no comparative forms corresponding to 'better' and 'worse'.[1] The only third possibility is that there is no relevant principle, in which case the action is neither right nor wrong but morally indifferent or neutral. The logic of the application of principles is thus different from the logic of the application of standards. Standards are fallen short of by greater or lesser degrees, but principles are either conformed to or not. The importance of this distinction will be explored in Chapter XI.

'Right' and 'wrong' differ, however, from 'ought' and 'ought not' respectively, in several ways. First, although what is wrong

[1] This is not meant to deny that it makes sense to speak of one action being 'more wrong' than another, as we might naturally wish to do in discussing (for example) Jesus and the Pharisees. But when we say that starving may be more wrong than violating the sabbath, we mean that starving breaks one rule and violating the sabbath breaks another, and that we may have to choose which rule we prefer to obey.

is what we ought not to do, and we ought not to do what is wrong, yet no such equivalence holds between 'right' and 'ought'. It is indeed, always right to do what we ought to do, but it is not always true that we ought to do what is right. For example, we might hold that there are certain circumstances in which it is morally right to commit suicide. But this is not the same as saying that, in such circumstances, it would be morally obligatory to commit suicide, one ought to do so. One cannot, of course, hold the second without also holding the first — 'ought' presupposes 'right' — and a Japanese, say, might hold both. But one can hold the first without also holding the second, as an Englishman might do. He might say that it would be right for someone to commit suicide, yet not that he positively ought to do it. Moore points out[1] that there may be several alternative possible actions, in a given situation, each of which would be right; but they cannot all be obligatory. For if we cannot do more than one of them, then, since 'ought' implies 'can', only one of them can be what we ought to do.

We can divide all possible actions, in a given situation, into three categories: (*a*) that which we ought to do; (*b*) those which we ought not to do; and (*c*) those which we neither ought to do nor ought not to do. Where there is no question of 'ought' — where no moral principle is involved at all — all actions will be of type (*c*). Now 'wrong' clearly applies to category (*b*); 'not wrong' applies, of course, to all the rest, namely (*a*) and (*c*). 'Right' also applies to (*a*) and part of (*c*). It does not apply to the whole of (*c*), because it would be absurd to say that any action was right just because it was not wrong: the most we could say of such an action, such as wearing silk pyjamas,[2] would be that it was '*all* right', not that it was right. The use of the words 'right' and 'wrong' presupposes some moral principle; and many actions, are 'morally neutral'. But, granted such a principle, it becomes fairly true to say that 'right' does mean the same as

[1] *Ethics* (H.U.L., 1912), p. 32 ff.

[2] This is not to say that there are no possible circumstances in which wearing silk pyjamas might be morally wrong. Any action whatever, in appropriate circumstances, can be the subject of moral censure. I am speaking, for the sake of an example, of ordinary circumstances.

'not wrong', and may even have to be so defined since, as we shall see,[1] 'being in accordance with' a principle is a less clear notion than 'being contrary to' one. This raises certain difficulties for ethics, which will be discussed later (VI, 12 and XI, 5).

With these brief remarks on the logic of the application of standards and principles[2] we must pass on to consider the philosophical status of the standards and principles themselves; in particular, the view that they can be said to exist or to 'hold good' independently of the actual people who adopt and profess them.

[1] P. 206.

[2] For a more adequate treatment of the logic of evaluation and prescription, see R. M. Hare, *The Language of Morals* (Oxford, 1952), and P. H. Nowell-Smith, *Ethics*.

CHAPTER III

# ETHICAL RELATIVISM

## 1. *The Independence of Moral Standards*

The question of Ethical Relativism is not so simple as it is often represented to be in ethics textbooks. It is easy to present the problem in the form 'Are there universally true moral judgments?' or 'Is there anything which is absolutely and unconditionally wrong?' or, more generally, in the favourite stock question 'Are there absolute standards in morality?' What is not so easy is to see exactly what these questions mean, indeed how many different meanings they can have. One purpose of my discussion of standards and principles was to put us in a better position to see what sorts of questions can be asked about them.

The chief reason why people want to say that there are absolute standards is the belief that without them there is no such thing as morality at all. I shall argue that there is indeed no such thing as morality without standards (or principles) but that there is no need for the standards to be 'absolute'. But first let us examine those features of moral thinking which seem to lend support to an absolutist view of standards.

In my analysis of evaluative moral language I suggested that moral (and also, for that matter, non-moral) evaluation involves the application of systems of preference. But in no case were these preferences mere personal inclinations. For instance, even in a non-moral context, my appraisal of a spade as a good spade meant not merely that I would prefer it to others, but implied that any other competent gardener would do so too; for my appraisal rests not on a personal whim or sentiment but on my knowledge or belief about characteristics of the spade which are open to inspection by other people, and it is powerfully supported by my knowledge or belief about the attitude of other people, of competent gardeners, whose competence is also a matter of qualities open to public inspection. Similarly in moral appraisals I do not merely prefer action A to action B; I rest my appraisal on certain characteristics of the action (such as circumstances and consequences) which I take as deciding the preferences of other people too. Moreover, just as a *soi-disant* gardener's choice of a spade I would reject entitles me to question his competence as a gardener, so a man's applause for an action which I would deplore entitles me to regard him as morally misguided, as adopting a perverted scale of values, the wrong set of standards, and the like. At least, it provisionally entitles me to do so: but, of course, I may revise my opinion, both about the gardener and about the moralist, provided that, if I do, I also modify my own attitude to the spade which I preferred, or to the action which I deplored. The same holds good, *mutatis mutandis*, of principles too: my principles of action, whether non-moral rules or moral principles, are not merely personal policies or programmes: they are principles which I regard as holding for others to the same extent as they hold for myself. And anyone who violates a principle which I adopt I am bound to regard as committing not a personal affront, but a moral offence. Again, I may revise my opinion of him, but not unless I also give up or modify the principles I originally held.

All this strongly suggests that moral standards and moral principles are independent of the particular individual people who actually hold them, or of the particular collections of people, such as societies, which collectively hold them. Even if we can never be sure that a particular set of standards is finally and indubitably the right set (since, as I have just indicated, there nearly always exists the possibility of revision) still, it may well be felt, there must be some irreducible core of moral conviction which cannot be altered.

Among moral philosophers who have upheld some kind of absolute theory, there are characteristic differences depending on whether they have taken standards or principles as fundamental. A standard which is universally applicable and independent of individuals and societies is called an absolute standard; a principle which is universally binding irrespective of who recognises or enforces it is called a moral law. Those who uphold an absolute standard theory tend to speak in terms of universally true moral judgments and of the criteria for their truth; they also make much of the supposed necessity of comparing one moral code with another, and ask how this is possible unless there is a fixed standard of comparison. Exponents of the moral law theories, on the other hand, tend to speak in terms of principles to which we subject ourselves in virtue of our nature as human beings, or as rational agents; such principles are contrasted (on the one hand) with, say, the laws of a state, to which we subject ourselves in virtue of something less than our full human capacity, say as citizens; and they are contrasted (on the other hand) with the provisional kind of principle, as in our ordinary moral code, to which we subject ourselves in virtue of our ignorance and fallibility: since we are only human, we cannot know for sure what the moral law actually is. The two kinds of theory have, of course, much common ground; both can speak of right and wrong, for instance, because, as we have seen, these words are grammatically similar to words of appraisal and logically similar to words having an imperative function.

Later we shall have to consider the rich and varied implications of the concept of law and its associated political terminology, and the analogy between moral and political authority. Until we have examined these concepts, and in particular the concept of authority, we shall not be able to give any precise meaning to statements about the universal bindingness of moral principles, since the notion of 'bindingness' is, by itself, obscure. Instead, then, of considering the issue of ethical relativism in relation to moral principles, it will be best to study it as far as possible in relation to moral standards, as indeed it usually is considered. There are several reasons why an absolute theory (and, accordingly, its rival theory) is more plausibly stated in terms of standards.

To apply an evaluative epithet (such as 'good') results in an expression which is remarkably like a factual statement, since epithets are usually descriptive. Because a factual statement is always either true or false, it is easy to conclude that an evaluative expression is also either true or false. But the question, whether an ordinary factual statement (such as that the window is broken, or that the earth is round) is true or false, is a question which is always in principle decidable; further, it is decidable by the application of one or other of certain well-accredited testing procedures (of which 'looking and seeing' is perhaps the simplest) and these procedures are always (save in most exceptional cases) universally accepted and unquestioned. Hence it looks as if there must be similar testing procedures for determining the truth of moral statements. Admittedly moral criteria are not so unquestioned and unquestionable as scientific ones; admittedly people do disagree violently about the truth of this or that moral verdict; but, it may be insisted, this does not necessarily mean that they disagree about fundamental moral criteria, since they may be mistaken about the (non-moral) facts, or about how the criteria properly apply to the facts; and even if they do disagree about fundamentals, it is still perfectly proper to say that one is right and the other wrong about these, or perhaps that both are mistaken, and this we can hardly say unless there *is* an absolute standard.

2. *Law and 'Necessity'*

In order to see how absolutism gets its most powerful support, however, we must bring in principles as well as standards. Though absolutism is most plausibly formulated in terms of standards, it is most deeply rooted in a certain attitude towards principles. To understand how this can be so, we must remember that both standards and principles can function as criteria for judgments. To say that something is good is to evaluate according to a standard, and a standard is a criterion of the 'more or less' type. To say that something is right is to apply a principle, and a principle functions as a criterion of the 'all or none' type. Both standards and principles, then, can be applied to the making of judgments subject to criteria. But to evaluate — to employ a 'more or less' criterion — is to perform an activity which is further removed from the direct control of behaviour than is the performance of issuing 'right' and 'wrong' verdicts. In others words, 'good' and its associates have a less directly regulative function than 'right' and its associates (which are themselves less directly regulative than advice-words such as 'ought'.) Standards are more sophisticated instruments of regulation than are principles. To put it a little crudely, it is necessary to command or prohibit before it is effective to commend or deplore. Moral imperatives precede moral evaluations.

The effect of responding to commands and prohibitions is to acquire a certain attitude towards the principles according to which the commands and prohibitions are issued. This attitude will tend to favour absolutism in two ways, one logical and the other sociological. The logical consideration is the fact that a command or principle is either obeyed or disobeyed; there are no degrees of compliance. If we have a principle, then, to the effect that one must not do X, then a particular instance of X is, in one sense of 'absolute', absolutely wrong. Accepting the principle, we are logically bound to condemn the action, and this applies to everyone whatsoever. The wrongness of X is a perfectly rigorous consequence of the principle, and is absolute in the sense that it is independent of whoever it is who makes the judgment, provided only that he accepts the principle.

But, of course, it may be objected, this 'provided that' begs the question. The logical absoluteness of the judgment is illusory; it is conditional on the principle, and anything conditional is by definition not absolute. The acceptance of the principle itself, on which the judgment depends for its validity, cannot itself be assumed to be beyond question. If someone doubts the principle, he may well doubt the wrongness of X. Such an objection may seem so obvious that the point it refutes is hardly worth making. Yet I suspect that people who like to speak of the 'necessity' of moral truths are falling into some such elementary trap.

There is an interesting parallel between 'moral necessity' and 'natural necessity', both of which have been upheld as constituents of an objective order, of the real universe. Some philosophers still find the notion of natural necessity indispensable. But many who acknowledge the force of Hume's critique of causation believe that necessity can be explained away. To speak of necessary connections in nature is merely a picturesque way of referring to the logical relation between a general law and a uniformity which can be deduced from the law. At one time it was thought that all bodies fall to the ground because there is a natural necessary connection between being a body and falling to the ground. Such a necessary connection becomes superfluous when it is possible to exhibit the generalisation 'All unsupported bodies fall to the ground' as a consequence of, that is a deduction from, the law of gravitation. The necessity in question is merely a logical one, the relation between premiss and conclusion, such that if one accepts the law of gravitation, and its applicability to stones and the earth, then the statement that stones fall to the earth, or that this one does or will fall, becomes a perfectly rigorous consequence. But if the law of gravitation came into disrepute, statements about falling bodies would become more precarious. Similarly the idea of moral necessity can appear less convincing, if it can be shown to be merely a picturesque way of referring to the logical relations between principles and judgments.

### 3. *The Force of Habit*

There remains, however, a sociological consideration which helps to explain the force of the absolutist theory of moral principles. It is possible for people in a society to be uncritical of the moral principles on which they act, advise and condemn. (I shall maintain in ch. VI that in such a case they may be not merely uncritical, but even unaware of them.) In another society people may not take for granted the principles on which they act, but may be prepared to question and criticise them. There are historical examples, which there are good sociological reasons for believing to be typical, of societies which have moved from the first stage to the second; in a society where rules of conduct remained unquestioned and unquestionable there eventually came a time when people were able to question the universal validity of those rules. Clearly the ability to question the unquestionable marks the rise of criticism and philosophy, and represents a very great intellectual advance. We date the rise of moral philosophy to the Sophist movement in ancient Greece, which is just such a stage.

Absolutism has its roots in tribal morality. Relativism represents the dawn of self-criticism, the achievement of an intellectual detachment, the ability to consider one's own moral code along with those of other societies, and to ask whether it is better or worse than they are, whether it can be justified or rejected. Absolutism as a developed theory, however, rather than an incoherent attitude, comes after Relativism as a natural reaction. Protagoras ('Man is the measure of all things') and Thrasymachus ('Justice is the interest of the stronger') precede Plato the absolutist. Of course, the Sophists denied that there were universal moral principles, and this might suggest that they rejected an absolutist theory, which must therefore have come first. But what came first was not absolutism as a theory, but only assumptions, ways of thinking and acting that were implicit in a traditional, unreflective morality and were not a theory because they were not consciously formulated. (They are represented by the old man Cephalus in the opening pages of the *Republic*.) Platonism is an attempt to rescue some of these assumptions from the attacks of the sophists and to reconstruct them into an alternative theory.

Relativism, then, stands between the absolute theory of morality and the untheoretical behaviour which was to provide the practical justification for the theory. Relativism rejects an uncritical acceptance of customary morality. Absolutism, being a philosophy, must needs endorse the rejection of an uncritical attitude, but retains the substance of the uncritical assumptions.

## 4. *In Defence of Relativism*

What we have to deal with, then, in the absolutist theory, is the formidable combination of (i) a deeply-rooted tendency, operative in uncritical moods and tempers, to act as if the theory were true; (ii) a powerful philosophical tradition in its favour; and (iii) an assortment of intellectual arguments for absolutism and against relativism. I pass now to a brief review of these arguments and counter-arguments, which I shall consider from the side of the relativist, marshalling them under the four headings set out below and giving some hints at the kind of arguments that typically occur in this notorious controversy.

(i) Stock arguments against relativism and their rebuttal.
(ii) Inconsistencies in the absolute theory.
(iii) Evidence for relativism and against absolutism.
(iv) Attempts by absolutists to make room in their theory for the evidence in (iii) which appears to contradict it.

I proceed to fill in a few details.

(i) Stock arguments against relativism can be found in almost any elementary textbook of ethics. An excellent example is W. R. Lillie's *Introduction to Ethics*. Lillie relies less on positive arguments for absolutism than on objections to relativism. 'The consequences of believing that there are no absolute moral standards,' he says, 'are such that it is difficult to believe that any sane person can accept them.' He distinguishes four such consequences.[1]

(*a*) We judge that one moral code is better than another; but 'if there is no absolute standard in morals we have no right to make such a judgment, for there is nothing in respect of which we can compare the two codes'. This is a *non-sequitur* and also contains a false premiss. If we wish to compare two things, but have no standard of comparison, is it impossible to compare them? Of course it is not. I can compare one stick with another and judge that the one is longer than the other, without having to use a standard of length, such as a ruler. Similarly, as far as that argument goes, I can perfectly well compare one moral code with another, without comparing them both with a third code. So much for the false premiss that we can only compare two things by comparing each with a third thing. But there is another flaw in the argument. Suppose I do wish to compare two things, but can do so only by comparing each with a third, which I take as a standard. For example, in the case of the two

[1] *Introduction to Ethics*, pp. 116–17.

sticks, if they cannot be brought together for direct comparison, then I must use some third object which can be carried from one to the other, such as a measuring-rod. We may call this third object a standard, but there is nothing 'absolute' about it. The measuring rod need not be, in fact cannot be, an *absolute* standard. Whether it is an extremely accurate or an extremely inaccurate replica of the standard yard does not make it more effective or less effective in measuring the comparative lengths of the two sticks. All that matters is that I should adopt it as my standard, and stick to it. Similarly in ethics, I can use a third code as a standard by which to judge the relative merits of two others; but whether it is like or unlike the absolute standard makes no difference as far as the comparison is concerned. All that matters is that I should adopt it — that it should be *my* code of ethics — and that I should stand by it. All that is needed, for me to judge that one moral code is better than another, is that I myself should *have* a moral code, not that there should be an 'absolute' code as well.

(Lillie evades this by a subterfuge. He says 'The ethical relativists say that we judge moral codes that are like our own to be superior to those that are unlike our own . . . this hardly seems to be the case as. . . .' and now what Lillie needs to say, to establish his objection, is that there are people who prefer some other moral code to their own — which is plain nonsense. Instead he says 'There are people who prefer some other moral code to that of their own *society*'. This looks so similar that the reader may be forgiven for being misled into thinking that Lillie has produced an objection to what the relativists say: but what he has actually said is entirely in agreement with the relativists. It is (logically) impossible for a man to prefer some other moral code to his own; but it is perfectly possible that a man may prefer some other moral code to that of his own *society*: and in that case he makes this other moral code his own, and rejects that of his society. Relativism does not insist that a man adopt the moral code of his society, though it may hold that he usually does.)

Lillie's other points are dealt with in the same way. (*b*) 'If there is no moral superiority of one code over another, there can be no such thing as moral progress or moral decline.' To this the short answer is that there can indeed by no absolute progress, but there can be relative progress. (*c*) 'As no moral code is better than another, moral effort becomes meaningless'. (*d*) 'No man is better than another, since each has a certain moral outlook, and one code is as good as another'. The answer to both these objections is that they beg the question. Relativists need not deny that one code is better than another, only that it is absolutely better.

(ii) The very argument used by the absolutists against the relativists can be turned back on itself. The argument insists on the need to allow for comparing one moral code with another, and claims that only the absolute standard allows us to do this. But if there were an absolute standard, this is just what it would *not* allow. For it is axiomatic that the absolute standard, being absolute, cannot be known, at least by human beings; for the actual standards which people adopt admittedly differ, so that either none of them is the absolute standard, or, at most, one of them is. And since there is no means of deciding who, if anyone, has access to the absolute standard, the situation is no better than if we admitted that no one has access to it. But this is fatal to the absolutist argument about comparison. For if no one ever had access to the standard yard, there would not *be* a standard yard; it would not fulfil any function at all. Similarly, if the only condition on which people are allowed to compare two moral codes is that they should refer them to the absolute standard, they never could do so, since the condition could never be satisfied.

Absolutists are not very careful about stating their case; and it may be objected that I have not done justice to their arguments. It is possible, for instance, that my counter-arguments about the nature of the comparison procedure might be deemed irrelevant. A believer in absolute standards might allow that they are not and cannot be like a sort of yardstick, but might still wish to hold that every assertion to the effect that something is right or wrong must, if it is to have its proper meaning, make a claim which presupposes the existence of absolute standards.

Now I allow (see Section 5 of this chapter) that such assertions do make claims, and that such claims do presuppose the existence of standards or criteria. But I do not understand what the force of adding 'absolute' could be, except what has already been sufficiently criticised.

(iii) Here it would be in place to review the kind of positive evidence on which relativists rely: but to do so at all adequately would require another book. Fortunately it is strictly superfluous, for if the theoretical arguments against absolutism are sound, there is no need to produce empirical counter-evidence as well. In any case, as we shall see in the next sub-section (iv), the facts alone are not decisive. The collection of factual observations is the province of descriptive ethics, which is itself a branch of anthropology. There is no strictly logical step from the facts of the world to a philosophical conclusion, such as relativism or absolutism. But the adducing of such observations can have, if not a logical, at any rate a rhetorical point; it is significant that very few absolutists are found among those who have made a detailed study of diverse societies, or of the history of moral attitudes within their own society. The more we attend to the correspondences between changes in moral outlook and changes in social conditions, the more likely we are to think of a given set of moral principles as itself a social fact, rather than something which necessarily calls for comparison with some natural moral law.

Slavery comes to be outlawed, duelling proscribed, capital punishment called in question, misgivings felt about the indissolubility of marriage and the ostracism of illegitimate children. This is called 'moral progress' by most of those who look back on the changes. But only, of course, by those who look back with approval. It is a truism, depending on a tautology, that people who come to adopt certain standards should regard the adoption of those standards, in place of others, as 'progress'. The facts entitle us to correlate such moral changes with changing social conditions; they do not entitle us to interpret them as convergences between actual moral codes and a pre-existing moral ideal.

(iv) Next we have to consider the attempts by the believers in absolute standards to make room for the historical and anthropological facts, without abandoning their theory. There are two common moves. The first is to say that of course people's actual moral principles differ from one another; this is only a consequence of our human limitations and the fact that no ordinary person can achieve direct insight into the true nature of the moral standard. Actual moral principles are only approximations, perhaps quite distant ones, to the true moral law. One answer to this would be to reiterate the objection that in that case the absolute standards are of no practical use; but that objection, though it refutes arguments appealing to actual comparison procedures, does not refute the theory itself, but only its practical applicability. It does not silence the Platonist, who speaks of the Soul pursuing the Good

> as the end of all her actions, dimly divining its existence, but perplexed and unable to grasp its nature with the same clearness and assurances as in dealing with other things.[1]

Again there is no short answer to this. But it seems legitimate to ask how, if the absolute standard (or the Good) is really unknown and unknowable, can we have any reason to think that our moral efforts are in fact tending towards the goal rather than away from it or in a different direction altogether? How can we know whether our actual moral principles, the best we can attain as yet, *are* 'approximations' to the ideal at all? But if we drop the notion of a pre-existing ideal, the notion of moral striving becomes more intelligible. Just as moral progress in the past is called progress because it has consisted in rejecting moral attitudes which according to our present ones are bad or wrong, and in adopting those which are good or right; so the moral progress which we envisage for the future — unless it be merely a stricter observance in conduct of the same principles we already uphold — must be our coming to adopt new principles which we do not at present accept, or to reject or supersede those we do hold now. Of course we cannot say what the new ones will be.

[1] *Republic*, 505 (Cornford).

Indeed, from our present moral standpoint, any conceivable change in moral attitude must be thought of as a change for the worse, and not as progress at all. We can only think of the possibility of future moral progress in the abstract, and by analogy with what we know has happened in the past. Thinking that I *may* come to hold to be right what I now hold to be wrong, is like thinking that I *may* come to believe something to be the case, even though I do not in fact now believe that it *is* the case. And just as in factual and intellectual matters, the lifelong series of our changes of mind does not imply that we are converging towards a fixed and eternal Truth, so in moral matters the history of moral change, either on the individual or the social level, does not imply an approximation to anything beyond itself. The notion of such absolutes is really a projection of the logical truism that, whenever I change my mind, I must regard my second opinion or attitude as better than my first.

The second move open to the believer in absolute standards is to minimise the effect of the evidence of diverse moralities, by distinguishing between fundamental and superficial elements in morality. To quote Lillie again,[1] 'Moral codes may differ as to whether a man may have one wife or four; all are agreed that a man may not have any woman that he likes whenever he likes.' Or as it is so often claimed, things like murder and stealing are always wrong, things like tolerance and charity always right. Thus it seems that there is at least some common content in the diverse moralities; and therefore there must be at least some moral judgments which are universally true, some moral values which are universally real, some irreducible core of moral conviction.

But this is an illusion. There is indeed something common to different moralities, but it is not in their content. Take murder for example. When we say that murder is wrong, we certainly say something that is universally true, and we get the impression that we are saying something positive and concrete. But we are not. For we are only saying that it is wrong to kill people in certain circumstances: of course there are other circumstances,

[1] *Introduction to Ethics*, p. 113.

such as a man's being guilty of murder or high treason, or being an enemy soldier, which make killing him not wrong, at least for some people. But of course people differ about the circumstances in which killing is permitted or forbidden. *Murder* is killing in circumstances in which killing is *forbidden*: so it is always true to say that murder is wrong only because it is always true to state a tautology. Murder is wrong, but what actions count as murder? Stealing is wrong, but what counts as 'rightful property'? The conclusion of this argument is that the absolutist's escape into generalities leads nowhere except into a barren formalism, which can be summed up as 'What is wrong is always wrong.'

5. *Against Subjectivism*

Although subjectivism is one form of relativism, it is an extreme form, and the position I am describing is certainly not subjectivistic. Subjectivism in ethics is not the view that there is no absolute standard of morality, but that there is no standard at all; that what is right is, say, what I happen to feel like doing, or that in saying that someone acted wrongly I am merely expressing my dislike of his action. The usual objection to subjectivism, and a perfectly convincing one, is that if subjectivism were true there could be no such thing as a moral dispute; for people do not dispute about what they like and dislike. On the contrary, there are standards to which disputes can be referred; and although these standards are not absolute, they are certainly not subjective. If we are to use the terms 'subjective' and 'objective' (which I don't find very helpful) we shall have to say that moral standards are 'objective': the sense in which they are 'objective' will, I hope, be made a little clearer in the sequel (Chapter V).

CHAPTER IV

# REASON IN ETHICS

## 1. *The Peculiarity of Moral Reasons*

In discussing the philosopher's three-tier model, in the first chapter, I distinguished between actors, critics and philosophers in general and, in the case of morality, between moral agents, moral judges or moralists, and moral philosophers. The contingencies of the moral life, it was noted, seem to call for two different kinds of activity, the activity of the moral agent, who makes choices and decisions, and the activity of the moral spectator, judge or critic, who issues moral verdicts on performances. We also explored, in the second chapter, the difference between evaluative expressions ('X is good') and imperative expressions ('You ought to do Y'). This is not the same difference; it cuts across the other. Evaluative language can be used both by agents choosing something, and by critics advising us what to choose; and imperative language can be used not only by those who advise us what to do, but by ourselves in deciding what to do: 'I ought' is a self-addressed imperative.

What is common to all these varieties of moral acting and moral thinking is that we can always ask for reasons. We can ask why somebody acted as he did, or why he chose what he did, or why he praised or deplored someone else's action or choice. And the reasons given will be reasons of the same kind. My reason for judging, say, that it is wrong to use gin-traps is the same as my reason for acting accordingly, say by signing petitions or boycotting certain ironmongers. Moral choices and moral judgments are both open to justification, and to justification of the same sort.

But what sort of justification is moral justification? It has its peculiarities; for the kind of justification we might produce, say, for asserting that Hitler was wrong to persecute the Jews, is obviously quite different from the kind of justification we might produce for asserting that Hitler did persecute the Jews. This is one ground for saying that moral judgments are not factual judgments, however, similar they may appear to be. But the peculiarity of moral justification is not that its reasons are different from those given as evidence for statements of fact. Rather it is in the procedure of giving — and asking for — reasons.

One of the most prominent differences, at first sight, is that moral justification, as compared with factual argument, suffers from a lack of finality. Moral questions do not seem to be decidable in the way factual questions are; in moral argument the notion of complete cogency seems to be missing. By contrast, there is a high degree of public agreement as to what is established as a fact, and a possibility of complete agreement; but this is clearly not so in ethics. Any reason I may advance in support of my moral choice or moral judgment can always be challenged. Take a factual statement, such as that Hitler persecuted[1] the Jews. If I produce all the relevant evidence, documents and witnesses, it would be senseless for somebody to ask 'Why is all that a reason for your saying that Hitler persecuted the Jews?'; but if I give my reasons for saying that Hitler was wrong to persecute the Jews, it always does make sense to ask 'Why is that a reason?' It seems as if moral reasons can always be challenged, whereas factual ones cannot, beyond a certain point. And it may seem that reasons which are always open to challenge cannot be *reasons* at all.

But is there not perhaps a 'certain point' in the chain of moral reasoning too? Some point where the moralist takes a final stand, where his reason is either accepted by the challenger, or the challenger must be written off as insane or irrational? This is the road to absolutism, for the point in question would be just where one would locate the relevant Moral Value, or the Moral

[1] If it be objected that 'persecute', like 'murder' (p. 45), is a quasi-imperative word ('treat as one *ought not* to treat'), then substitute a purely factual description of what happened in concentration camps.

Law. Must we accept the dilemma: either absolutism or undecidability? We need not. Without committing ourselves to absolutes, we shall find that the antithesis challengeable — unchallengeable is overstated, and cannot serve to distinguish moral from factual argument, or justify the exclusion of reason from morality.

2. *Kant versus Hume*

The chief exponent of the thesis that ethics is a rational activity, that moral reasons *are* reasons, is of course Kant; and although Kant is an absolutist, and a representative of the Platonic, finalistic, systematic style of philosophy, much of what he says about reason in ethics is so very nearly right, and the points where he goes wrong are so illuminating, that it is worthwhile considering what he has to say. Now with Kant, as with so many other philosophers, the point of his thesis can best be understood by thinking of it as a polemic: as a reaction against, and a criticism of, some other thesis. In metaphysics, Kant explicitly acknowledges his chief adversary as David Hume. There is a parallel, though less explicit, opposition between the two men in the field of ethics. Hume professes — in both fields — a profound scepticism about the power of reason to support belief; Kant regards himself as 'roused from his dogmatic slumbers' to mount a counter-attack. Hume's attitude to the question of reason in morality is expressed in the celebrated dictum: 'Reason is, and ought only to be, the slave of the passions.'

To prove his point, Hume[1] considers an oak-tree in the forest, which drops an acorn close beside it; the acorn germinates, and grows into a sapling which starves, overshadows and finally kills the parent tree. If you translate this story into human terms, you have the situation of parricide, one of the worst conceivable sins. Yet there is nothing sinful about the botanical instance. Morality has obviously come in; but where has reason come in? Reason, for Hume, is the power of analysis, discovering similarities and differences among our ideas. It will note the simi-

[1] *Treatise*, III, i, 1.

larities between the botanical and the human situation; the relations between the terms are identical, just as the arithmetical relations between a set of numbers remain unchanged if you make the numbers enumerate people instead of trees. But one instance is an instance of morality, and the other not: therefore morality cannot lie in the relations between the terms, discovered by reason. What about the differences? But the only difference that reason can discover, according to Hume, is that we feel differently, when we contemplate the one case, from the way we feel when we contemplate the other. He concludes, then, that Reason can only show that morality does not rest on reason, but on feeling.

Hume is nowadays regarded as one of the pioneers of the movement in more recent philosophy known as Logical Positivism; and the logical positivists certainly adopted and developed this view of Hume's about morality. It was said, for instance that so-called moral judgments do not assert anything and are *not* judgments: *a fortiori*, cannot be reasoned judgments. All they do is to evince or express our feelings; when I say that stealing is wrong, all I do is to give vent to my feeling of horror at the thought of stealing.[1] Stevenson[2] has toned down this extreme scepticism in regard to reason; but he holds that moral judgments consist of two aspects, a factual aspect and a persuasive aspect; in saying that stealing is wrong, I may be saying something about the actual effects of stealing, or even the effects of those effects, and of course I can produce *reasons* to support my forecast of the effects of stealing. But these will be the ordinary factual reasons. In saying that stealing is *wrong*, I must also be trying to dissuade or deter someone from stealing, and this is what I cannot produce reasons for; I can only threaten, coax or cajole. Such activities can be more or less effective, but they are not rational. So this comes to the same sceptical position in the end; for the specifically *moral* part of the judgment is placed beyond the range of rational discussion.

[1] A. J. Ayer, *Language, Truth and Logic*, Ch. VI. It should be added that Ayer no longer holds the views there expressed.

[2] *Ethics and Language*, Ch. VII.

All these views are examples of the subjectivist type of doctrine and are open to the same type of objection; namely that they make it impossible for there to be such a thing as a moral dispute. In a moral argument, people are trying, or think they are, to convince their opponents that they are right and their opponents are wrong; but, if moral judgments are merely expressions of feeling, this is just what they cannot be doing. Some indeed, have not hesitated to assert this paradoxical conclusion; holding that we really never do dispute about moral issues, but only about facts of the case; if we are agreed about the facts, but still unable to agree in our moral verdict on the facts, the argument is simply closed. But even if we are able to digest this paradox, there is another still less digestible. Normally we draw a distinction between liking something and approving of it; we think it perfectly possible to disapprove of something we want to do, and perfectly possible to dislike doing something we regard as our duty. Yet if the positivists were right we could not do this. If moral judgments are merely expressions of feeling, then it will be logically impossible for me to say that something is wrong if I personally feel an inclination to do it.

### 3. *The Role of Reasoning in Moral Argument*

In the rest of this chapter and in the next, we shall be concerned with two general features of morality and moral discourse which provide the most formidable (and in my opinion conclusive) objections against any subjectivist theory of ethics. The first is the one I have already introduced, namely that we are prepared to discuss reasons for and against moral decisions and moral judgments. The second, which will be discussed in the next chapter, is the fact that we are prepared to discuss the truth of moral judgments, or at least to speak of moral statements and assertions, which imply some criterion of acceptability analogous to that of truth and falsity. Both these features of moral discourse have to be explained away, on a subjectivist theory, and with highly paradoxical results. (Moral reasons are not *reasons*, but emotional promptings; moral judgments are not *judgments*, but are pseudo-statements.) The general thesis I shall be developing is that there are important similarities between moral discourse and discourse of the fact-stating or informative type, similarities which the objectivists emphasise, though often to the exclusion of the equally important differences; these differences, however, are not wide enough to justify the subjectivists' attempt to deny a place for truth and rationality in morality.

To illustrate some features of ethical reasoning, let us take a simple conversational example. There are two speakers, A and B.

A. You did wrong to tell the patient that he would recover.
(A gives an adverse moral judgment on B's action.)

B. Why?
(B asks for a reason for A's judgment.)

A. Because it wasn't true.
(A gives a reason by pointing to a certain characteristic of B's action, namely untruth-telling. Fully explicit, the reasoning would run as follows:

(i) 'It is wrong to say what is untrue,' *or* 'One ought never to say what is untrue.' This is a universal rule prohibiting actions of type T (untruth-telling).

(ii) 'Your action was of type T.' This is a statement of fact, the force of which is that the action in question falls under the rule (i) and allows a conclusion to be drawn about it.

(iii) '(Therefore) your action was wrong.' This is a verdict arrived at by drawing a conclusion from (i) and (ii) as premisses. Only (ii) and (iii) were explicit in the dialogue, (i) being tacitly supplied by one or both parties.)

B. What has that got to do with it?
(B brusquely challenges A's 'reason'. He tacitly admits the truth of the statement embodied in A's last remark (i.e. (ii)), but he makes it clear that he is not a party to the acceptance of (i), the general principle of truth-telling, and so does not accept the conclusion (iii).)

B. (continuing) I told him what I did because, for a man in his condition, the sudden revelation that his case was hopeless would profoundly distress him, aggravate his suffering, and accelerate the progress of the disease.
(B not only rejects A's principle as a reason against his, B's action, but supplies an alternative principle as a reason for it. He points to a different characteristic of the action, perhaps unnoticed by A or judged irrelevant, thus replacing (ii) and bringing the action under a different rule, namely 'One ought always to avoid unnecessary suffering, to prolong life, etc.', in place of (i).)

A. I'm sorry, I didn't realise that. Of course you were right.
(A accepts B's reason, and by adopting it revises his own judgment on B's action.)

*Or*, I realise that, but I still think it was wrong to tell a falsehood.
(Accepts B's statment, but refuses to accept it as a reason, and reaffirms his own reason for condemning B's action.)

*Or*, Why is that a reason for doing what you did?
(A neither accepts nor rejects B's reason, but asks for a *further* reason. Since both A's and B's reasons, so far, have been principles from which verdicts or decisions could be derived, the new reason must be something from which the principle itself can be derived, and this will have to be a more general principle. Can the principle here — the avoidance of unnecessary suffering — be derived from some more general principle?)

B. I just think that avoiding unnecessary suffering is more important than avoiding false statement. Don't you?
(B refuses to give a further reason, suggesting that no more general principle is available. He also indicates that, unless A agrees with him on what is for him a fundamental and independent principle, no further progress in argument is possible.)

*Or*, It would be contrary to the teaching of Jesus Christ to inflict needless pain.

(B is willing to quote a further reason, and supports his principle about avoiding pain by mentioning a more fundamental principle from which this can be derived, namely the principle that one ought to observe the teachings of Jesus Christ.)

This simple example already suggests that giving reasons in ethics is rather a complex process. One can give, and accept, a reason for acting, or not acting, in a certain way; for deciding so to act; one can give a reason why it was right so to act, and one can give a reason for saying that it was right so to act. All these, which can be roughly divided into giving reasons for decisions and giving reasons for verdicts, involve a reference to some general principle which, in conjunction with a minor premiss giving the principle an application, provides a reason for the decision or verdict. But one can also give reasons for accepting or rejecting the principles themselves, or for preferring one principle to another, such as the principle of truth-telling to the principle of avoiding suffering.

### 4. *Reasoning and Consensus*

An important point which emerges from this example is that a discussion of reasons is only possible on some basis of agreement between the parties to the discussion. What is put forward as a reason, either for saying something or for doing something, is put forward with a claim, or at last an expectancy, for recognition by other people, especially our interlocutor, as a good or valid reason, that is, as a *reason*. Of course such a claim or expectancy may be disappointed. If, on meeting with opposition, we withdraw our claim, we thereby withdraw our claim to give a reason. If we insist on our claim, we thereby insist on the further claim that our opponent is mistaken, and perhaps go on to try to convince him of his mistake. It is essential to distinguish between situations where no claim is made, and situations where it is made but not met.

Consider first the following conversation:

A. Don't you like rice pudding?
B. No: do you?

A. Yes, I do.
B. Why?

B's final question is silly, because in matters of taste, such as liking or disliking rice pudding, rational justification is necessarily out of place. If A were to answer B by giving a 'reason' for his liking rice pudding, this would also be a 'reason' against disliking it, and A would be inviting B to consider it as a valid reason for giving up his dislike of rice pudding. But *de gustibus non disputandum*. Contrast the next case:

A. Rice pudding is very nutritious.
B. Why?
A. Because it contains plenty of starch.

Here B's question is not silly, because on matters of factual opinion, such as on the nutritive value of rice pudding, rational justification is completely in place. A gives a reason with a claim on B's assent. But if B disagrees with the general statement that whatever contains plenty of starch is nutritious, the discussion must proceed further until either agreement is reached, or there is nothing more to be said. Arguments are conducted with a view to securing general agreement on some proposition, on a presumption of agreement about some *other* proposition. Without such a presumption, argument cannot proceed, and nothing can count as a reason. No debate is possible between adversaries who deny each other's premisses.

Our examples have shown that such a presumption of agreement is not always substantiated. But it is tempting to misinterpret this. The correct interpretation is just that, in the last resort, people will be found to agree and disagree about everything under the sun. This is inconvenient for theory, and also smacks of philosophical scepticism. A simpler and more appealing position, and a metaphysical one, invites us: we are tempted to say that, despite the existence of disputes in practice, whether in science, history, ethics or religion, there is always a correct answer, even if we may not happen to know it. We may not know it, but we could know it if only we were wiser, more discriminating, more impartial, and so on. We may dispute about a certain view, but one or other party must be right, or if neither is, then some third party could be in possession of the truth, and correct us both. There is such a thing as Truth, whether or not individual human beings actually attain to it in any particular matter. Either the corpuscular theory of light is right, or the undulatory theory is; either there are exactly 120 mountains over 30,000 feet high on the unseen face of the moon, or else there are some other number; some action or other, in a given situation, would be absolutely right. This is a persuasive metaphysics, not only because it seems to underlie our unphilosophical talk about truth and the world, but because it affords us the satisfaction of holding that people who disagree with us are downright mistaken and not just of a different persuasion from ourselves.

I shall want to give an account of reason and truth in ethics which does not presuppose this easy but false metaphysical doctrine, but only a humbler, if less satisfying, alternative. This is, that all criteria of truth, validity, moral rightness and so on, are functions of the degree of agreement among classes of human beings.

Kant certainly does not hold the crude metaphysical view of independent reality, just sketched out, but much of what he says about reason involves something rather close to it; for he holds that Reason is the same for everyone, and is what qualifies a human being as a rational agent; so that men would all think alike, know the truth and act morally, if only . . . , just as we have seen that they would if our metaphysical caricature were true.

5. *Two Dimensions of Universalisability*

We may begin with Kant's distinction between duty and inclination. What is the difference between approving or disapproving of something and liking or disliking it? Or, what is the difference between doing something because I ought to do it and doing it because I want to do it or feel like doing it? There are two important differences.

If I do it because I ought to do it, I should have to be ready to say that, if ever the same circumstances recurred, I ought to do it on this other occasion too. *What* I ought to do depends, as we have seen, partly on my moral principles and partly on my situation; but, having applied my principles to my situation and decided that I ought to do X, I am bound to say that I ought to do X not merely on this occasion but on any other occasion on which the situation recurred. I ought to do it on any future occasion which may recur, and I ought to have done it on any past occasion which may have occurred. But this is certainly not the case with feelings. If I do something because I feel like doing it, there is no reference to other occasions. I can't tell what I shall feel like on future occasions, and in any case even if I could it would not make any difference to what I am to do now; nor does what I felt in the past make any difference. This difference between the moral situation and the feeling situation is what I shall call the characteristic of Universality: what I ought to do now is what I always ought to do. In other words, moral judgments and moral decisions carry with them moral principles, and moral principles are universal in one direction at least: they apply to actions of mine whether past, present or future, while feelings of course do not. This *is* the difference, or at least part of it, between principles and feelings.

But there is another direction in which moral principles are universal. If I do something because I ought to do it, and not because I feel like doing it, I should be ready to say, not merely that *I* ought to do it whenever circumstances of the same kind recur, but also that anyone else ought to do it. Conversely, if I say that some other person ought to do something, I must be prepared to say that I ought myself to do it, if I were in his situation. In other words, moral principles are universal in that I regard them as applying to people other than myself. But it would be absurd to say that, if I feel like doing something, other people should feel like it too, or that what other people like or dislike need make any difference to what I myself like or dislike. Moral principles, then, are universal, and moral judgments and decisions are universalisable, in at least these two ways, and that is what distinguishes them from feelings. The question now is, can this double feature of Universality be described as a function of Reason?

6. *The Principle of Non-Self-Contradiction*

Kant himself was much less interested in this question than in a different and much more exciting one, namely the question, can every actual moral duty be demonstrated as a deduction from some absolute principle, recognised by Reason? The concept of Reason invoked in the discussion of this question is a positive and substantial one: Kant thinks of Reason as an active principle of insight, in the true rationalist style. But he also works with a much more modest and less controversial concept of Reason, which has a bearing on our question. Consider what is the very least we should require of a piece of thinking or arguing that is to be called reasoning. The very least we require is that it should not contradict itself. Consistency is a necessary condition of rationality.

Kant in his ethical system makes great use of the Principle of Non-Contradiction. Very briefly, his argument is that what all moral agents have in common is that they are rational; so, if there is to be a universal moral principle, it will have to be a principle of reason. If a moral action can be shown to be somehow self-contradictory, that will itself be a ground for condemning it; conversely, any action that passes the test of non-self-contradiction will be right. In this way Kant hoped to deduce what is right and wrong from the principle of non-self-contradiction.

But how can an *action* be self-contradictory? Obviously actions cannot contradict themselves: only statements can contradict themselves. What we must look at, then, is not just the action but some verbal formula concerning the action. (This is what Kant calls a *maxim.*) For only something we can put into words can be self-contradictory. If I want to ask whether this particular action is right or wrong, I must not consider it in itself, as a unique action, but as one of a class of actions of the same type, which I may have to consider doing whenever circumstances of the same type recur. In other words, I must consider not just doing something, but doing it, as we say, *on principle*; and I must ask whether the 'principle'[1] of the action (Kant's 'maxim') is right or wrong. Reference to a principle, rule, maxim or class of actions is what I called in the last section the first dimension of universalisability.

But how am I to decide whether the principle is right or wrong? I still cannot use the standard of non-contradiction. As long as my principles are *my* principles, that is, are regarded as applying only to my own actions, I am free to choose what principles I shall adopt, and, providing that I follow them conscientiously, no self-contradiction will appear, however monstrous the principles may be. The answer is that I must universalise in the other direction as well. I must consider my principles as applying to other people too — all other people. Kant's way of putting it is to say that we must act only on those 'maxims' which we could wish to be adopted as universal laws for everyone whatever. If we find that we could not universalise our principles in this way without involving ourselves in a contradiction, the principles must be immoral and actions in accordance with them wrong.

Kant's attempts to illustrate his own thesis[2] by giving examples of actual moral duties as deductions from his Universalisation Principle are badly stated and unconvincing. To take two of his examples: the duty to make truthful promises, and the duty not to commit suicide. He has to prove that it is wrong to make a promise without intending to keep it. The action must first be generalised into a private principle or maxim as 'I will always make a lying promise when it suits my convenience'. Then this maxim has to be converted into a public principle by being universalised as 'Everyone is to make lying promises when convenient'. Now this universalised principle is supposed to be something I cannot possibly assert because it involves a contradiction. And the contradiction is supposed to arise from the fact that if this principle were to be accepted, the institution of promise-making and contract would collapse because no one

[1] In what follows, I use the word 'principle' in this ordinary, though non-Kantian, sense. Nor do I claim to state Kant's own position, which is notoriously controversial, with complete accuracy.

[2] *Groundwork of the Metaphysic of Morals*, ed. H. J. Paton, p. 89.

would put any trust in other people's promises. But while this is no doubt true, there is nothing self-contradictory in willing such a state of affairs to exist. It may be difficult to will it, but it is not self-contradictory; indeed it may not even be difficult for a man in debt, for instance, who would be considerably better off for the abolition of the contract system. As for suicide, the objection is clearer still. It is supposed to be self-contradictory to assert that everyone may take his own life whenever he feels like it, because such a system would allow human life to die out; but even it it would (which is itself doubtful) there is nothing self-contradictory in wishing the human race to exterminate itself. It may be difficult, but it is not logically impossible, and may at times be only too easy.

Some such defects were bound to follow the attempt to deduce what is actually right or wrong from an absolute principle of pure reason. Reason alone cannot prove that certain things are right or wrong. Yet reason does enter into our knowledge of what is right and wrong: and it enters in the form in which Kant looked for it, at least part of the time, that is in the form of consistency or non-contradiction, though the job it does is less exciting than Kant hoped. Let us take his example of lying and (assuming without question that lying is wrong) consider what we should think of someone who made statements like these:

(*a*) 'It would be wrong for me to tell a lie just now, but for all I know it might be quite all right tomorrow, even in the same circumstances.'

(*b*) 'Lying is always wrong, but it is all right for me to tell this lie.'

(*c*) 'I disapprove of lying myself, but I don't object to other people telling lies.'

(*d*) 'No one ought to tell lies, except myself.'

Would it not be clear that each of these statements did involve a self-contradiction, a lack of consistency? Is it not inconsistent of me to disapprove of lying and yet to hold that a certain lie is right, or to disapprove of it in other people but not in myself? If so, this suggests that Reason, in the form of consistency or non-contradiction, does enter into morality; it is involved in

of universalisation I described — an extension
al act into all acts of that kind performed by
er extension to all acts of that kind performed by
e generalisation of act into maxim, and a further
of maxim into universal law. Where Kant went
rying to show that this possibility of universalisation actually made the act right, while impossibility of universalisation made it wrong. All that he was entitled to say was that if the act is to be either right *or* wrong, there must be this possibility of universalisation. In other words, we cannot deduce any actual moral duties from the possibility of universalisation, but *given* any moral duty *or* moral crime, we can say that it must be universalisable; that is, we cannot say that if something is universalisable, it is right, if not, that it is wrong (as Kant wished to say): but only that if it is not universalisable it is *neither* right *nor* wrong, but outside the range of morality altogether. Universalisation is a necessary condition of morality, not a sufficient condition of right (as opposed to wrong) action.

We have now briefly stated part of an ethical theory — the universalisability of moral judgments—which is closely associated with Kant's own theory, though in the interest of historical accuracy it ought to be stressed that it is at best presupposed by Kant and would have been regarded by him as little more than a platitude. But a platitude it certainly is not, as is shown by the hostility not only of a Hume, but of an Existentialist (p. 193).

7. *Reasoning as a Second-Order Performance*

We must now consider a little further what sort of reasoning is involved in this universalisation. To bring out a little more of the nature of reasoning, let us consider an example from geometry. If we can show that in spite of the big differences between geometry and ethics, the same features of reasoning are to be found in both, we shall have answered Hume and at the same time avoided falling into Kant's mistake.

Reasoning has to do with criteria — and with criteria which are taken as applying universally. To give a reason is, as we have seen, to make a claim to universal recognition. Reasoning is the application of criteria to certain kinds of performance. It is not itself a performance; or, if preferred, it is a second-order performance which presupposes a first-order performance.

Consider, for example, a candidate and an examiner in a paper on geometry. Let us suppose that the candidate is asked to prove a certain theorem of which he has not yet been given the proof, but he knows enough to work out the proof. Now it might be supposed that the reasoning is done by the candidate, who does the actual thinking out and writing down of the theorem; what the examiner does is merely to check the reasoning. But this would be a mistake. Reasoning is not the same thing as thinking or writing: it is the application of certain universal standards to the thinking and the writing: in this case, the principles of valid deduction. Obviously this is what the examiner does: he asks whether this proposition follows from that, whether there is a contradiction or inconsistency somewhere, whether what is claimed as a proof really is a proof. But this is not just what the examiner does. It is what the candidate does too. And he does it not merely in checking over the final written answer; he does it in the thinking out; in so far as his thinking is reasoning, it is the weighing and criticising of concepts and propositions which come into his mind. The examiner judges someone else's performance; the candidate judges his own; and that is the only difference there is. That is why it would make sense for the examiner to say 'The right answer is the one which I should have given if I were doing the paper', and for the candidate to say 'The right answer is the one I should mark correct if I were examining the paper' and similarly for the wrong answer. Significantly enough, it would be a self-contradiction for the examiner to say 'This answer is wrong, though it is the one I should have given' and for the candidate to say 'This answer is wrong, though I should have given it full marks if I were the examiner'.[1]

What I wish to extract from this example, as a basis for com-

[1] These two statements would not be self-contradictory on a special interpretation, namely that the candidate and the examiner are each confessing that, had he been in the other's place, he would have made a mistake. This is a complication that need not concern us here. See, however, pp. 173 and 174.

parison with moral examples, is this. Whether we are engaged, as geometers, in *doing* something, or in *judging* what someone else has done, we apply the same kind of reasoning in both cases. If we call the person who acts the agent, and the person who judges the judge, we can say that agents and judges cannot be regarded, and cannot regard themselves, as distinct persons performing distinct functions. Each is complementary to the other. The agent must not merely act, if he is to act reasonably — as a rational agent — he must also judge his action, he must be judge as well as agent; and the judge must not merely pronounce, if he is to make a reasonable pronouncement — he must judge according to the same principles that he applies, or would apply, to his own performances.

What I have said of geometrical performances is equally true of all rational performances. If we can show that it is true of moral performances, we shall have established a very strong case for the rationality of ethics, without falling into the errors of rational*ism*. But we have already seen that it is true of moral performances; at least we have seen that moral principles are universalisable in two directions, they apply to all actions of mine, of a certain class, and also to all such actions on the part of other people. All that remains is to connect this with the point that moral experience consists of decisions and judgments. In terms of the concepts of 'agent' and 'judge', we say that the person who makes a moral decision or performs a moral action is the moral agent, while the person who makes a moral judgment, who comments on and criticises other people's actions, is the moral judge. And the universality or moral principles then appears in a new form. The moral agent does not merely act, if he is to act as a moral agent; he judges his action, he applies to his own performance the criteria which he uses in judging other people's performances. And the moral judge or commentator or moralist does not merely utter pronouncements on people's conduct: he makes them in the light of the same moral principles which he uses, or would use, to guide his own moral decisions. In my discussion of the three-tier model (I, 6), I said that the roles of agent and judge, actor and critic, can well be combined

in practice. We can now add that, for rati
judgment, not only can they be combined, they m
bined. In ethics, as in geometry or any other rational p
there is no minding your own business: both action an
ment, performance and criticism, must be referred to a se
principles which are taken as applying universally.

8. *Universalisability without Universality*

One formidable-looking obstacle remains. The following objection may be raised against any proposal to establish a rational basis for morality, on the lines I have suggested. Reasoning such as we use in geometry, according to this objection, does in fact refer to principles which really are universal: there is no dispute about the principles of valid deduction. But this is notoriously not the case in ethics. The moral principles which form the moral code of one society differ from those of another; even within the same society there are marked differences between the moral standards of different groups and even individuals. Surely this demolishes the whole case for the rationality of ethics; how can there be reason where there is disagreement about fundamental principles? Surely (according to this objector) this puts you in a dilemma: either Platonism or Hume. Platonism, if you insist that there *is* a standard of rational morality, despite the disagreement about what it is; Hume, if you admit that reason is not to be found in fundamental principles but only in working out ways and means of achieving one's purposes whatever they happen to be.

My answer to this objection falls into two parts. I entirely agree with what the objector says, but I claim that it is not an objection. As will appear from Chapter VI, I regard the existence of disputes, controversies and differences of opinion on moral principles as not merely something that has to be allowed for by any theory of morality which is to do justice to the facts, but as very much more important: as something that actually makes morality what it is, and has to be a central feature of a moral theory. The objection is not, however, an objection to the rationality of morality, because it does not affect my comparison

er true it is that moral principles
s do not, this leaves things just as
gnificant parallel between moral
es. Why the parallel remains, de-
stion which must be postponed to
1.

his. One may disapprove of another
he himself does not disapprove of it,
would refuse to disapprove of it. Indeed this
banal truism. In order to judge other people by the
standards as those by which we judge ourselves, there is not the slightest need to judge by the same standards as theirs. Morality requires that we universalise the principles on which *we* act and judge: not that the principles be in fact universally accepted. Universalisation is perfectly consistent with a diversity of actual moral principles. One man has his set of moral principles which he universalises, another has another set which he universalises. There is no more need for rational beings to have a common morality than there is for them to have a common language: yet morality involves a common element of reason, as language involves a common element of intelligence. In fact, as I hope to show, it is not merely permissible for moral beings to have different moralities; it is in a way actually necessary. If the principles and standards to which we appeal in our moral choices and moral judgments were indeed universal (in the sense of being in fact universally accepted), as the principles of deduction in geometry are universal, then morality would *be* a sort of geometry. Having found a common ground between morality and mathematics, we must of course look for differences too, which remain to be explored. Something we call reason distinguishes moral choices from choices of taste, liking, inclination and so on, and moral judgments from judgments about what satisfies our wants. But not all reasoned choices and reasoned judgments are moral ones.

9. *Self-Criticism and Moral Education*

Implicit in my discussion of reason and criteria is a point

which is of special interest from the standpoint of education. I have spoken of morality as a sort of self-criticism — the same sort of self-criticism as any rational conduct involves; namely the application to one's performances of standards and criteria which one applies to other people's performances. Criticism and self-criticism in morals is commenting on performances, but it is not mere commenting. Its purpose is to make a difference to performances: at least to one's own performances. One does not merely assess one's conduct in the light of certain standards: one tries to make one's conduct *conform* to those standards; and the purpose of self-criticism is to make conduct conform more closely to the standards one professes. In terms of my geometrical example (for the same is true here) there is a difference between the examiner on the one hand and the candidate and teacher on the other: the examiner, as a rule, criticises not with a view to *altering* the candidate's performance, but merely in order to assess it; the teacher, on the other hand, applies the same standards of criticism, but this time with a view to improving the candidate's performance; and the same is true of the candidate's self-criticism: this is aimed not merely at self-assessment, but at self-improvement.

And so in ethics. Theoretically there is no reason why there should not be moral examiners, whose function would be merely to allot marks in accordance with some conventionally agreed standards; but in practice there are only moral teachers and moral pupils; moral teachers, that is, moralists and preachers and all those who are concerned with the moral training of the young; and moral pupils, that is, people who are either learning what moral principles to adopt, or learning to improve their performance in accordance with the principles they do adopt, or both. Criticism aims at improvement; self-criticism aims at self-improvement.

But why should the standards I adopt make any difference to my performance? Why should I not merely recognise certain principles, according to which I judge conduct, but also try to model my conduct on them? These questions are various ways of putting the one big question with which I introduced the discussion of regulation in Chapter II. Why does recognising standards make a difference to conduct? The facile answer and perhaps the most immediately satisfying one is to say that there must be some specifically moral 'faculty' in man — some inner sense that doesn't just recognise the moral principles and doesn't just appear in consciousness as a feeling of approval for some actions and disapproval of others, but actually prompts and motivates the individual to act. A famous example of this is Kant's *Achtung* or 'sense of duty' which is for him the mainspring of all moral action.

Another is Butler's 'Conscience'. Conscience just is, for Butler and for many ordinary people, the faculty in us which both apprehends moral principles and prompts us to act conformably with them, for instance by making us feel that special sort of discomfort which we call remorse whenever we fail to act conformably with our principles. Conscience has fallen into disrepute nowadays; mainly, I suspect, because it is thought of as a sort of motive and yet psychologists, whose business it is to tell us about motivations, cannot locate it; or, if they can, all they can say about it is that it is just another conditioned response to certain situations, produced by a certain kind of training in youth. Agnostics and atheists, again, take exception to it because it smacks too much of theology; for Butler, indeed, it was the voice of God; and we may well want our ethical theory to be independent of our theological beliefs — as even Butler himself did.

Conscience does not deserve this stigma. I think it is still a very useful concept. It incorporates a great deal of moral educational theory. For instance, children are not supposed to have consciences, except in a qualified sort of way. If we say that a small child has a bad conscience, we mean something like this: that it feels it has displeased its parents, anticipates punishment, or knows it has fallen short of what was expected of it. Yet although children do not have consciences in the full moral sense, they are in a way just as much concerned with morality as adults, in fact more so: they have got to learn what the adult already knows. But the crucial difference is this. A child begins to learn what he ought to do by being told what he ought to do. But who tells him? Certain people who stand in special and close relations with him, such as parents and teachers; and what is important about them is that they have *authority* which the child recognises, and which other people do not have. A child begins to learn his moral principles, the ways in which he ought to behave, in the same way as he begins to learn most other things: by being told what to do by people whose authority he respects. He is a moral pupil and these people are his moral tutors.

But although he *begins* to learn his morality this way, he certainly doesn't *learn* it this way. A child doesn't learn arithmetic by being told the answers to certain arithmetical examples, nor does he learn French by parroting examples of French sentences. Until he has learnt at least some principles of arithmetic, such as the principles of addition and multiplication, and some rules of the French language, such as the principles of French grammar, he certainly hasn't really learnt any arithmetic or French. Furthermore his learning the principles must not be merely learning to enunciate things like 'twice two is four', or 'adjective agrees in gender with noun': he must learn to apply the principles, not to recite them but to employ them. Learning the principles in the proper sense *is* learning to apply them. And to apply principles is to criticise. It is at least one purpose of education to teach criticism. But it is more than that; one very important purpose of education is to teach not just criticism, but self-criticism. Whether in mathematics or morals, the pupil must learn not merely to apply standards to performances, but to apply them to his own performances; and while the teacher can give examples of criticism, he cannot give examples of self-criticism; this is what the pupil has to achieve.

But when he has achieved it, the authority on which he relied for being told what to do, in the beginning, is now no longer needed; or, rather, it is transferred to a different place. To put the matter somewhat picturesquely, and to anticipate Chapter IX, it is no longer external, in the person of the teacher, it is internal, in the pupil himself. By internalising the authority behind the principles of criticism, whether in mathematics or morals, the pupil ceases to be a pupil: he achieves autonomy and independence. And in the special case of morality, we can say that the internalisation of the authority behind the principles of conduct, marks the emergence of the moral agent as an autonomous, independent, adult human being. Morality depends on the recognition of some authority: moral maturity requires that one should be one's own authority. And this internal authority is just the feature of Conscience which Butler emphasises most strongly, and which I think has to be kept, even if we dislike its other attributes. A full discussion of conscience will be conducted in Chapter VIII. In the meantime, this concept, or something like it, is what we need to describe certain essential features of moral action, but especially these two:

(*a*) Applying to one's own performance the criteria one applies to other people's — being judge as well as performer, as it were two persons in one, an 'inner' as well as an 'outer' — Conscience being the name of the 'inner' man.

(*b*) Not merely recognising and using the criteria, but making one's conduct conform to them, trying to do what one is told to do by an authority one respects — this authority being no longer visible in the person of a moral tutor, but somehow transferred to oneself; so that one is again as it were two persons in one, but this time (to borrow Kant's terminology) both legislator and citizen: in one's capacity as citizen one obeys the laws which one enacts in one's capacity as legislator.

CHAPTER V

# TRUTH IN ETHICS

## 1. *Matters of Fact and Matters of Taste*

The deepest issue, and the most violent controversy, in contemporary moral philosophy is between those who assert, and those who deny, that moral judgments can be true or false. This difference can indeed be taken as the simplest way of defining the meaning of the pair of correlative terms 'objective' and 'subjective'. What is objective is capable of being true or false, of being a statement, a belief or opinion; what is subjective is not capable of taking a truth-value, but is an expression of some psychological state. (It is not a *description* of a psychological state, which would, of course, be true or false.) 'Rice pudding is nutritious' is a statement, which is either true or false; 'Rice pudding is nice' is an expression of the speaker's liking for rice pudding, having much the same force as 'Rice pudding, yum! yum!' or 'I *do* like rice pudding'; not, however, if the latter is taken as a statement — as it could be — for it would then be a description of a certain individual's taste in food, which would be true or false in exactly the same way as the third-personal statement that Mr. X likes rice pudding.

The two sentences 'Rice pudding is nutritious' and 'Rice pudding is nice' have the same form; and in view of the difference just noted, it has to be said that the similarity of form is misleading, and that a sentence can have the form of a statement without having the force of a statement. Of course the distinction is not as clear-cut as I have suggested. Part of what is involved in making a statement, asserted in the ordinary way as a true statement, is that one invites, or at least counts on, agreement by the listeners. If it turns out that nobody agrees with me that rice pudding is nutritious, I shall be somewhat bewildered; I am not compelled to withdraw my statement, but my confidence in it may be shaken. And since this *could* happen with any statement whatever (excluding analytic statements which are true by definition), I must be prepared to admit that, in the end, anything I assert could conceivably be mistaken. Matters of truth and falsity are always matters which involve the possibility of error.

But somewhat similarly, in saying 'Rice pudding is nice', I am surely issuing a tentative invitation to my listeners to endorse my utterance, and this is partly the reason why the sentence has the same form. Yet the two cases diverge, for if it now turns out that no one agrees with me, my confidence in what I said will not be in the least shaken: rice pudding is just as nice as it ever was. And I shall certainly not be prepared to admit that I could have been mistaken. Matters of taste and distaste, unlike matters of truth and falsity, involve no possibility of error.

### 2. *Cambridge Objectivism*

A notable and characteristic brand of objectivism in ethics is associated with the Cambridge philosophers Moore and Broad. This type of theory involves the controversy between Naturalism and Non-Naturalism, which in turn arose out of the attempt to define certain characteristic words of moral discourse, such as those we examined in Chapter II — 'good', 'bad', 'right' and 'wrong'. Can these ethical words be defined in non-ethical terms? Now it was taken for granted that these words, being adjectives, referred to qualities or relations as ordinary adjectives do; and the question was, whether these qualities or relations could be specified without using moral language. Do the qualities actually exist in the world (are they 'natural') whether or not we have occasion to invoke them in our ethical judgments, as ordinary qualities like *red* exist in the world, whether or not we have occasion to say of something that it *is* red? Many ethical theories have been naturalistic in this sense. The Epicureans held that good means pleasant, the Utilitarians that right means what conduces to maximum general happiness.

Theological Naturalism holds that right means what is in accordance with the will of God.

But all such definitions were thought to be ruled out once and for all by Moore's classical refutation of the so-called Naturalistic Fallacy.[1] The refutation may be paraphrased as follows. If *x* means the same as *y*, then it will be self-contradictory to say that something is *x* but not *y*; if it is not self-contradictory to say so, then *x* cannot mean the same as *y*. Now even if it is true that what is good is always pleasant and *vice versa*, yet it is certainly not self-contradictory, in the normal usage of words, to say that something good is unpleasant, or something unpleasant good; therefore good and pleasant cannot mean the same, as they must if one defines the other. And the same argument holds against all other possible definitions of 'good' in terms of something else. So the only alternative is to reject Naturalism and embrace Non-Naturalism. 'Good', 'right', and so on, are not definable (except perhaps in terms of each other). They refer to 'non-natural' qualities or relations. The main difference between Moore and Broad is that one takes as his fundamental ethical characteristic a quality (goodness) while Broad takes a relation ('rightness', or 'fittingness')[2]. Both claim what is at the heart of objectivism, that such characteristics exist, and that moral judgments ascribing them to actions or situations are true or false in a perfectly ordinary way.

Objectivist theories of ethics, then, tend to assimilate moral judgments to statements of the subject-predicate type such as 'Rice pudding is nutritious' — or, rather, to acquiesce in and to develop the assimilation which is already embodied in the linguistic structural similarity of the sentences. Subjectivist theories, on the other hand, tend to emphasise the contrast instead of the similarity, to say that the linguistic structure of moral judgments is misleading, and to develop an alternative comparison with sentences of the type 'I *do* like rice pudding', to which the epithets 'true' and 'false' are inappropriate.

### 3. *The Problem of Moral Disputes*

Such an issue cannot be settled without a preliminary study

[1] *Principia Ethica*, pp. 11–14. [2] *Five Types of Ethical Theory*, p. 219.

of what is involved in the decision to allow or to withhold the epithets 'true' and 'false' in the first place. We have already seen that part of what is involved when a sentence is employed assertively, that is, as a true statement, is an expectancy of agreement. Now the notorious lack of agreement on many ethical issues, indeed the very existence of ethical *issues*, of different moral codes, of differences of conscience, creates a *prima facie* difficulty for an objectivist theory of ethics: if ethical judgments are statements, how is it that the criteria for their verification and falsification are so elusive? It might be objected that this is no objection: for surely there are factual statements of which the truth or falsity is equally undecidable. It is unlikely that we shall ever know who was the executioner of King Charles I. And we cannot, at present, know whether it is true that there is living matter on any other planet. But as to the second example, we presumably shall be in a position to verify it, when suitable techniques have been developed; whereas the obstacle to ethical agreement does not seem to be the absence of any observational technique. As to the first example, it can be replied that an historical example is not a case in point, for in ethics we are concerned with disputes about whole classes of action ('Is war ever right?') and not just with isolated instances. Whatever may be the difficulties of deciding the truth of singular statements about the past, there is no such difficulty about deciding the truth of general statements of a factual sort, corresponding to general moral judgments. Questions like 'Is sugar soluble in water?' are always decidable; or, more precisely, there exist always (save in quite peculiar and untypical cases on the fringe of an advancing science) decision procedures for such questions.

But if the existence of moral disputes constitutes a difficulty for an objectivist theory of ethics, the same fact, paradoxically, proves a still worse obstacle for subjectivism. For, as we have seen, matters of taste are just what we do not argue about; there is no dispute between people who express differences of taste; but when A says that wars are sometimes justified and B says that war is always wrong, it seems too drastic a revision of common sense to say that there is really no dispute between them because each is merely expressing his own attitude to war (and perhaps coaxing his opponent to change his mind). It is an irreducible demand of an objectivist theory, first, that moral judgments should be true or false, and second, that contrary moral judgments should be strictly incompatible. The second demand, at any rate, is amply met. Judgments which are ostensibly contrary or contradictory (such as 'Wars are sometimes right' and 'Wars are always wrong') are genuinely incompatible.

All the same, while the existence of moral controversy helps to refute subjectivism, it does not help in more than this negative way to establish objectivism. In particular it does not suffice to meet the first demand of objectivism. Moral judgments may be incompatible, but truth and falsity are not the only incompatibles. I shall try to show that there are indeed extensive similarities between moral judgments and other judgments of a fact-stating type, though not quite enough to justify the application of the terms 'true' and 'false' in moral discourse. For these concepts themselves stand in need of analysis; and when this is undertaken, it will be seen that they refer to criteria (of verification and falsification) which are a special sort of criteria of appropriateness, and that the criteria for deciding moral judgments are also a sort of criteria of appropriateness — but a different sort.

What is analytically prior to truth and falsity is the acceptance and rejection of statements. We do not accept statements because they are true and reject them because they are false. Rather (though this is too crude) we call statements true which we accept, and false which we reject. We accept and reject statements because they satisfy or fail to satisfy the criteria which we apply in testing certain linguistic performances, namely assertions. (There are other linguistic performances, such as commands, questions and expletives, to which we apply quite different criteria, or none at all.)

The task in this chapter is to consider whether the criteria for the correctness of moral judgments are sufficiently analogous to truth criteria to justify the extension of the terms 'true' and 'false' to moral discourse.

4. *Appropriateness, Criteria and Conventions*

But in order to say more about the criteria behind moral language, we must begin further back with some observations about the nature of language in general.

I shall suggest that there is a very general property of statements which I shall call appropriateness; that factual truth and moral 'truth' are each of them a special kind of appropriateness; and that appropriateness depends on the recognition of certain conventions or rules. More explicitly: to say that a statement is true (or false) is to say that it is appropriate (or inappropriate) in one way, while to say that a moral judgment is sound is to say that it is appropriate in another way. Truth is not the only kind of appropriateness. But the appropriateness of anything is not a simple property which that thing just possesses, or a simple relation between one thing and another. Black is appropriate to mourning, but its appropriateness is not something that just belongs to blackness, nor even a relation between blackness and death. To be sure, a relation of similarity can be found between blackness and death, or between our emotional reactions to these; but the relation of appropriateness is quite different from this, though connected with it historically. To say that black is appropriate mourning attire is to imply that there is a rule or convention in force according to which it is correct for the mourner to wear black and incorrect to wear, say, yellow. A remark can be appropriate, or a gesture, or a dress.

The rule or convention need not be explicit; it need never have been formulated by anyone. We might find it extremely difficult to formulate the rules governing the matching of colours, say, or the choice of hats. But even dress fashions are rules, though notoriously short-lived ones. Any judgment of 'correct' or 'incorrect' involves a latent, if not explicit, rule; even if the rule in question can only be extemporised in the form 'Anything resembling X in certain respects (but not, of course 'anything exactly like X', which would make the rule empty) is correct (or incorrect) in situations of type Y.' (Compare our discussion of moral pioneering in II, 5 and 6.) We have already seen that a moral judgment refers to a moral standard or principle: 'X is wrong' means that X is contrary to a moral principle or rule. We have now stated a more general form of this thesis, namely, that any judgment of 'right' and 'wrong', not merely a judgment of moral right and wrong, refers to a principle or rule of some kind.

5. *Criteria of Meaning*

We shall now proceed to compare simple factual statements (which are true or false) with simple moral judgments (where the claim to the epithets 'true' and 'false' is in question). What sorts of rule or convention are at the back of a simple factual statement like 'There is bread on the table'? The first point to notice is the distinction between meaning and truth. The sentence just quoted has a meaning, whereas the sentence 'There is bread between the table' has not; we can express this by saying that the second sentence is not a statement, that is, it cannot be used, under present linguistic conventions, in order to assert anything at all, whether true or false. One set of conventions, then, must determine the correctness or incorrectness of a sentence purporting to state something, and these will be conventions of meaning. But in any actual context in which the sentence first quoted is used to make an actual assertion (as it was not, of course, in the present context), it will be either true or false: true if there is bread on the table, false if there is not. And the rules of meaning do not suffice to determine this kind of correctness. So we shall need another set of rules governing the appropriateness of statements to certain kinds of situation.

A full discussion of these two kinds of rules would take us too far into the philosophical theory of meaning and truth; but something must be said about what kind of rules they are. Rules of the first kind include the rules of grammar and syntax. They also include the 'rules' which determine the meanings of words, such as dictionary definitions: the definition of 'square' as 'equal-sided rectangle', for instance, is a rule to the effect that the word 'square' is properly used to describe the shape which is also described by the defining expression 'equal-sided rectangle'. That this is a rule is shown by the word 'properly', and by the fact that we speak of using words correctly and incorrectly, and that the dictionary gives the 'correct' meanings of words. One of the most prominent of the first kinds of rule, then, is the rule correlating words and things: part of what is involved in getting the sentence 'There is bread on the table' right is using the word 'bread' in accordance with the rule that 'bread' means *bread.*

### 6. *Criteria of Truth*

The second kind of rule is involved in getting the sentence right not in the sense of getting it to mean something, but in the sense of getting it to be true. This kind of rule enjoys less publicity than the other kind, but it is just as genuine. Under what conditions do we get the statement 'There is bread on the table' right or wrong in the sense of being true or false? Simply when there *is* bread on the table, or when there isn't. At the cost of being ponderously trite, we can formulate the rule as follows. 'The sentence "There is bread on the table" is to be used only when there is bread on the table.'

Notice two points about this 'rule'. In the first place, it is not a rule which is universally in force for all linguistic performances. If it were, I should have broken it and, consequently, asserted what was false, when I wrote it on page 75, there being at the time no bread on my table. For the same reason, the whole corpus of fiction writing would be a mass of untruth. We say, of course, that in such cases the question of truth or falsity does not arise; and this means that sentences which have the appearance of statements or assertions need not necessarily be *asserted*; or, in terms of rules, that the rules determining appropriateness of the true-or-false kind do not always apply.

Secondly, the rule is negative rather than positive, a prohibition and not an injunction. It does not tell us what to do. Rather it forbids us (at the cost of saying what is false) from saying that there is bread on the table (when there isn't any). It does not instruct us to say that the bread *is* on the table, when it is. For we break no rules by keeping silence. There is no general injunction to say what is the case, but there is a negative injunction to refrain from saying what is not the case. It should be noted that this is by no means the same thing as the moral principle forbidding lying. It is a purely linguistic rule determining what counts as a correct statement. There is a further and quite distinct question, in what circumstances one is morally permitted or forbidden to utter statements which are correct or incorrect according to the linguistic rules. Breaking a linguistic rule (of this sort) counts as falsity, and falsity may or may not be morally reprehensible. Breaking a moral rule counts as a moral wrong and is always, of course and by definition, morally reprehensible.

### 7. *Singular and General Statements*

We can generalise the rule, which we have so far formulated only for a particular kind of situation ('bread and table'), as follows: 'A sentence describing X as Y is to be used only when X is Y.' Difficulties arise when we pass from simple to more complex sentences, such as from particular statements or descriptions to general statements; but we must consider these if we wish to find parallels for moral assertions, since a moral judgment may commend or condemn not merely a particular action but a whole class of actions, such as executing criminals. The former judgment is of the type 'This X is wrong', while the latter is of the type 'All Ys are wrong'. We have already seen that even a particular moral judgment is not, despite its formal similarity to a description, a singular statement about an individual, such as 'This cat is black'; rather it is an application, to a particular case, of a general assertion about all cases of a certain sort. This X is wrong because all Xs are wrong and it is an X; such an assertion, then, is completely different from a description; 'This cat is black' or 'There is bread on the table' certainly does not depend on any general statement about the blackness of all cats or the bread-bearing properties of all tables. Even singular moral judgments, therefore, will depend for their correctness on rules which cannot be compared with those governing the correctness of singular descriptions. We must look for a comparison with the rules governing the correctness of general statements.

What, then, are the rules governing the truth of a general statement about all things of a certain sort, such as 'All birds lay eggs'? Here we seem to be precluded from stating a general rule mentioning conditions of applicability, since the conditions are themselves general; any situation of the bread-on-table type justifies a singular statement 'There is bread on the table', but what type of situation is the 'all-birds-lay-eggs' type, of which a particular situation could be an instance? Obviously no situation whatever can be an instance of *all* birds. We can point to no particular state of affairs with which a particular utterance of 'All birds lay eggs' can be matched. The correspondence theory of truth, which works well enough with singular statements (provided we remember that the 'correspondence' is entirely conventional, depending on the kind of rule discussed on p. 76) breaks down altogether over general statements.

We can deal with the discrepancy as follows. In the case of a singular statement ('There is bread on the table') the rule is to the effect that the sentence is not to be asserted *unless* the situation is of a certain type (bread-on-table type); the rule lays down a necessary condition for the assertion, but not a sufficient one (since we break no rule by refraining from speech). However, if someone does assert the statement, then the condition mentioned in the rule as a necessary condition of the assertion of the statement becomes, in our verdict on the statement once it is made, our evidence for saying that the rule has been observed, that is, a sufficient condition for the verdict 'true'. In the case of the general statement ('All birds lay eggs') we must say that the rule is to the effect that the statement is not to be asserted *if* there *does* occur any situation of a particular type, namely a non-oviparous bird. The rule lays down not a necessary condition for the assertion of the statement, but a sufficient condition for its non-assertion.[1]

[1] Logicians may be inclined to object here that to specify a necessary condition for something is the same as to specify a sufficient condition for its absence. There being bread on the table is a necessary condition for asserting that there is bread on the table, and there being no bread on the table is a sufficient condition for not

Neither necessary nor sufficient conditions can be given for the assertion of a general statement. Sufficient conditions cannot be given, for the same reason as before, that we break no rule by saying nothing at all. Necessary conditions can indeed be mentioned, such as that there should be oviparous birds; but that *all* birds should be oviparous is not an identifiable condition, being merely the generalisation itself (see footnote); and though it is necessary that this, that and the other birds should be oviparous, this necessary condition cannot be converted, as it was in the previous case, into a sufficient condition for a truth verdict on the statement when made. That some birds are oviparous does not verify that all are. Only one possibility remains. This is to take the rule as laying down a sufficient condition for the *non*-assertion of the statement: we must *not* say 'All birds are oviparous' if there *is* a viviparous bird; if we do say so, we break this rule, and our verdict on the general statement will be that it is false.

Generalising again, we may say that the rule governing general statements is as follows: 'A sentence of the form "All As are B" is not to be asserted if there is an A which is not B.' We have thus arrived at a conclusion which is in full agreement with the orthodox logical theory of general statements, namely that while a singular statement can be conclusively verified or refuted, a general statement can be conclusively refuted but not conclusively verified: it only permits of degrees of confirmation.[1] A single non-oviparous bird upsets the statement that all birds are oviparous, but a number of instances of oviparous birds supplies only partial confirmation of the statement.

asserting that there is. But this put-it-whichever-way-you-like device works only when both positive and negative forms describe some possible situation, as 'bread on table' and 'no bread on table' do. In the case of general statements, the only relevant situations are the occurrence of birds which are either oviparous or viviparous; an oviparous bird, or a collection of them, will not do, as stated in the text; a viviparous one constitutes a sufficient condition for not asserting the generalisation. But no corresponding negation constitutes a necessary condition for asserting it, for the *absence* of all viviparous birds is not a possible 'situation'.

[1] It may seem paradoxical that the rules for general statements should be decisive only for non-assertion and falsity. The explanation is that the positive conditions of acceptability are not truth conditions; but this subject belongs to the theory of induction and philosophy of science.

8. *Meaning-Criteria in Moral Language*

From this analysis of truth-and-falsity rules in empirical discourse, we can pass to moral language. What conventions are we to look for here? The first type of convention, such as the rules governing the meanings of words, has the same part to play, though with a number of modifications. For instance, not all nouns in moral discourse refer to things or actions, as the words 'bread' or 'walking' do. 'Murder' means not a certain kind of killing, but killing which is forbidden by certain moral rules. Secondly, as we have seen, the characteristic terms of moral discourse, words like 'ought', 'right', 'good', and so on, have rather complex functions, such as commending or evaluating with implied reference to a standard or principle. Thirdly, ethical words are contextually linked with a number of extra-linguistic factors such as feelings, attitudes of approval and disapproval, remorse, and so on. But even in such cases there are criteria of appropriateness, that is to say, implicit rules and conventions. The word 'virtuous' is an epithet of commendation, and people who use it, as is common today, in order to disparage conceit or smugness (which are moral defects) are breaking the rules according to which the word is (or was) 'correctly' used, and setting up new rules of correctness. Again, anyone who said 'Torturing is wrong' in a tone expressive of glee, or whose actions manifested an attitude at variance with his professed moral view, would be held to be saying something inappropriate.

9. '*Truth*'-*Criteria in Moral Language*

But what of the truth-governing conventions? Is there a criterion of appropriateness for the judgment 'It was wrong to torture that prisoner' analogous to the criterion of appropriateness for the statement 'There is bread on the table'? There is not, if what we want is a conventional correlation between type of assertion and type of situation. There is no correspondence theory of truth for moral discourse. We cannot deal with singular moral judgments in isolation, but only by affiliating them to the general principles from which they are derived and on which they rely for their support. 'It was wrong to torture that prisoner depends on the general principle that torturing is wrong.

But what of the conventions for the appropriateness of this general assertion itself? We might follow the pattern of our analysis for empirical general statements and say that the rule prescribes a sufficient condition for its non-assertion, and is broken if we assert the judgment in face of a counter-instance. But this will certainly not do, and the reason why it will not do is instructive. We are always prepared to withdraw a general statement like 'All birds lay eggs' in face of a counter-instance, such as a viviparous bird. But we do not withdraw our moral judgment that torturing is wrong in face of an instance of torture which is not wrong. (At least, the cases where we do are very special.) As we have seen, an instance of 'torture which is not wrong' is not a datum or simple fact of the world, but is itself the application of a general moral principle. So far from being a counter-instance forcing us to withdraw our general moral assertion, it is a situation which we refuse to recognise at all; as long as we adhere to our moral principle, there cannot *be* a counter-instance. (Such a contrast between moral and empirical general statements is illustrated by the well-known story of the professor who refused to look through Galileo's telescope; his refusal to admit a counter-instance to his 'theory' that the number of the planets was seven is more characteristic of moral than of empirical procedure.)

'Torturing is wrong' expresses, among other things, our refusal to admit the possibility of a situation which would force us to withdraw it. Of course we *may* withdraw it, but we are never forced to by the facts. And in practice it is much more likely that we should qualify rather than withdraw. A Utilitarian might hold that, if we became convinced that a certain act of torture produced results that were signally beneficial and far outweighed the victim's pain, we could resort to the qualified principle 'Torturing is always wrong except under conditions C' — but this is no less a universal rule, and it still expresses our resolution to reject any alleged counter-instance which does not fall in the general class of exceptions. (I could not myself adopt this procedure in the case of torturing; in the case of lying I might.) Another expedient is to manipulate the operative word — say 'lying' — and to refuse to call the act 'lying' ('It's not lying, it's just being tactful'), so saving our principle intact by a suitable adjustment of a definition. This procedure has its exact analogy in the case of empirical statements; it would be possible to save the general empirical statement 'All birds lay eggs' in the face of a counter-instance, by suitably redefining 'bird', so that no viviparous creature can be called a bird. (Indeed this may be what the zoologist does.) But then the empirical statement is transformed into a definition.

The rule or convention which we are looking for to guarantee the correctness of a general moral judgment and, in turn, of singular moral judgments, turns out, then, to be identical with the moral principle itself. When I say 'It was wrong to torture that prisoner', the relevant rule which guarantees the appropriateness of the judgment is the general judgment 'Torturing is wrong' which expresses a moral rule. When I say 'Torturing is wrong', the relevant rule for the correctness of this assertion is nothing other than the moral rule which it expresses. We have just seen that general moral assertions have much in common with definitions. The rule governing the correct use of a word is given by a definition; but if we ask for the rule governing the correctness of the statement which forms the definition, this rule can only be the definition itself. Similarly the correctness of a moral verdict can be governed by a moral principle, but if we ask for the rule governing the correctness of the formula expressing this principle, such a rule can only *be* the principle.

Moral rules apply not only to actions but to judgments about actions. The rule in accordance with which I abstain from theft, the rule in accordance with which I condemn another's act of theft, or he mine, and the rule in accordance with which I either pronounce a singular moral verdict, or enunciate a general moral judgment about thieving, are one and the same rule. Such rules are the criteria of correctness in moral discourse, as truth-criteria are in factual discourse.

10. *Actual and Implied Consensus*

Now I wish to argue that, despite appearances to the contrary (p. 72), moral discourse, just because it involves criteria of correctness, presupposes a general agreement, a *consensus*, among moral speakers. We shall, indeed, have to distinguish between an actual and a hypothetical consensus, but so we must in the case of factual language too. When I make a matter-of-fact assertion, say that this pencil is yellow, I make a claim on my hearers' agreement; I appeal to certain truth-rules about statements of this kind, and claim that the truth-conditions are in fact satisfied and that others agree that they are, or would agree if they were suitably placed (near the pencil, not suffering from eye defects, etc.). If I did not wish to make such claims and appeals, I should have to limit myself to saying that the pencil *looks* yellow *to me*. Similarly, when I express a moral judgment, say that a certain act of torture was wicked, I make a claim on my hearers' agreement; I appeal to a moral principle which I expect them to hold too. If I did not wish to make such moral claims and appeals, I should have to limit myself to saying merely that I didn't like it.

Hume makes the point when he says

> The notion of morals implies some sentiment common to all mankind which recommends the same objects to general approbation and makes every man, or most men, agree in the same opinion or decision concerning it. It also implies some sentiment, so universal and comprehensive as to extend to all mankind, to render the actions and conduct even of persons the most remote, an object of applause and censure.[1]

In both cases, of course, my claims may be rejected, my expectations falsified. Assertions may be significant yet false; moral judgments may be intelligible yet perverse. Hume overstates his case by using the word 'implies', as if the actual existence of moral discourse allowed us to infer the actual existence of a universal feeling. The 'implies' should be 'presupposes': moral discourse does not make sense unless moral speakers can count on some sort of support.

[1] *Enquiry Concerning the Principle of Morals*, IX, i.

Both 'factual' and 'ethical' language, then, imply (in this special sense) which I may call an assumption of hypothetical consensus. When I make any factual statement, it seems to be a necessary part of the situation that I can assume that either in these circumstances, or in suitably arranged ones, anyone else would agree in making the statement. Our disposition to speak of truth in ethics rests on our recognising such an assumption about general agreement, just as our disposition to speak of reasoning in ethics depends on an assumption about general agreement as to what counts as a good reason (Chapter IV, pp. 53–5).

But what are these 'circumstances'? It looks like a platitude to say that a statement, 'X is Y', is either agreed to by everybody, or would be if only everyone were placed in suitable circumstances. For it will be easy to make this true by definition: if someone happens to disagree with 'X is Y', we merely say that the circumstances are not suitable. The light is bad, you must be colour-blind. In ethics the objection is still more serious: the platitude is positively dangerous. It seems to be suggested that the only obstacle to universal ethical agreement is unenlightenment. If only people were suitably educated, suitably informed and suitably situated, they would all agree that torture, polygamy, suicide, etc., are wrong. For the objectivists, no doubt, this is no objection, since they are already committed to holding that unenlightenment is indeed the only obstacle to ethical unanimity. But for those who wish to allow for irreducible differences of moral opinion in the world, the statement that people would agree if only they were suitably circumstanced, will seem a truism, and not even a trivial one, because of its dangerous implications. It smacks of intolerance: either you agree with me or you are morally backward.

To see that these unwelcome consequences do not follow, let us look again at the general theory of language on which Hume is relying for his theory of moral language.

> In order, therefore, to prevent those continual *contradictions*, and arrive at a more *stable* judgment of things, we fix on some

*steady* and *general* points of view; and always, in our thoughts, place ourselves in them, whatever may be our present situation.

*Treatise*, III, iii, 1

General language, being formed for general use, must be moulded on some more general views, and must affix the epithets of praise or blame, in conformity to sentiments, which arise from the general interests of the community.

*Enquiry*, p. 186

It were impossible we could ever make use of language, or communicate our sentiments to one another, did we not correct the momentary appearances of things, and overlook our present situation.

*Treatise, loc. cit.*

All these features of language, though here ascribed specifically to moral language, occur even more prominently in fact-stating language. We do not say that the penny is elliptical, even though it presents an elliptical shape to the eye in most if its positions; we do not say that grass is black, though it may appear so in a red light. We adopt what Hume calls 'general points of view' which are so chosen as to be neutral for different observers. In speaking of pennies we speak as observers from a standard viewpoint, located at right angles to the surface of the penny; whatever shape the penny happens to present to the eye, we explain as a deviation from the standard shape according to the laws of perspective. We could have chosen, as our standard shape, any of the other possible shapes ranging from a thin rectangle (the penny seen edgewise) through ellipses of decreasing eccentricity (the penny seen more or less obliquely) to the circle (the penny seen full face). We choose the circle because it proves the most useful for correlating the experiences of different observers in terms of a common language. This is not to deny that a common language could exist with some other viewpoint taken as standard. It only means that in such a case the laws of perspective would have been more complicated. The possibility of language depends only on the choice of *some* standard or other. We do adopt conventions as to standard conditions of observations. In speaking of the colours of things, for instance, we adopt a convention as to standard conditions of illumination, namely, white light above a certain degree of intensity.

Even so, the existence of suitable conventions does not guarantee that all observers will in fact agree. Someone may insist on describing a penny as elliptical, if for instance the conditions are such that all he can make out is a brown shape which he does not recognise as a tilted penny; someone else may refuse to call a green card 'green' even in normal daylight, if, for instance, he is colour-blind. There are abnormal observers claiming to be normal, such as colour-blind persons unaware of their defect; and there are abnormal conditions mistaken for normal ones. Any statment about a material object (the size of a mountain, the shape of a penny, or the colour of a card) always presupposes a consensus of observers, but it is always possible for the presupposition to be false in a particular case. When the Swiss guide was deceived as to the size of Snowdon, the proposition embodied in his mistaken belief (that Snowdon is too high to be ascended in a day) received no support from other observers who adopted a different standard as to viewing conditions, and were able to explain his mistaken estimate in much the same way as the mistake of the man who thought the penny was elliptical would be explained. The adoption of conventions, standards or 'points of view', then, is a necessary condition for the existence of 'general language' — and that is, of *language*. But they do not, of course, suffice to establish actual and complete unanimity among speakers of that language.

And the same is true in moral discourse. Moral judgments are also couched in 'general language', which presupposes a consensus of moralists, just as factual statements presuppose a consensus of observers. Let us see how Hume's general theory of language, explicitly applied by him to moral language in the following passage, is in fact (as its metaphors of 'approach' betray) drawn from a theory of observation-language.

> All sentiments of blame or praise are variable, according to our situation of nearness or remoteness with regard to the person blamed or praised, and according to the present disposition of our

mind. But these variations we regard not in our general decisions, but still apply the terms expressive of our liking or dislike, in the same manner as if we remained in one point of view. Experience soon teaches us this method of correcting our sentiments, or at least of correcting our language, where the sentiments are more stubborn and unalterable. Our servant, if diligent and faithful, may excite stronger sentiments of love and kindness than Marcus Brutus, as represented in history; but we say not, upon that account, that the former character is more laudable than the latter. We know that, were we to approach equally near to that renowned patriot, he would command a much higher degree of affection and admiration.

*Treatise*, III, iii, 1

I shall now re-write this passage, substituting terms referring to material objects for the original ethical terms.

All *impressions* of *size, shape, etc.*, are variable, according to our situation of nearness or remoteness with regard to the *objects observed, described, etc.*, and according to the present disposition of our *bodily organs*. But these variations we regard not in our general *reports, descriptions, etc.*, but still apply the terms expressive of our *sensations*, in the same manner as if we remained in one point of view. Experience soon teaches us this method of correcting our *impressions*, or at least of correcting our language, where the *impressions* are more stubborn and unalterable. A *tree, if close at hand*, may excite stronger *impressions* of *size* and *colour* than *a mountain in the distance;* but we say not, upon that account, that the former *object* is *larger and more brightly coloured* than the latter. We know that, were we to approach equally near to the *mountain*, it would *produce* a much *stronger impression* of *size* and *colour*. Such corrections are common with regard to all the senses. . . .

It is easy to see that the terms of ethics and the terms of epistemology are, for Hume, completely interchangeable within the same general framework, and that this framework is a social theory of language which emphasises the importance of publicly agreed conventions and standards. In speaking of trees and mountains we adopt the convention of public space — the Newtonian three-dimensional continuum in which the size and shape of bodies is constant and independent of their position relative to the observer; we adopt this in preference to the private visual space in which the size and shape of bodies varies according to their position in the field. Quite similarly, in speaking of the moral worth of great men and of personal servants, we adopt the convention of a fixed standard, according to which the value of persons and their actions is constant and independent of their temporal relation (distant or recent past or present) to the assessor; and we adopt this convention in preference to whatever would correspond to private visual space, namely a system of choices in the light of personal preferences and inclinations. What we call objectivity in the former case, we call impartiality in the latter, and impartiality is what justifies us in saying that morality too can be objective. But just as there was no need for three-dimensional public space to be the sensorium of a supreme Observer, as Newton said it was, so there is no need of a supreme Assessor having standards over and above the moral standards we actually adopt. All that matters is that some standard should be adopted, not that it should be any given standard taken as absolute. To quote Hume again:

> When a man denominates another man his *enemy*, his *rival*, his *antagonist*, his *adversary*,[1] he is understood to speak the language of self-love, and to express sentiments peculiar to himself, and arising from his particular circumstances and situation. But when he bestows on any man the epithets of *vicious*, or *odious*, or *depraved*, he then speaks another language, and expresses sentiments in which he expects all his audience are to concur with him. He must here, therefore, depart from his private and particular situation, and must choose a point of view, common to him with others.
>
> *Enquiry*, p. 222

Despite the extreme opposition between Hume and Kant over the place of reason in morality, they are here very close; for Hume's step from 'private situation' to 'choosing a common

[1] Hume, it may be noted, has fallen here into the error of confusing two kinds of utterances, namely, those which express sentiments and those which describe them. To 'denominate a man my enemy' is not to express sentiments, but to state a fact, to describe a man, and to state something, by implication, about my sentiments towards him. An utterance *expressing* these sentiments would be not 'X is my enemy', but 'I hate X!' or (since even this could be a description) 'To hell with X!' This does not, of course, affect Hume's main point.

point of view' corresponds with Kant's step from 'maxim' to 'universal principle'.

It is worth repeating that the difference between my account and Hume's is that Hume tends to suggest that there actually is a consensus of moral principles, while my account requires only that such a consensus is implied or presupposed on any given occasion of moral discourse — not that it actually exists: the implications may be mistaken. No doubt Hume agreed with Butler that there is one uniform standard of morality throughout the world, to which the conscience of mankind testifies, and such a belief can hardly be maintained in the face of the moral controversies of today, and of our knowledge of the dependence of moral codes on social conditions. But Hume is not committed to a belief in uniformity of conscience. When he contrasts the 'language of self-love' with the language of morals, he explicitly says that the moral speaker 'expresses sentiments in which he *expects* all his audience are to concur with him'. And this is true. Such expectations, however, may at any time be disappointed. But moral discourse would be impossible, just as empirical discourse would, if no kind of agreement could be taken for granted at the outset.

Mr. Hare has suggested[1] as an analysis of 'You ought to do X' the following: 'If you do not do X, you will be breaking an "ought"-principle to which I hereby subscribe.' This is entirely in accordance with what I have said about the dependence of singular moral judgments on general moral principles. But Mr. Hare's analysis does not bring out the point that, in saying 'You ought to do X', I am also appealing to a principle which I assume my hearer to adopt too. Even if I say '*I* ought to do X', if I say it aloud and to a listener, I am appealing to something presupposed by the speaker-hearer community. Consequently I should want to add to Hare's analysis and to say 'If you do not do X, you will be breaking an "ought"-principle to which I hereby subscribe, and to which I assume you to subscribe.' Or, if it turns out that my assumption is mistaken, or if I know or suspect in advance that my listener does not subscribe to it, I shall add, in

[1] *The Language of Morals*, p. 191.

effect, 'and which I invite you to adopt'. I shall be prepared for opposition and argument, but argument cannot proceed except on the assumption that agreement can be reached.

11. *A Third Dimension of Universalisability*

The upshot of this long discussion of truth and criteria of appropriateness is that there are both similarities and differences between the criteria of correctness for empirical statements and for moral judgments. Are these similarities close enough to warrant the ascription of truth-values to moral assertions as well as to empirical ones? My view is that they are not; but to say that the similarities, though close, are not quite close enough is very different from saying that they are insignificant or misleading. It is an easy, but false, step from the proposition that moral judgments are not true or false to the proposition that they are meaningless. Our distinction between meaning-criteria and truth-criteria is enough to discredit this step. But in the heyday of the Verification Principle it was frequently taken, because the principle defines meaning in terms of truth; consequently moral judgments, being admittedly not statements of fact, were thought to have been proved strictly without meaning and were dismissed to the limbo of 'emotive' language, pseudo-statements, utterances evincing our own feelings and stimulating those of others. What happened was that, in the interests of eliminating metaphysical statements from philosophy, a criterion of meaning was set up according to which only certain sorts of assertion, especially those occurring in scientific reports and theories, were to be accepted as genuine statements; and since this criterion was supposed to be universal, it eliminated not only metaphysics but theology, aesthetics and ethics as containing nothing but pseudo-statements.

But this was far too drastic. All that follows, from the fact that moral judgments do not satisfy a certain criterion of meaning, is that moral judgments do not have the kind of meaning that satisfies that criterion. They are not scientific statements, but neither are they pseudo-statements. To show how arbitrary this procedure is, we could claim with equal justification to set up a criterion for a genuine moral judgment and then proceed to criticise empirical statements in the light of it. Suppose we said, for instance, that in order for an utterance to be a genuine moral judgment, it must tend to induce a change of attitude in the hearer, and suppose we called such an utterance a 'directive'. Then we could examine empirical statements and ask whether they are directives. We might decide that statements like 'The cat is black' do not have any directive force and therefore are only 'pseudo-directives'. Or we might persuade ourselves that even giving information is a way of altering people's attitudes, so that empirical and theoretical statements are a sort of directive after all. Such a procedure would be clearly absurd. The plain fact is that the functions of language are many and various, and so, accordingly, are its rules and conventions.

Next, it is worth noticing that my 'hypothetical consensus' is involved not only in the assertion of moral judgments, which we have been considering in this chapter, but also in the deployment of moral argument in support of such assertions, which we considered in the last chapter. Ultimately, indeed, the two combine. Disagreement about the reason for a moral decision (cases, that is, where the consensus is found to fail) nearly always involves disagreement about premisses, that is, assertions.

Finally, I want to link up my 'hypothetical consensus' with the doctrine of universality of moral judgments. We have seen (IV, 5) that a moral judgment must be universalisable in two dimensions; and we are now in a position to add a third. A moral judgment must be universalisable, firstly, in the sense that it applies not to a particular action, but to a class of actions; this is involved in the meaning of 'principle' or rule. Secondly, it must be universalisable in the sense that it applies not only to me but to you; not only to you but to me; not only to us but to everybody; this is involved in speaking of *moral* principles as opposed to maxims or private policies. And now thirdly: a moral judgment must be 'universalisable' in the sense that others besides the speaker are assumed to share it. To illustrate: when I say 'It was wrong of you to torment that animal', I must be be prepared to extend my judgment to all cases of tormenting animals (universalisability 1); I must be prepared to apply the principle, not only to give a verdict on your action, but also upon my own, and to come to decisions in the light of it (universalisability 2); and I must expect, or at least invite, assent to the principle on your part, and on the part of an indefinite community of moral beings like ourselves.

*PART II*

# THE MORAL LIFE

*Mankind hath the rule of right within himself.*

JOSEPH BUTLER

CHAPTER VI

# COMMITMENTS AND ISSUES[1]

## 1. *What is the Distinctive Feature of Morality?*

One of the main tasks of philosophy — indeed the only task of philosophy in its synoptic aspect — is the mapping out of the relations between different regions of human activity. Rough-and-ready distinctions between such regions exist in our every-day use of such terms as art, religion, law, science, politics, morality. The philosopher's task is to show the bridges and the barriers that exist between them. To take a simple example, the gist of the Platonic theory of Values is that each of these regions of activity is a region where men are pursuing something which is the same within that region and different in another region. What they are pursuing are Values: Truth, Beauty, Goodness and the like. 'Pursuit of value' is the bridge; the differences between values are the barriers.

Other philosophers have drawn the bridges and the barriers very differently. So far we have been concerned with the bridges between morality and other activities. For instance, the discussion of reason in ethics, and of truth in ethics, were designed to establish bridges between morality and fact-stating discourse, in opposition to certain rival cartographers who have obliterated these bridges and given prominence to others, such as those leading to 'Behaviour in response to stimulus'. But the marking of bridges always leads to a question about barriers. No amount of bridge-building leads to complete integration; and however we emphasise similarities, it always remains to describe differences. Even if moral judgments are very like assertions of

[1] Much of the material of this chapter has appeared in an article, 'Ethics and Moral Controversy', *The Philosophical Quarterly* (Jan. 1954) and is here used by kind permission of the Editor.

fact, they are still different, or, if you like, there are still differences between moral facts and other facts. Even if moral judgments are expressions of feeling, we can still enquire what distinguishes them from other, non-moral, expressions of feeling.

To take examples of philosophers who have adopted these particular bridges: Moore takes moral judgments to be statements of fact, and expresses the difference between moral facts and other facts by saying that moral facts are 'non-natural'. This is, indeed, the only escape for a philosopher who assumes that a word like 'good', because it is an adjective, must therefore stand for a property. It is *like* 'yellow' in standing for a property, but *unlike* 'yellow' in standing for a 'non-natural' property. Ayer, whose bridge was between moral judgment and behaviour-in-response-to-stimulus, dealt with the question 'What characteristic *sort* of behaviour?' by dismissing the question as irrelevant to philosophy and relevant only to psychology.

The question 'What is the distinguishing feature of morality?' is perfectly legitimate, and I shall deal with it by considering the difference between moral principles and other kinds of principle. We have already seen that the characteristic function of morality is the regulation of conduct. We want to enquire how moral regulation differs from other kinds of regulation. What is the distinctive feature of moral rules?

We may briefly anticipate the answer in terms of the notion of consensus discussed in the last two chapters. We have seen that moral discourse, like mathematics and fact-finding, involves a hypothetical consensus among a community of people. We shall now see that, unlike mathematics and fact-finding, it involves a hypothetical dissensus as well.

## 2. *Rules and Regulation*

Rules can be classified on the basis of several features: for instance, the sort of actions they enjoin, or the kind of authority recognised in the regulators. But there is one characteristic of rules which is of special interest for a classification of moral rules. The function of rules is to regulate, and the function of moral rules is to regulate certain parts of human behaviour. But regulated behaviour is different from unregulated behaviour; however much they may happen to coincide, there is a difference of type. People may act as a law prescribes, even though they are ignorant of the law. But people acting in accordance with rules are acting differently from people acting spontaneously, even though outwardly their actions may be precisely similar. (In such a case, the actions might be similar, but the full descriptions of the actions would be different, if one were rule-guided and the other not. To say that an action was performed in accordance with a rule involves telling a longer and more complex story than saying merely that an action took place.)

But even if regulated behaviour sometimes coincides with unregulated behaviour, it cannot always do so. For the point of regulating behaviour is to make it different, in general, from what it would be if unregulated. If unregulated behaviour always coincided with regulated behaviour — if everybody for whom a certain rule is supposed to be in force, behaved just as they would have behaved anyway, even without the rule — then the rule in question would be not merely practically superfluous and due for scrapping; it would be logically redundant. But if it is true that people left to their own devices would not, in general, behave as they would behave in observance of some rule, it seems to follow that the imposition of a rule — the regulation of behaviour — must involve a certain degree of coercion. The coercion may of course be very mild, as for example in the regulation of play by the rules of a game.

This suggests a further basis for the classification of rules. Rules can be classified according to the degree or type of coercion involved in their imposition; or in the degree or type of resistance or opposition to be expected from those who are to be regulated. I shall contend that the distinguishing feature of moral rules is to be looked for by examining this element of resistance or opposition. Moral principles are not merely framed with a view to possible opposition, but are actually created in the process of dealing with opposition. And this means, I shall maintain, that moral controversy enters into ethics very much more deeply than is allowed for by any of the familiar theories.

We saw in the last two chapters that moral discourse involves a 'hypothetical consensus' which nevertheless does not exclude the possibility of moral disputes. We shall now see that the possibility of such disputes is not merely a factor that has to be allowed for, but is actually an essential feature of morality. Morality involves not merely a hypothetical consensus but also a hypothetical dissensus.

### 3. *Moral Philosophy and Moral Controversy*

Moral philosophers often used to write, and some still do, as if people's moral behaviour consisted in ascribing to certain actions, things or states of affairs, certain characteristics connoted by words like 'good', 'right', or 'obligatory'. The primary task of ethics was to analyse these characteristics and their relations with one another. Of course, there were other ethical topics. It was recognised, for example, that people do not merely describe things by means of these ethical words; they are not content with ascribing characteristics: they also act, and they act in ways which are somehow correlated with the ways in which they use the words, or attribute the qualities: they tend to seek the good and avoid the evil, perform acts of self-exertion, try to do what they believe to be their duty, conform to principles, and so on. But the explanation of this was conceived as a secondary task in ethics, allotted, perhaps, to the uncomfortable borderland of moral psychology peopled by motives, inclinations, decisions and acts of willing. And perhaps it was also recognised, more dimly, that people do even more than this: they do not merely seek the good and try to do their duty, but they also recommend the good to others, try to get them to seek it too, try to alter the ethical views of people who disagree with them, and so on. But this was not conceived as the proper object of study for ethics at all.

The result is that a long line of moral philosophers, say from Aristotle to the modern Intuitionists, have failed to treat the occurrence of ethical disputes as anything more than a consequence of people's moral views; or, in other words, they have regarded the analysis of disputes as subsidiary to the analysis of the terms occurring in the disputes. But a more modern school, whose chief exponent is Professor C. L. Stevenson, has made the occurence of ethical disputes an explicit feature of its moral philosophy. The main question I want to ask in this chapter is whether controversy is a peripheral or a central feature in ethics. For Stevenson himself is careful not to commit himself on this question. He tends to say that the examination of typical examples of ethical disagreement is useful for exhibiting the characteristic features and functions of ethical language; but he explicitly states that his first object is 'to clarify the meaning of the ethical terms — such terms as "good", "right", "just", "ought", and so on',[1] and he ostensibly puts agreement and disagreement on the same level, saying that the positive term is to be treated by implication.[2]

I want to question this parity of status between agreement and disagreement. The first step is to formulate a simple statement of a contrasting view. The one I shall adopt is certainly only partially adequate. Its merit lies in drawing more attention to certain comparatively neglected features of moral situations. Its chief limitation is that it confines us to the ethics of regulation. It has less relevance to the ethics of evaluation, and still less to the ethics of inspiration. In a later chapter (Ch. XI), however, I shall try to redress the balance by saying something about these other moralities.

Let us consider, then, the view that all moral matters are controversial matters; the study of ethics is the study of moral conflict; the data for ethical theory are the facts of moral controversy; the incidence of ethical disputes is not a peripheral topic in ethics, it is not even an interesting and illuminating aspect of ethics; it is the whole of ethics.

## 4. *Mill on Ethics and Teleology*

This view finds a limited and indirect support in certain writings of J. S. Mill, which could serve as a starting-point for discussion, although Mill himself would certainly have rejected

[1] *Ethics and Language*, p. 1.
[2] *Op. cit.* p. 2.

the thesis as a whole. In the closing chapter of his *System of Logic*[1] Mill discusses the relation between the sciences and the applied sciences, and brings in the concept of a Teleology or Doctrine of Ends; this he divides into three departments, Morality, Prudence and Aesthetics, or the Right, the Expedient and the Beautiful. Subsequently, in dealing with the point that many people think a scientific training entitles them to say not only what *is* but what *ought* to be, Mill says: 'In this respect the various subordinate arts affords a misleading analogy. In them there is very seldom any visible necessity for justifying the end, since in general its desirableness is denied by nobody, and it is only when the question of precedence is to be decided between that end and some other, that the general principles of Teleology have to be called in.' Thus the absence of controversy about the desirability of, say, curing disease and improving communications suggested to Mill that the occurrence of disputes distinguishes cases where critical teleology has to be invoked from cases where a teleological proposition is merely presupposed and left unquestioned. But this suggestion in turn suggests another, going well beyond Mill: that the occurrence of disputes distinguishes between the various departments of teleology itself, because it is the special concern of one of them, namely morality; it distinguishes the Right from the Expedient and the Beautiful. Morality is not just a department of teleology, but that department which is concerned with controversies. What is right or wrong is always a matter about which there is either an actual controversy or (as I shall argue later) a possible one (in a stronger sense of 'possible' than that of logical non-self-contradiction). This is not to deny that there are disputes about expediency or beauty, but only to deny that the existence of controversy in the fields of expediency and aesthetics is a necessary condition of things being called expedient or beautiful.

### 5. *'Acting on Principle'*

We speak of moral principles and of moral judgments. Neither of these expressions appears to suggest a moral controversy. We

[1] Book VI, Ch. xi, Sec. 6.

tend to assume that there may be a contingent connection, but not a necessary one. For an example of a contingent connection: an actual set of moral principles never in fact forms a wholly self-consistent system, either for an individual or for a society; sooner or later, therefore, we are likely to be faced with a situation in which an action required or permitted by one principle is forbidden by another. Disputes will then arise when one person appeals to one principle and another to the other; perplexity or internal conflict will occur when an individual is faced with incompatible decisions each supported by a principle which he accepts. But the occurrence of such disputes, external or internal, would be a merely contingent fact, depending on the lack of self-consistency in the particular moral system. A perfectly self-consistent system is not logically impossible, and in such a system, it might be claimed, disputes need not, and indeed could not, arise.

Yet there is a sense in which disputes are a necessary (perhaps even a logically necessary) feature of moral principles. To bring this out we must first attend to certain logical peculiarities of words like 'principle' and 'rule'. We say that a person is guided, or fails to be guided, by certain principles. But a person may be said to act in accordance with a principle, or to break a rule, in more than one sense. He may break a rule either deliberately or inadvertently; he may act in accordance with a principle either attentively or inattentively, either conscientiously or accidentally. And there is a third possibility, which applies only to compliance and not to infringement. He may comply with a rule 'dispositionally': that is to say, he may comply because he has the sort of character that disposes him to act in that way, because that is the way in which he always or usually does act in situations of that kind.

This third sort of compliance ought to be of special interest to moral philosophers, because it offers an answer, essentially an Aristotelian answer, to the question: 'What is the relation between good character and good conduct?' The two other sorts of compliance yield unsatisfactory answers. Is a good man one who deliberately makes every action conform to some rule or principle, who always thinks before he acts? Or does this make goodness too formal and unspontaneous? On the other hand, could a man achieve goodness by never thinking at all, if by a providential series of coincidences his actions always happened to coincide with what would be morally right or good? Obviously not. The truth is in between: the good man conforms to moral principles not because he is always thinking about them, certainly not because he happens to conform without thinking, but because he has a disposition towards certain kinds of action, because he always or usually does act in a certain way whether he thinks about principles or not.

But how can the principles be operating, if he is not thinking about them? The answer is that they are not operating. When a person's acting in accordance with a moral principle is of this third sort, as it may well be in the majority of so-called moral actions, a description and explanation of his action can be as adequate as need be without introducing the moral principle itself. What I mean is this. In order to describe and explain the acting, there is no need for any story about a man giving consideration to certain ethical propositions (perhaps with the aid of a faculty called Reason), and somehow translating his intellectual cognisance into practical action (perhaps through the intervention of an organ called Will); there is no need for any specifically moral concept at all, except in the obsolete sense of the word 'moral' in which it meant 'concerned with character or disposition' (*Concise Oxford Dictionary*).

6. *The Creation of Moral Principles*

Now when a moral principle in this (obsolete) sense becomes a *moral* principle (in the current sense) and a moral *principle* (as opposed to a way of talking about someone's character), it is because, as we say, a person has been 'forced to reflect' on his principles. But what I am suggesting is that the principles are not, as it were, there all the time, always guiding his conduct but sometimes reflected on and sometimes not: they are actually created (or re-created) by his 'reflections'. In the intervals between 'reflections' they do not 'guide' his conduct, any more than the rules of arithmetic 'guide' the multiplications of a competent reckoner. But, unlike the multiplication rules, which are not created by being thought about, the moral principles are positively and creatively asserted and affirmed, not merely followed, assented to or recognised. Thus to speak of 'reflections' is both to understate and to misreport the situation: to understate, because creation, affirmation, even self-affirmation, is more than reflection; to misreport, because 'reflecting on' implies the existence of something about which reflection is made, but moral 'reflection' does not involve 'objects' of this sort, is not 'about' anything. In short, moral principles operate only when they are thought about, which is to say that they are either created or re-created by reflection on certain special occasions.

The next point is to ask what these occasions are. It is already suggested that they are occasions when we have to think deliberately about what ought to be done. To go further than this takes us to the main point. The occasion of moral reflection and re-affirmation, and perhaps not merely the occasion but a necessary and even sufficient condition, is always an actual or possible dispute ('possible' in a stronger sense than logical non-self-contradiction).

To bring out both these points, let us consider, as a simple working model, an imaginary social group which is such that no one of its members breaks any rules of conduct or engages in any ethical dispute. Their behaviour, of course, exemplifies my third sort of compliance with rules, neither deliberate nor fortuitous but 'dispositional'. A scientific observer could describe and explain the activities of the group and of its members, however complex, in terms of purely descriptive formulae (tendencies, habits, dispositions, general patterns of behaviour). He would not need any terms like 'rule' or 'standard', still less 'moral' (in the current sense). The function of rules is to make people's behaviour different from what it would be in the absence of the rules; but if people left to themselves always acted in a certain way, there would be no place for a rule to the effect that they *should* act in that way. Our ideal social group would, to the observer, have no morality because it would have no rules;

and it would have no rules because there would be nothing to regulate.

But next suppose that eventually somebody 'breaks a rule'. At this stage such an event could not even be called, strictly, 'breaking a rule' (since there are no rules) but only, say, 'non-conformity to established procedure'. Let us also suppose that the rest of the group object. (Of course they need not do so, but if they do not, the question of morality has not yet arisen.) A new phenomenon would now have appeared: for the members of the group would no longer be merely acting in certain ways, they would be trying to coerce the non-conformist into acting in conformity with those ways, or taking other steps to ensure that the non-conformity should not be repeated; in other words, to re-establish the ways of acting. But in order to take steps to re-establish the ways, they would need to become conscious of them, and of the need to re-establish them. And this is the point at which the observer would need to introduce the concept of a morality: for this is the difference between a mode of behaviour and a principle of conduct. Becoming conscious of the mode of behaviour, in such circumstances, is what makes it a principle of conduct.

### 7. *Actual and Potential Controversy*

But even if this establishes my subsidiary point, that moral principles have to be positively asserted and not merely reflected on, have we yet established the main point, that the occasion for asserting such principles is necessarily a dispute? It might seem that we have to follow our model society to a further stage of moral evolution. There is a stage at which a rule is not merely broken, but deliberately broken. At this stage a moral principle is not disregarded, but is actively challenged and criticised. (Perhaps the most familiar example of this is the Sophist movement in ancient Greece.) Challenging a rule is very different from breaking one. To break a rule is merely to perform an action which the rule forbids. To challenge a rule is to raise the question, whether what the rule forbids *ought* to be forbidden.

It might seem that a dispute, in the proper sense of the term, can only occur at this stage: when, that is, an action which other people condemn on one set of moral grounds is not merely committed by the non-conformist, but is committed and also approved, justified and defended on another set of moral grounds. Disputes only occur when somebody adopts principles which somebody else rejects.

It is probably true that an actual, full-dress ethical dispute would occur only in these circumstances. Nevertheless, the conditions for a dispute are already present in the earlier stage of simple non-conformity. The two stages should not be contrasted, because we are envisaging a controversial situation where the dispute is either actual or possible. The sense in which I speak of a 'possible' dispute will be clarified when I come to deal with moral judgments in Section 12: I shall want to say that the assertion of a moral principle, in the form of a moral judgment, is an act of commitment, not a statement but a declaration, a participation on one side or the other of a moral controversy, actual or possible. What can be said now is this. Although a breach of a moral rule will lead to an actual dispute only if the offender is prepared to defend his action on moral grounds, still a breach always creates the actual conditions for a dispute. People object to moral non-conformity, adopt an attitude of opposition, are prepared to take up the quarrel if the offender should attempt to justify his action. And the principles they would assert, merely in drawing attention to the breach, would be the same as the principles they would assert if they were actually challenged. Conversely, although an actual dispute is not always preceded by an actual breach of a moral rule, still it is always preceded or accompanied by the consideration of a possible breach. If I argue against someone's moral principle, I at least contemplate the possibility of my infringing it, I am prepared to do so; if I argue in defence of my own, I contemplate the possibility of his infringing it.

## 8. *Commitment and Belief*

It is perhaps a commonplace to say that morality involves commitment. Indeed this could be regarded as an example of the bridge-mapping procedure I mentioned at the beginning of the chapter: for we commit ourselves to many things and in many ways outside the field of morality. Reasoning, for example, involves commitment. The acceptance of certain beliefs, formulated as premisses, commits the believer to certain other beliefs which can be formulated as conclusions from these premisses. If I believe that the earth is round, I am committed to another belief about what happens to explorers travelling long enough in the same direction. Closely connected with this is the avoidance of inconsistency; we saw in Chapter IV that universalisation in ethics can be regarded as a function of reason, in the form of consistency. It is inconsistent of me to say that something is wrong for you, if I do not also think that it is wrong for me; and this could be expressed by saying that my moral principle according to which something is right for me commits me to the view that the same thing would be right for you.

However, I want to consider another kind of commitment which, though still paralleled in non-moral thinking, points also to the distinction we require between moral and non-moral thinking. Accepting certain beliefs commits us, in one sense, to the acceptance of certain other beliefs. But what of the original beliefs? It is a commonplace that not every belief can be justified by adducing some prior belief from which it follows; the ultimate premisses of our thinking must stand unsupported by reasons. The theorems of a geometry follow from the axioms, but the axioms do not follow from anything. Accordingly, if we are to have any beliefs at all, there must be some beliefs such that we are not committed to them *by* anything else, we just commit ourselves to them. (This does not mean a jump in total darkness; it means a stance without demonstrably adequate grounds.) The sense in which I wish to speak of moral commitment is the sense in which we commit ourselves to certain fundamental moral convictions. These are the principles beyond which we refuse to be pressed by the questioner who insists on asking 'Why?'

So far, this kind of commitment is common to moral and non-moral beliefs. What is characteristic of moral commitment is that it is commitment *on an issue*. It is what I propose to call 'taking sides'.

## 9. *Taking Sides on Moral Issues*

Moral principles, I have suggested, are in some sense inseparable from the occasion of moral disputes. But they are invoked, or rather reaffirmed and re-created, not only in the heat of moral controversy, but, more important, in preparation for it.

In taking sides either in a competitive game, or in politics, or in a war (to take some obvious examples), we are overtly preparing to take steps, committing ourselves to taking them, to bring something about against opposition: scoring goals, the adoption of a party policy, unconditional surrender. The opposition may be actual or potential. The analogies, however, cannot be pressed very far; in Section 11 I shall indicate some important aspects in which they seem to diverge from the moral situation.

There was a special reason for considering the imaginary social group in the last section — the group in which all the members rallied together against the non-conformist. For this represents the ideal or limiting case of the operation of the moral consciousness. Many actual situations approximate to it fairly closely; in many ethical issues of practical life (though not the most spectacular ones) there is an established set of moral principles which is fairly widely adopted throughout a society; public opinion is fairly unanimous in condemning the delinquent. (This, of course, though roughly true of our own society, would not be true of all possible ones. It would not be true of a society on the brink of a revolution.) But in other cases there is a sharp cleavage. On issues like capital punishment and racial segregation there may well be two sets of opposed principles of fairly equal weight. In still other cases there may be ethical views which are strongly held by small minorities, such as conscientious objectors to military service. But in all these cases those who hold the views hold them in common with others; they are taking sides with a view to action on behalf of their side. Morality involves both consensus and dissensus.

A further reason in favour of this view of morality is that it corrects a prevalent mistake, even if it is itself liable to err in the opposite direction. Emphasis on moral controversy in contemporary writing is often misleading (if not misled) because it tends to be reserved for a special kind of controversy, namely altercation or personal dispute between protagonists. Stevenson's examples, in spite of their impressive variety in other respects, agree in this. Such emphasis is unfortunate for two reasons. First, it draws attention to the way in which disputes are terminated or resolved, rather than to the way in which they get started. Stevenson's examples are alike in that they illustrate the passage from conditions of initial conflict to or towards a state of reconciliation or mutual readjustment. But the initial conditions can be set much further back. Disputes do not occur spontaneously; they occur between people who are already prepared and equipped for them. Disputes are not a contingent consequence of the fact that people hold moral views which happen to conflict; on the contrary, people's moral views just are the ways in which their holders are committed to act or argue in possible controversies. I shall develop this when I come to deal with moral judgments in the next section.

Secondly, the emphasis on altercation as the typical dispute-situation suggests, if it does not imply, an ultra-individualistic morality, in which people have strong views on all moral matters, and strong motives for getting them adopted, or at least considered, by other people. This suggestion of a strong-minded morality is reinforced by an incautious use among philosophers of the family of terms 'imperative', 'command', 'demand', and 'directive'. A typical example is what Reichenbach called his 'democratic principle' and formulated as follows: 'Everybody is entitled to set up his own moral imperatives and to demand that everyone follow these imperatives.'[1] This strong-minded morality has, to say the least, little empirical evidence in its favour. But the question is not, of course, an empirical one, to be settled by a sociological enquiry into people's moral judgment-making behaviour. Rather it is a question of what con-

[1] *The Rise of Scientific Philosophy*, p. 295

cepts to use in discussing such behaviour; and the words belonging to the 'imperative' family require careful handling. Moral language certainly has an imperative function, but this does not mean that moral judgments are commands. Morality is not to be described in terms of setting up directives or making demands. We must speak of accepting standards, subscribing to principles, following recognised ways of acting, acknowledging certain values, espousing causes, and so on — though always in the face of possible or actual opposition. Consequently, controversy enters into ethics not merely in the form of man-to-man altercation but, more important, in the form of commitment to action for or against some publicly recognised object, where the dispute is something that is envisaged but not necessarily engaged in. Ryle, in one of his rare and tantalisingly laconic references to ethics in the *Concept of Mind* (p. 128) says something close to this when he describes moral judgments as 'warrants addressed to any potential givers of behests and reproaches' or as 'licences to give and enforce orders'. What I feel uneasy about in Ryle's suggestion is that it, too, smacks of a strong-minded morality; warrants and licences have to be issued by competent authorities. Perhaps what Ryle means is not that when we make ethical statements we are in the position of people who issue licences, but only that we are in the position of people who quote them. If so, all I should want to add is that holding a licence to command or condemn is being equipped not merely for the giving of behests and reproaches, but also for controversy and dispute with the recipients of our behests and reproaches, as well as with their sympathisers.

## 10. *The Importance of Importance*

A third reason for regarding morality as a matter of taking sides springs from the argument about triviality and importance. Examples in standard ethics textbooks, about borrowed books and unposted letters, are often felt to be unsatisfactory.[1] Are

[1] 'The question whether I shall return a book to the man I borrowed it from, or keep it and deny having borrowed it if he asks me to give it back, raises no serious moral problem.' — R. G. Collingwood, *Principles of Art*, p. 289.

they not, perhaps, a little too humdrum or commonplace to serve as useful examples of genuine moral problems or genuine moral issues? We can agree that a moral problem is necessarily an important problem, that is, one which it is more or less vitally important for me to solve, not one which I can afford to lay aside as too bothersome; while a moral issue is an *issue*, that is, not something about which people can 'agree to differ' but something which they are prepared to 'make an issue of' as we say. And there is a further reason for rejecting the textbook examples. A moral decision, whether it be to comply with a moral principle, or to act in pursuit of some 'focal aim' (Stevenson's phrase), must be a difficult decision. There is of course no answer to the question 'Just how difficult must an action be, if it is to count as a moral action?' But there is a rough-and-ready distinction between difficult and easy decisions which goes with the distinction between acting in pursuit of an important aim and acting in discharge of a routine obligation; it also goes with the difference between principles which we are prepared to uphold at the cost of effort and self-sacrifice, and principles which we are prepared to abandon in the face of moderate inconvenience. To speak in Aristotelian terms, the good is not just what is pursued, but what is pursued against obstacles, and achieved, if at all, by effort; similarly, and perhaps more forcibly, evil is not just what is avoided, but what is avoided in the face of temptations and despite the weakness of the flesh. In these efforts, as Aristotle himself rightly said when speaking of Friendship, we need, unless we are superhuman, fellow-workers or at least well-wishers; in our own idiom, we need 'moral support'. And this we get, in some sense or other, just because our principles are public, even though it may be only to a small minority. But the textbook examples do not bring this out. Even in a roundabout way they lead us only to issues which are not issues at all, such as the general obligation of promise-keeping, payment of debts, avoidance of self-seeking, and so on — matters on which no one takes sides because no one feels strongly about them; and no one feels strongly because no one seriously entertains the possibility of a challenge.

This is not to say that these matters are unimportant; for there is a discrepancy between the notions of importance and of strength of feeling. While an issue on which people feel strongly is always an important issue, at least to the extent that people are prepared for considerable self-exertion to forward a cause, the converse is not true. In many senses of that very ambiguous word 'important', the paying of debts (for instance) is of course important; and to deny this would be to adopt a positive moral standpoint which most people would reject. But although the principle of debt-paying is certainly important, it is not a live issue on which people feel strongly, or on which they are divided into factions, because it is not an issue at all. Again, this is not to say that issues do not arise in connection with debt-paying: although no one makes an issue of the general principle of the repayment of money debts, moral controversy might arise over the admissibility of various kinds of excuse for not paying debts of various kinds; or, again, over debts which are not money debts, but (for example) debts of children to parents, or of parents to children. In the case of promises, too, although no one makes an issue of the general principle of promise-keeping, moral controversy may well arise over the question 'Ought I to keep promise P, in situation S?' where the situation contains a counter-obligation. The moral issue, in such cases, is over the question 'Ought one to keep a promise of type P in a situation of type S?' All I am concerned to point out is that there are some situations in which a principle of conduct is regarded as beyond challenge, while in others it is still a matter of dispute. Text-book example tend to conform to the first type, but it is the second type which brings out the real nature of morality.

## 11. *A Misleading Model*

An analogy between participation in a moral issue and participation in other kinds of issue like wars or competitive games can, however, be seriously misleading. For instance, it might suggest that there must actually exist, in any given society, opposing groups segregated into hostile camps divided by a moral frontier; and that, in adopting a certain moral principle,

I am deliberately choosing to join the group whose members, so to speak, wear the right uniform or fly the right flag. On the contrary, moral partisanship is perfectly compatible with a high degree of actual moral unanimity, even, in fact, with the degree of unanimity envisaged by the classical moral theorists, who certainly underestimated the extent of moral diversity. Hume's morality which 'implies some sentiment common to all mankind': Kant's morality for all rational beings; Butler's morality with its presupposition of uniformity in the deliverances of conscience; it would only be necessary for these philosophers to admit, as in their various ways they actually did, that common human sentiments can be ignored in action, rational beings can behave irrationally, conscience's voice may fall on wilfully deaf ears, and so on: such offences would already be enough to constitute the challenge to established morality which (as I suggested in Section 6) creates the conditions for the assertion of moral principles. The modern philosophers who criticise the assumption of moral unanimity in Hume, Kant and Butler are thinking of opposition to a given morality as deliberate as well as impulsive. The difference is only that, in their case, moralists are regarded as taking sides against actual opposition and not merely potential opposition.

To bring out the complexity of the opposing groups, and the futility of the 'camp-and-frontier' model, it is necessary to postulate a different pair of opposing groups for every distinct moral principle. It may be the case that in practice a number of moral principles form a coherent system, so that a person who adopts principle P will always in fact adopt principle Q and never principle R. In some cases these coherences and incompatibilities will be of a logical nature; for example, a Conscientious Objectors' Tribunal might hold that a person cannot, in logical consistency, allow himself to be employed by an armaments firm and object to military service. But even if some moral principles logically entail others, yet, in the first place, it is certainly not the case that any given morality must consist of logically interdependent principles. Even if two principles are in fact shared by everyone we may know of, it still remains possible for someone to adopt the one and reject the other, that is, to regard them as logically independent. Secondly, even if some moral principles logically entail others, yet, except in the simplest cases, opinions may differ on the question whether a principle is or is not entailed by some other principle; so that we may have to allow for people refusing to commit themselves to principles to which others regard them as logically committed by their espousal of other principles. In short, we must postulate different pairs of opposing groups for each distinct principle, whether logically independent or not.

There remains a rather obvious question. Who are the people with whom and against whom we take sides on a moral issue? According to the 'camp-and-frontier' model, they would be actually enumerable. But this is not so. Our supporters cannot be enumerated, since they are definable only in terms of the particular moral principle concerned. We usually know, to be sure, that certain enumerable persons do share our views. But if we regard ourselves as forwarding the cause of a particular group, our actions and judgments will no longer be of the moral kind: which follows, in any case, from the Kantian thesis, here adopted, about the necessity of universalisation in moral judgment.

I have already suggested that adopting a moral principle is not deliberately choosing to join a faction. It is certainly not true that people first have moral views and then take sides with others who share their views, or that people take sides with certain other people because they hold similar views to their own. On the contrary, holding certain views and being on one side of a controversy are inseparable aspects of a person's morality. Politics provides an analogy here, for the same feature is found in that field, where it is perhaps more easily detected. When we say that a man is a Conservative, we mean both that he holds certain political views and that he sides with other people who hold similar views; but we do not mean that he sides with them in consequence of their holding views similar to his; on the contrary, his holding certain views and his taking sides with certain people are inseparable aspects of his being a Conservative. Similarly in ethics we should not speak of people holding moral views and naturally or consequently associating with others who share them; the association is not natural and contingent but logical and necessary. Having a moral principle is being on a side, and, as I try to show in the next section, stating it is putting oneself on that side.

## 12. *Moral Judgments as Acts of Commitment*

So far I have not said much about moral judgments. But if moral principles function in the way I have described, there will be a related function for moral judgments. There is a difference between being on one side of a controversy, and putting oneself on that side. This is the difference between being ready to exert oneself in certain ways, and making it clear to other people (or to oneself) what are the ways in which one is ready to exert oneself. Morality involves not merely participation in a struggle, but commitment to participation. Moral judgments are acts of commitment — and re-commitment.

When I say that a certain course of action X is wrong, I am certainly not (or not merely) giving vent to my feelings, as the primitive Emotive Theory used to claim; I am not (or not merely) expressing my disapproval of X, as a more sophisticated Emotive Theory has held. The very least that I am doing, even if I am also 'expressing' something, is committing myself to a future policy with regard to X. I am, for example, disclosing my readiness to avoid X myself, to resist any inclination towards X, to condemn it on other occasions, to reproach those who have done it and to deter those who propose doing it, to deplore its historical instances, to try to secure other people's disapproval, and so on. But this list of possible actions, which can be continued indefinitely, is not a list of personal resolutions. I am not announcing, not even in a very general way, what I intend or propose to do in certain future contingencies, though I am certainly doing something which entitles others to rely on my future actions, in those contingencies, being of a certain sort. In a rather similar way, though a much simpler one, my wearing a shirt of a certain colour entitles others to predict that I shall try to cause a ball to move in certain directions and not others.

When I say that X is wrong, I commit myself to the kind of policy with regard to X to which others have committed themselves who have also said that X is wrong.

Now it may be that no one else has ever said that X is wrong. In that case I shall indeed be an example of that strong-minded moralist whose appearances, as I have suggested,[1] are comparatively rare. To what extent such cases do occur is a difficult question. It is often argued that what we call moral progress is possible only if and when they do occur. And if and when they do — if I am the first, and (for the time being) the only person to hold that X is wrong, it seems obvious that I cannot be taking sides with anyone. Not, at least, with any actual people. But if the opposition on a moral issue may be potential as well as actual, as I suggested in Section 7, then so may the defence. But I should not press this, because the question: 'What about the first person to say that X is wrong?' does not seem to me to be at all a crucial question for ethics. Take the issue of slavery: the question suggests that some one individual, as a matter of 'historical' but unrecorded fact, first formulated the moral judgment that slavery is wrong. And such a suggestion seems to conceal a theory which bears a strong family likeness to theories about a 'social contract'. Certainly in cases which concern us practically, the rightness or wrongness of X is not a personal discovery (thought it may well be a personal conversion — which is different). It is an issue, already in the air, with people and their arguments already marshalled for and against; and in making my own contribution in the form of a moral judgment, whether supported by argument or not, I come in on one side or the other.

One advantage of this account is that it helps to remove a certain air of paradox about our analysis of 'right'. So far, I have suggested that 'right' means the same as 'not wrong', since to be in accordance with a principle means to be not contrary to it.[2] This may strike us as unplausible, since 'right' seems to be a word of praise, while 'not wrong' is merely a witholding of

[1] P. 108.
[2] P. 31. The point is further developed in XI, 5.

blame. Indeed it may be pointed out that the colloquial expression '*all* right' does duty for 'not wrong', and is quite different from 'right'. But this is misleading. 'All right' is very seldom used in moral contexts at all. I ask the boss if it will be 'all right' to take the afternoon off. But if I raise a moral issue, such as taking the afternoon off without permission, then I ask not whether it is 'all right', but whether it is *right* to do so. If I say of someone else that it was 'all right' for him to take the afternoon off, then I imply that he had somebody's permission to do so. But if I say that it was right to take the afternoon off (without anyone's permission), then I do not mean that he did something of positive value which 'right' expresses but 'all right' does not. What I do is to shift the discussion from a non-moral context to a moral one; and to imply that there are circumstances (such as illness) which defeat a verdict of (morally) 'wrong', irrespective of what the boss might say or think. But in order for a verdict to be defeated, there must have been a verdict. 'Wrong' is thus logically anterior to 'right'. Just as in saying that X is wrong, I oppose myself to anyone who practises X, so, in saying that X is right, I oppose myself to anyone who says that X is wrong.

### 13. *Commitments and Fulfilments*

How does the relation between the moral agent and the moral judge fit into this? When a man decides that he ought to do X, acting as a moral agent, it is essential to the ethical nature of the situation that he makes a universal judgment: anyone else, in the same relevant circumstances, would be under the same obligation to do X. Conversely, when a man approves of another man's action as right, acting as a moral judge, it is essential to the case that he includes himself in the universal judgment; it would be equally right for him if he were in that situation. An agent, when acting, puts himself in the position of a judge, and a judge, in judging, puts himself in the position of a possible agent.

Now the agent's considered action and the spectator's judgment are both acts of commitment or re-commitment. People take sides on moral issues, and commit themselves to certain ranges of action in certain possible contingencies. Some contingencies call for personal action, others for comment and criticism. But both the action and the comment, when they occur, themselves function as further acts of commitment. They reaffirm and perpetuate what we call the person's moral principles or moral views on the subject in question.

Of course, there are differences in the way moral decisions and moral judgments function as acts of commitment. For instance, while a moral judgment is, generally speaking, unambiguous, it is often difficult or impossible to tell from a person's action in a particular case in what way he has committed himself, or whether he has committed himself to anything. It may even be objected that a moral decision need not be an act of commitment at all, since a commitment is something public, while many of our moral decisions are made and executed privately. The answer to this objection is that moral commitments do not require external witnesses: we may be our own witness; we affirm our principles to ourselves, we commit ourselves in our own eyes.

But there is still the difference between judgments and decisions. It is tempting to say that a moral judgment just is an act of commitment, while a moral decision is an act of commitment only if it is accompanied by a moral judgment. But this will not do, for we hold that a moral decision is always accompanied by a moral judgment. What we have to say, I think, is that a moral judgment is indeed an act of commitment, while a moral action is both an act of commitment and, more importantly perhaps, an act of fulfilment. It is not merely committing oneself to something, but doing something that one is committed to. Sometimes, indeed, 'actions speak louder than words': for example, resignations. Such an action is called a 'gesture'. For both gesture and spoken language can be used not only to convey information, but also to commit oneself on an ethical issue.

CHAPTER VII

# THE NATURE OF MORAL PROBLEMS

## 1. *Kinds of Moral Problem*

The difference between a moral issue and a moral problem is that the first involves an open dispute between different moralists, each of whom adopts a different set of principles, while the second is a kind of internal dispute in which a man is, as it were, divided against himself. For the sake of simplicity, we shall assume that in either case the difficulty is about what ought to be done; that it is a question of decision, not of passing judgment on something already done. A moral problem has to do with an individual decision, and a man is 'in two minds' how to decide. We shall have occasion to examine at length the implications of this suggestion that there are 'parts of the soul', an ancient doctrine which receives its most powerful support from the facts of moral perplexity.

Moral problems are of different types, and it is not always easy to decide to which type a given case belongs. To take some obvious differences. In the first place, a man may not know what moral principle to adopt; he may have become acquainted for the first time with a class of cases outside his previous moral experience, and he requires a moral principle, or a set of principles, in order to deal with them. Now we have seen that moral principles belong, in an important sense, to a community rather than to an individual, and he may accordingly have the requisite moral principle at hand in the general moral lore of his society, other members of which have experienced the cases in question and formulated moral principles accordingly. But it may happen that the cases are altogether new and the requisite moral principles are totally lacking. A situation approximating to this might have been the problem of dealing with 'war criminals' in 1945.

Secondly, a man may have difficulty in coming to a moral decision in a particular case because, although he has the requisite principle, he does not see how to apply it, or because another principle seems to conflict, in this case, with the first. The problem of the conscientious objector to military service is usually of this type. Thirdly, a man may have come to a moral decision, but finds it difficult to carry out. An example of this would be the man who cannot bring himself to carry out an unpleasant task which he recognises to be his duty.

We can distinguish between these three cases according to the kind of assistance that would be appropriate in each of them. The third man needs fortification or encouragement. The second man needs advice or reasoning. But what the first needs is something like a sermon.

We can also distinguish the three cases according to the kind of verdict that we should pass, as critical spectators, in the event of failure; that is, by noticing the three different ways in which it would be possible to go wrong, to fail to solve one's moral problem. The third man is in danger of failure through 'failure of nerve' or some other weakness; his moral principle and his moral decision may be irreproachable, yet he fails because his decision is not executed. The second man is in danger of coming to a wrong moral decision, not because his moral principles are at fault, but because he has failed, through lack of insight or discrimination, to apply them correctly to the situation as it is. The first man is in danger of failing through adopting a wrong moral principle, or none at all.

These three different ways of going wrong on the part of the moral agent will be discussed in more detail in the next chapters. It must be emphasised at once that the distinction between them is a strictly logical one and, from the point of view of actual practical life, somewhat artificial. Very few actual moral problems lend themselves to a straightforward classification into one of the three types; in practice they will be found to involve a combination of two or more. But as a theoretical model for the understanding of moral perplexity, the three types are indispensable.

## 2. *Moral Problems and Personal Problems*

It may be questioned whether a problem of the third type is a *moral* problem at all. It is plausible to suggest that a moral problem must be concerned with coming to a decision, and not with any practical difficulties which may supervene when it comes to carrying out the decision. Indeed this is supported by what we have said about the place of reason in morality. One can give reasons for or against any moral decision; we saw that a decision for which no reason can be given cannot be a moral decision. ('Reason' here includes the procedure of referring the decision to a moral principle which may not itself admit of further supporting reasons.) But one cannot give reasons for doing or not doing something, over and above the reasons one has already given for *deciding* to do that something. Whatever difficulties may intervene between decision and action, they are not difficulties which attention to reasoned advice or argument tends to diminish. Rather they are psychological obstacles. The process from principles to decision is a logical one; but the process from decision to action is not; it is a psychological one.

A person may be convinced that he ought morally to befriend and assist someone whom he happens to dislike, and he may find it extremely difficult to take the requisite steps. If he fails to take them, a critic is likely to ascribe his failure not to moral blindness but to a defect of character, to weakness of will, a personal failing. And so, it may be suggested, the problem, of which this failure is an outcome, is a personal problem rather than a moral one. The moral problem ends with the decision; thereafter one may or may not have a personal problem on one's hands, according as one is weak or determined, timid or resolute.

This suggestion that we should separate personal problems from moral ones has a good deal of force. All the same, it must be resisted, because the result of following it would be to cut ourselves off from a good deal that is interesting and important in moral philosophy. It would be, in effect, to draw a sharp line between ethics and psychology; but the sort of question which we took, at the outset, as characteristic of an ethical enquiry — namely, 'How is it possible for the acceptance of certain moral truths to make a difference to our behaviour?' — demands a bridge, and not a gap, between ethics and psychology. Ethics is not a self-contained discipline, as those who confine it to the analysis of moral discourse seem to think. It must take account of extra-linguistic factors, such as the characteristics of human beings which make it easy or difficult for them to execute the decisions to which reason and discourse may have led them. It must also be capable of contributing to a wider study, the philosophy of human nature; and later in this chapter we shall see how a major theme in classical philosophy originates at just this point, the problem of connecting moral decision with moral action. And finally, even if personal problems are indeed distinct from moral problems, those personal problems that crop up in moral contexts tend to be of such a striking sort, and are so difficult to isolate from such contexts, that we cannot relegate them to a different study.

### 3. *A Specimen Problem Analysed*

As an example of the complexity of a typical moral problem, I shall consider various interpretations, all plausible but very different, of the moral problem presented in the story of Mr. Coward's play, *Brief Encounter*.[1] A situation presented in a story is necessarily, of course, simpler than a real-life situation, if only because the limited resources of language compel the writer to select certain features and ignore others. A real-life moral problem, then, might well be still more complex than the one in our example.

The story is about the love-affair of two married people on the verge of middle-age, and is told by the woman, Laura. She is happily married to Fred, who is affectionate but dull. They have two children. On her weekly expeditions to the local

[1] Selected as the central topic for a series of talks and discussions organised by the University of Birmingham, 1952. I am indebted to several speakers in the series.

market town she meets Alec, a doctor, who is also married. They fall in love and continue to meet clandestinely. After a series of crises, in the course of which they narrowly avoid adultery and contemplate going away together, they decide to part. Laura comes near to suicide, but eventually returns to Fred, who has suspected nothing.

A religious moralist might say that this is an example of a person who is exposed to the temptations of the flesh, but vanquishes them perhaps with the aid of spiritual guidance, in obedience to the seventh Commandment.

Another moralist might classify the alternative courses of action under some convenient abstractions, such as fidelity and affinity, and describe a conflict between the two ending in the victory of fidelity.

A metaphysical philosopher might interpret the conflict more generally as a problem of choice among values, among which would be numbered happiness, truthfulness and kindliness.

A social philosopher might wish to look behind statements of value or judgments of right and wrong, and to explain Laura's problem as the outcome of social pressures acting contrary to personal inclinations.

An anthropologist might emphasise the dependence of the moral judgments on the type of conjugal relationship taken as normal in a particular culture-group.

Finally an analytic philosopher might wish to emphasise the distinction between personal problems and moral problems, in accordance with the suggestion I considered in Section 2; he might suggest that there is really no moral problem at all in *Brief Encounter*; that Laura knows all the time that she ought not to commit adultery or suicide (the fact that she does not *say* so is irrelevant, for knowing what one ought to do can be a matter of conducting oneself in a certain way, and is not necessarily a matter of uttering moral judgments). She knows what she ought to do, but her inclinations and aversions make it difficult for her to do it; but this (according to our analyst) is a personal problem and not a moral one; it would have been just the same sort of problem, if the policy she has difficulty in following had not been a moral policy at all, but something she wished to achieve or avoid on quite different grounds: for example, the (hygienic) policy of regular visits to the dentist.

All these interpretations agree in referring to a conflict or issue, but they differ in their further analysis of this supposed conflict in Laura. The first three interpretations also agree in speaking of values or laws determining our moral decisions; the social philosopher goes behind these and explains their practical effect on conduct by the dynamic hypothesis of social pressures; the anthropologist emphasises the relativity of such values and norms as conditioned by social institutions.

But none of this is quite sufficient to characterise the conflict in Laura, and for this purpose the distinction between moral problems and personal problems, proposed by the analytic philosopher, must be considered. It is, of course, too wildly paradoxical, as it stands, to say that there is *no* moral problem in the story at all. But some distinction is needed. Consider three possibilities of conflict between duties and inclinations. (These words are to be regarded as mere abbreviations for 'what we ought to do' and 'what we want to do' respectively.)

(1) An inclination to play tennis may conflict with another inclination to sleep in a deck chair. The problem here, such as it is, could not be called anything but a personal problem.

(2) A duty to tell the truth may conflict with a duty to avoid unnecessary suffering. The problem here is without any doubt a moral problem.[1] But

(3) A duty to befriend and assist a certain person may conflict with a disinclination for that person's company. Is this a personal or a moral problem? It will not do to say that it resembles (1) — and is therefore a personal problem — because there is a conflict of inclinations here too, only one of them happens to be the inclination to do one's duty. This will not do, because it violates the essential distinction between knowing that one ought to do something and wanting to do something; whatever prompts us to do our duty, even against inclination, is not another inclination. What it is, will be discussed in detail

[1] Considered in detail at IV, 3.

later (Sec. 11–13). In the meantime, we can perhaps classify our three conflicts by reserving 'personal problem' for the first; allowing 'moral problem' for the third; and introducing a new term 'ethical problem' for the second, in which there is a genuine ethical issue irrespective of any difficulties about executing a decision.

The classification is still not quite satisfactory, because it seems to leave no room for the kind of problem, hinted at by our *Brief Encounter* analyst, in which one has difficulty in translating into action a decision which is not a moral decision, but, say, a prudential one, such as the decision to visit a dentist. This kind of problem can be accommodated by temporarily extending (or, rather, reverting to the old-fashioned sense of) the term 'moral'. Failure to execute a moral decision (in the narrow current sense) through weakness, timidity, etc., is a manifestation of a defective character; the difficulty is, as we say, temperamental. But so is failure to execute any decision whatever — at least, any decision arrived at rationally. And conversely, the ability to carry out such decisions, whether moral (narrow sense) or non-moral (such as the decision about the dentist) is the mark of a different temperament, and on the whole a laudable one. It is through character or temperament, once the main subject-matter of 'morality', that practical knowledge and practical decisions fail or succeed in altering behaviour. And this is the point where ethics must both borrow from, and contribute to, the general philosophy of human nature.

4. *Moral Language and (Un)philosophical Language*

So far, much of our enquiry has been about moral language, that is, about the kind of language that we use in giving moral advice or in formulating our moral decisions. Giving advice and formulating decisions are linguistic activities, and a linguistic study is essential to their understanding. But responding to the advice or the decisions is not a linguistic activity. In studying this part of moral behaviour, therefore, the analysis of moral discourse will not take us very far. We shall still be concerned to a great extent with questions of language; but it is language of a very different sort. Instead of studying the language which moralists use, we shall be studying a descriptive language which has been bequeathed to us, enriched and also distorted by ancient philosophical theories — the language in which we talk about human behaviour in general and moral behaviour in particular. In terms of the three-tier model with which I proposed to illustrate the nature of philosophy (I, 6), the language of morality itself occurs mainly on the second level, that of the moral judge or spectator; what occurs on the lowest level is not language but action. But the language in which we talk *about* morality and moral behaviour belongs to the third level of the philosopher. This is not to say that all talk about morality is philosophical. But even our unphilosophical talk about people's behaviour often involves concepts which raise awkward philosophical questions, or are themselves embodiments of the philosophical wisdom — or unwisdom — of earlier ages. One big difference between moral language proper, or second-level language, and this third-level language, is that our job was to study, analyse and display the workings of the one, but we shall need to criticise, correct and improve the other.

5. '*Self-Control*'

Perhaps the most prominent constellation of philosophy-provoking and philosophy-embodying concepts in everyday discourse occurs in just the context we were considering, namely the situation where a man has difficulty in carrying out a moral (or, for that matter, a non-moral) decision, and either succeeds or fails to act accordingly. At the centre of this constellation is the concept of *self-control*, and very close to it is the metaphor of *conflict* (which cropped up so irresistibly in the discussion of *Brief Encounter*). Our everyday use of these concepts is perfectly unembarrassed. We speak frequently and quite intelligibly of the exercise of self-control, of a man controlling himself or bringing himself to do something; or, alternatively, of a failure of self-control, of letting his temper get the better of him, of being tempted to act against his better judgment, of being a slave to drugs or unable to master his craving for alcohol or money or power. All this seems perfectly transparent good sense, and we seem to know just what sort of conduct in other people, or just what sort of experiences of our own, we are talking about. But on second thoughts we may be puzzled about this sort of talk, and many of the great philosophers certainly have been, notably Aristotle, Hume and Kant.

What sort of 'control' is this? Plato shrewdly remarked that if a man is really master of himself, then he must also be a slave of himself, which is absurd. So we are driven to ask 'What controls what?' Some of the examples suggest that it is the man who controls things like anger, lust or ambition. But what sort of control is this? It cannot be the sort of control which a man exercises over his motor-car. Anger, lust and ambition are not remotely like bits of machinery equipped with levers which the man operates or fails to operate. They are something internal to the man himself. And so we are driven to the examples which speak not of a man controlling himself or a part of himself, but of part of the man controlling another part of the man. Judgment or reason or intellect are what control or fail to control things like anger, lust or ambition. To revert to the 'conflict' of duty versus inclination, duty wins or loses according as the sense of duty is in control or not.

This is the basis of Plato's doctrine of the Parts of the Soul;[1] since there are such conflicts, there must be different agencies at work in the psyche. It is also the basis of Aristotle's further elaboration[2] of the doctrine: since a man can know what is right and yet not do is, there must be both rational and irrational elements in the soul; yet, because very often a man does do what is right just because he knows it to be so, there must be some internal connection between the parts.

### 6. '*Reason*' and '*Passion*'

I propose to call the two elements involved in this division by the names Reason and Passion. The names are taken from Hume's ethical theory, and call for some explanation. So far we

[1] *Republic*, 435–40.
[2] *Nicomachean Ethics*, I, xiii.

have spoken of reasons and reasoning, but not much of Reason. Reason may be understood as a compendious way of referring to a person's capacity for deducing conclusions, avoiding inconsistency and weighing evidence; but (as we noted in connection with Kant's theory) it is often understood not merely as a capacity, but as a positive agency in the human psyche. This tradition we owe largely to Plato and Aristotle.

The word 'passion' I use in a sense which is unfamiliar today. In its original sense it was an exact translation of a term in Aristotle's moral philosophy, *pathos*; and this sense it retained in English (as in Hume's *Treatise*) until, as I suspect, it was finally corrupted by the film industry. According to the old meaning of 'passion', as Aristotle and Hume used it, there were very many different passions; according to the film industry, there is only one, namely the sexual one. A similar narrowing-down of a generic concept to a specific one — again with a sexual connotation — occurred somewhat earlier with the concepts of 'virtue' and 'vice'. In Victorian English 'virtuous' meant 'chaste', and both have now practically disappeared, to the great detriment of moral philosophy, which cannot afford to dispense with 'virtue'. As for 'vice', this can no longer be used to mean a general moral defect, on account of its strong association with homosexuality and noxious drugs.

This drastic narrowing-down of the sense of 'passion' is deplorable, because it was an admirable and useful word for which there is now no substitute, at any rate in ordinary speech (there may be in psychological jargon). What I mean by a 'passion', in this old-fashioned sense, is simply whatever activates us when we act, as we say, 'on impulse'. Indeed, 'impulse' is perhaps the nearest we can now get to this sense of 'passion'. Examples of 'passions' are anger, fright, joy, lust, envy. What is characteristic of such 'passions' is that they lead, if unchecked, to the sort of actions which we call 'impulsive' and which, in fact, we often do check. An immediate response to anger might be a blow; to fright, a scream; and so on. Yet we sometimes, perhaps often, succeed in witholding the blow, in suppressing the scream, even though we experience the 'passion' of anger or fright.

A passion, then, is something which, if it were operating alone, would issue in an action which does not in fact always ensue. Therefore, it seems, there must be something else operating as well, something which holds the passions in check and either prevents them from issuing in action altogether, or else modifies the ensuing action in a certain way. Very commonly this inhibiting effect occurs when the agent is 'thinking what he is doing' and fails when he is 'not thinking'. Very commonly, again, such 'thinking' may take the form of attending to reasons for or against acting in a certain way. Accordingly the inhibiting agent is plausibly identified with Reason. In cases where the 'passion' is one which issues not in action, but in inaction (such as fear, in some cases) the contrary principle must be a stimulating one rather than an inhibitor. Reason and Passion, then, are the two agencies or principles supposed to be related in such a way as to explain the obvious facts (1) that we do abstain from doing things which we feel strongly impelled or inclined to do, and (2) that we do succeed in doing things which we feel strongly disinclined to do. The difficulty is to say just what the relation between Reason and Passion is.

### 7. *Classical Puzzles and Classical Paradoxes*

The classic philosophers thought it must be some kind of control, a view which is still embedded in our unphilosophical language. But the problem of saying what sort of control it was, presented itself very differently, according to the place which these two elements (Reason and Passion) already held in certain philosophical systems. For the Greeks, Reason was very important; Plato called it the divine element in man, and Aristotle made it the defining characteristic of humanity. So for the Greeks the question tended to present itself in the form 'How is it possible for Reason to fail to control Passion?' This question came to a head with the famous paradox attributed to Socrates, that 'No man does wrong knowingly'; and it was the challenge of this paradox that helped to shape Aristotle's theory of moral psychology, in the Nicomachean Ethics.

For the seventeenth-century European philosopher, Reason

was still very important, as it was for Descartes; but the rise of British empiricism, and particularly the empirical approach to psychology, caused a great change of attitude towards the concept of reason. It is a difficult concept to clarify in terms of an empirical psychology. And for Hume, the question of the relation between Reason and Passion presented itself in just the opposite way to the Greeks' version. It was 'How is it possible for Reason to exercise control over Passion at all?' This question, in turn, came to a head with an equally famous paradox, that reason is the slave of the passions and cannot pretend to any other office than to minister to them; and it was the challenge of *this* paradox that helped to shape the moral philosophy in Kant's *Groundwork*.

8. *Facts and Metaphors*

Now a question which is formulated in terms of 'parts of the soul' can only be answered by a doctrine of 'parts of the soul'. But perhaps the question is wrongly formulated in the first place; perhaps it already embodies a mistaken philosophy. I shall suggest that if we can trace the way in which the language of 'control' and 'conflict' has developed, we may be able to take these metaphors for what they are, and see how alternative locutions, and perhaps better ones, could be devised for describing the same facts.

What are these facts? First, the simple ones. We know what it is like to feel an impulse to do something (a 'passion', in my sense), and we believe more or less confidently that other people feel the same. We recognise the symptoms of anger and fright in other people, even when no action ensues, such as swearing or screaming. And when we say that somebody screamed because she was frightened, or swore because he was angry, both kinds of event, the screaming and the fright, are to some extent open to inspection, and we have no need to resort to metaphors or analogies in describing these facts.

But there is another set of facts which is not so easy to describe. We know that people can exhibit genuine symptoms of fright, and yet not scream or run away; or all the symptoms of anger, yet not explode into violent language or action. We know that we ourselves can feel a strong impulse to act, and yet not act on it. And we must describe these facts in a way which will distinguish them satisfactorily from the other facts. We feel forced to say that some factor is present here which was not present there. But what factor can this be? And if we decide that it is Reason, what is its mode of operation? This is where the notion of 'control' provides such a useful metaphor, analogy or model. It seems to have just the features required. Control in the literal sense has two characteristics which seem to be exactly paralleled in the Reason-Passion situation. Control involves, firstly, some specific activity or set of activities which are more or less persistent or self-maintaining; and, secondly, some specific means of modifying the activity (including its origination and cessation) in accordance with the wishes of the controller. The standard activity of a motor-car, for instance, is to move persistently in a straight line, and the purpose of the controls is to enable the driver to modify this activity in accordance with his wishes. He turns the steering wheel in order to make the car go round a corner, and he presses the footbrake in order to introduce a deceleration. These are ends he wishes to achieve, and they consist in modifications of the original activity, brought about by the exercise of bodily power.

Similar features can be found in human conduct. Impulses and passions just do produce their characteristic responses if they are left to themselves, just as the driverless car plunges straight ahead. The life of automatic response to impulse corresponds to the standard activity of the motor-car. But we do not wish to live the life of automatic response to impulse, any more than the driver wishes to leave the moving car to its own devices. Moreover, we often succeed in not living that kind of life, just as the driver often succeeds in not being transported in that kind of motion. Further, just as the good driver is more successful than the bad one in making a car do what he wants it to do, rather than what its engine, transmission and road conditions alone would make it do — though the best driver in the world cannot make it do exactly what he might like it to do — so in the matter of conduct some people are more successful than others in achieving a life other than the life of automatic response to impulse — though here too no one achieves perfection. And so the analogy fits only too well. We cease to think of it as an analogy, or of the language as metaphorical. And when we begin to ask what corresponds to the motorist and what to the car; where to look for the intervening machinery; what controls and what is controlled; then we are puzzled because we have already become slaves to our metaphor.

9. *A Para-Political Myth*

So far I have suggested that there is only one sort of control, which supplies our metaphors. But there are really at least two sorts, and our approach to the problem of Reason and Passion varies according to which sort we have in mind. Modern philosophers, such as Hume, tend to think in terms of mechanical control. My example of the motorist is typical of our machine age. But the ancient Greeks had no machinery, and their philosophers were precluded from using mechanical analogies. The sort of control they had in mind when they discussed our problem was not mechanical control at all. It was political control.

Political control is exercised not over machines but over other men. Even today, though we may think more readily of mechanical control, our language is still richer in the more ancient political metaphors than in the more recent mechanical ones. We 'yield' to temptation, or we 'overcome' it; we 'master' a craving; we 'listen' (or refuse to listen) to Reason; we experience a 'conflict' between the 'claims' of reason and desire; our desire 'gets the better of' our judgment; we recognise, or reject, the 'authority' of conscience: all these familiar expressions are borrowed from political (and a few from military) language. We do indeed have a few words like 'outweigh', 'preponderate' and 'counteract', which can be used in similar contexts and are borrowed from the language of mechanics, but they are outnumbered by the earlier intruders from the language of politics. As Ryle has put it,[1] the 'para-mechanical myth' of the Cartesians

[1] '*Concept of Mind*', p. 23; also *Dilemmas*, p. 64.

about the human mind superseded the 'para-political myth' of the ancients and medievals; but the more ancient myth is still firmly embedded in our language.

Political control has the same features as mechanical control which form the basis for an analogy with human conduct. The standard activity of the subject-matter on which political control is exercised is, of course, the ordinary unregulated behaviour of human beings; by 'unregulated' we must understand 'subject to no external regulation'. A political controller, that is, a ruler, exercises control because he wishes, and is able, to modify this unregulated behaviour on the part of his subjects. His methods involve the familiar organs of government: commands, laws, penalties and so on. The difference between the behaviour of people left to themselves, and the behaviour of people subject to government, is explained (if 'explained' is not too extravagant a term) by pointing to the ruler and saying that he controls his subjects. Mechanical and political control, then, are to some extent alike. But there are also differences, just because political control is exercised within an organisation, such as a state, which is a different thing from a machine. According to the political model we are encouraged to think of the human psyche as a sort of organisation, while according to the mechanical model we are to think of it as a sort of machine. As a satisfactory way of answering our problem about Reason and Passion, each of the models has one big advantage, and one big drawback, as compared with the other.

According to the political model, the human psyche is like an organisation, and the various principles in it, such as Reason and Passion, stand to one another like different parts of a state. In the simplest form of this model, the two elements, Reason and Passion, stand in the relation of ruler to subject, or master to slave. Now the great advantage of this model is that it does enable us to say something in answer to the question 'How is it possible for Reason to fail to control passion?' We do this by making a distinction which Bishop Butler made in his very deliberate development of this analogy between man and organisation. We distinguish between power and authority. A ruler may have absolute authority, but he cannot have absolute power. He can command, but he cannot always compel, for human power is not irresistible. Similarly Reason can command Passion, but Passion may ignore the command. When Butler said of Conscience 'Had it power, as it has manifest authority, it would govern the world', he was clearly thinking of the failure of Conscience to control conduct as a kind of disobedience, a defiance of authority. Impulsive action contrary to Conscience (or to self-interest, for that matter) may be unnatural, but it is certainly possible. Similarly for Plato in the *Republic*, where the soul is again compared with a political organisation in the explicit analogy of the Large and Small Letters, passion may defy reason, and this is a violation of the true nature of man, but it is not impossible.

The analogy of political control, then, does give some sort of account of loss of self-control. But the big drawback of this way of talking is that it is so very obviously analogical. We know that the soul is not really a miniature commonwealth, in which officials give orders which are either executed or disobeyed. And even if it were, the same problem would arise all over again, because acting in compliance with orders is itself (as a rule) a case of acting contrary to inclination. It would be very awkward if we insisted on asking what happens when Passion obeys Reason: must Passion itself have a rational as well as a passionate component, which 'listens to' Reason? But this would go on *ad infinitum*. Aristotle actually takes the first step in this infinite regress, saying that the irrational part of the soul 'has a share in' reason.[1]

## 10. *A Para-Mechanical Myth*

We might be tempted to say at this point that, after all, the political model was the only one which was available to the ancients; that it does suffer from a glaring inadequacy, and that we have a much better model in the mechanical one. At any rate the misfit here, if there is one, is not so glaring. Human beings are certainly not republics, but it is not quite so obvious they are not machines.

[1] *Nicomachean Ethics*, I, xiii, 15.

According to the mechanical model, the human psyche is a system of interacting forces. Whatever a man does is the result of a set of component forces. There is nothing in this model which corresponds to the distinction between authority and power. If Reason and Passion are distinct principles in the psyche, the only relation between them can be the relation of co-action or counter-action. Since the cases we are considering are cases where an impulse does not issue in the action which it tends to produce, there must in these cases be a counteracting factor, and if this is to be called Reason, we must say that Reason and Passion are opposed forces. In other words, the only way in which the force of impulse can be resisted is by another force acting in the opposite direction and of at least equal strength. Reason must be such a force.

The objection to this is not so much that it is obviously an analogical myth. (Though as a matter of fact it is.) It is an objection which Hume himself notices, despite his own preference for the mechanical model. The objection is this. It is a tautology that the stronger force must prevail over the weaker, and if passions are forces then a stronger passion must prevail over a weaker one. But Hume notices that there are 'calm' passions and 'violent' passions, and that the calm passions often prevail over the violent.[1] Patience prevails over anger, though it has none of the violent feeling we associate with anger; similarly a sense of shame may prevail over an acute pang of fear. For Hume, of course, Reason is not a passion or anything that can be matched against a passion, but for anyone who stops short of Hume's paradox (that Reason cannot conflict with passion at all) his point about the calm and violent passions seems to offer a serious difficulty. For Reason above all is associated with 'calmness' in strong contrast to the violence of the passions which it can defeat. The mechanical model of counteracting forces seems incapable of explaining this.

### 11. *Disposition-Words and Occurrence-Words*

It seems that we must abandon both the models and look for a

[1] *Treatise*, II, iii, 3.

different terminology in which to characterise the situation. We can start from Hume's point about the calm and violent passions. The military metaphor of 'conflict' suggests that the conflict between Reason and Passion must be a conflict between two parties which are capable of being matched against each other. One football team can only be matched against another football team, and not against a cricket side. One force can only be counteracted by another force, and not by a colour. Hume was perfectly right in saying that Reason cannot conflict with Passion because the only thing that can be matched against a passion is another passion. But he was wrong in saying that there are calm passions which can defeat violent ones. Where he went wrong was to call the calm passions *passions*. The examples he gives ('Benevolence and resentment, the love of life, and kindness to children; or the general appetite to good, and aversion to evil') are not examples of passions at all. Indeed he himself seems to have been uncomfortable about this because he refers to them as 'calm desires and *tendencies*' and also as 'principles'. It is not only Reason, but also these so-called 'calm tendencies', which are incapable of being matched against the passions.

The solution which just eludes Hume at this point turns on the logical distinction between dispositions and occurrences. This is by no means a discovery of modern logic. Aristotle had a great deal to say about it. There are two categories of words which we use when talking about human beings and their behaviour. We use words from one category when we are talking about what happened or is happening to somebody, or about what he did or is doing at a particular time. We use words belonging to the other category when we are talking not about what happens or what he does on a particular occasion, but about what might or would happen, or what he may be expected to do or would do on certain sorts of occasion. Examples from the first category are the following: angry, sad, excited, frightened. Examples from the second category are: short-tempered, melancholy, excitable, timid. To say that someone is frightened is to say that something is actually happening to him now — he is experiencing feelings of fear — or that he is actually doing something now — he is running away or screaming. But to say that someone is timid is not to say that he is frightened; it is to say that he tends to get frightened easily, or that he would be frightened if . . . ; to say something about the sorts of occasions on which he would be frightened, namely that they are more frequent or less dangerous than those which would frighten the ordinary man. An occurrence-word tells us what is happening; a disposition-word tells us what tends to happen, or would happen if. . . . Some words are ambiguous in this respect, and belong to both categories, for example: affectionate, passionate, and (Hume's example) resentful. To say that a man is resentful can mean either that he is feeling or showing resentment, or else that he tends to feel or show resentment too frequently.

Now the class of disposition-words is a very large and indispensable part of our vocabulary for describing human beings in ordinary life. The use of disposition-words tells us very much more about people than the use of occurrence-words does. We know a lot more about a man when we are told that he is timid than we know when we are merely told that he is frightened. For we can predict nothing of his future behaviour from the mere knowledge that he is frightened, and very little even if we also know the occasion of his fright. But if we know that he is timid, then we can predict with some confidence what his behaviour will be in a whole range of possible situations. When we do wish to give concise information about people, as in writing testimonials, for instance, we talk in terms of dispositions and not of occurrences. A testimonial is not a section of biography. And if we do insert a mention of some occurrence, something which our acquaintance has done or some event in which he has participated, this could only be relevant as manifesting in a striking way some character-trait which we wish to ascribe to him.

It would be misleading to suggest that the contrast between dispositions and occurrences, and the greater information-valuc of disposition-words, applies only to people. What has been said so far applies also to all sorts of other things. A salesman's description of a motor-car is much like a personal testimonial in its ascription of dispositions (reliable, economical, powerful, etc.). Indeed, all knowledge which is capable of being put to practical use is knowledge of this sort: knowledge, that is, not of events, episodes or states of affairs, but of the tendency of things to behave in certain ways on certain sorts of occasion. Learning from experience means acquiring this sort of knowledge.

### 12. *Disposition-Words and Human Character*

But though disposition-words as a class are not peculiar to the description of human beings, there are of course certain disposition-words which are. Let us consider a list of disposition-words which is specially relevant to our original problem. Patient, resolute, indefatigable, diligent, assiduous, conscientious, equable, faithful, trustworthy. Such disposition-words have certain peculiarities.

(1) They are unlike those so far mentioned (short-tempered, melancholy, excitable) in that they tell us, on the whole, what a person would *not* do on certain sorts of occasion, rather than what he would do. A patient man is not one who tends to do certain things, but rather one who tends not to do certain things: he would not get angry or exasperated under the sort of provocations which would anger or exasperate another man. Similarly a resolute man is one who would not be deterred from his purpose by dangers which would deter another man. A conscientious man is one who would not be tempted off the path of duty by inducements which another man would follow. And so on. We can see already where this is leading. The sorts of things which a person would not do, if he possesses one of these dispositional characteristics, are the sorts of things which issue from passion or impulse.

(2) Another feature of these disposition-words applies to the others too, but is notably absent from disposition-words applying to things other than people. It is that a person can be said to have the disposition in question (such as bad temper, or resoluteness) even though he does not in fact always act in the appropriate way when the sort of occasion, on which we expect him

to act in that way, occurs. This is not true of simple non-human dispositions. Take the 'solubility' of sugar in water. To say that sugar is soluble is to say that pieces of sugar always dissolve when immersed in water, and (what follows strictly from this) that a given piece of sugar would dissolve if it were placed in water. If pieces of sugar sometimes failed to dissolve, when the appropriate occasion occurred (immersion in water) we could not attribute the characteristic of 'solubility' to sugar at all. But when we say that a man is irritable, meaning that he tends to get angry on certain sorts of occasion, we do not rule out the possibility that, on an occasion of that sort, he might not get angry. And if he unexpectedly keeps his temper on such an occasion, we don't necessarily withdraw our disposition-word 'irritable' from our estimate of his character. People do, after all, act 'out-of-character'. The point is that human dispositions are essentially elastic; there is always an implied 'more or less' about them. Otherwise we could not speak of them at all. There are some provocations which anger patient men; some dangers which deter resolute men; some temptations which the conscientious man fails to resist.

(3) The third point to notice about this list of disposition-words is that, unlike the first, they refer to virtues. Both lists refer to qualities which can only describe human beings; but of the first list some (timidity, short temper) describe defects of character, others (melancholy, excitable) are on the whole morally neutral; but the second list contains only virtues; virtues, moreover, which are associated with an ability to avoid impulsive action: with what we are tempted to call self-control.

## 13. *Solution of the Classical Puzzles*

We can now exploit these three features of this class of disposition-words in an attempt to answer our original problem about Reason versus Passion. First, the question as Hume saw it: How is it possible for Reason to control Passion at all? We need only reformulate this question in our new terminology so as to avoid the political or mechanical metaphor: 'How is it possible for human beings to acquire character-dispositions like patience, resoluteness and conscientiousness?' For we have seen that having dispositions of this sort *is* having a tendency to act otherwise than on impulse. But when we think of feature (3), this question 'How?' begins to look less formidable: for the ability to acquire dispositions of this sort is part of our being men and not children, animals, or vegetables.

Next, the question as Aristotle saw it: 'How is it possible for Reason to lose control of the passions?' We reformulate this question so as to bring in feature (2): 'How is it possible for statements about dispositions to admit of exceptions?' and this, too, is no longer embarrassing if we remember that the dispositions we attribute to human beings, unlike those we attribute to chemical substances, are always of the 'more or less' type.

But is this a 'solution' at all? Does it not merely shelve the original difficulty? It may be felt that the translation of a question from one sort of terminology into another does not *answer* the question. Are not the facts of 'self-control' as puzzling as they ever were? Part of the reply to this is that, even if there are residual problems still demanding solution, it is at any rate some achievement to have rejected false answers, especially when these are disguised in plain descriptive terminology concealing an obsolete metaphysics. I have tried to show that a traditional and commonplace way of stating the problem involves the use of language which already contains philosophical theories, and mistaken ones, about the nature of the soul. The question which demands an answer at the outset cannot receive one because the language in which it is formulated already embodies the wrong answer to a prior question. It is like asking 'What is the colour of Smith's motor-car?' when Smith has no motor-car; the question embodies the wrong answer to the prior question, 'Has Smith a motor-car?' The correct answer being 'No', the original question does not arise and no possible answer can be correct. Similarly, the question 'How can Reason control Passion?' embodies the wrong answer to a prior question; each of the three key-words in it incorporates a whole philosophy of human nature. It is only by going back to the prior questions and, if necessary, adopting or inventing a different set of concepts, that we can progress. And the result of progress is not to answer the original question, but to supersede it.

The rest of the reply to our critic is that any residual problems about the facts of 'self-control' can be handed to the psychologist in a form suitable for investigation, being no longer wrapped up in the relics of a false theory.

### 14. *The Brake and the Accelerator*

There is a final point concerning feature (1) of the 'virtuous' disposition-words. This was a negative feature; the words in the list pointed to what a person would not do rather than to what he would do on certain sorts of occasion. This might suggest that virtue, moral goodness, is necessarily a matter of restraint and inhibition; and though this may accord with a somewhat puritanical moral code, it is rejected by other codes and is not implied in my argument. When discussing cases of Reason 'controlling' Passion, I have tended for the sake of simplicity to concentrate on the type of case where Passion leads to impulsive action and Reason to the restraining of such action. But I have hinted at the other type of case, where a passion (such as fear) tends to inaction and the victory over passion issues in positive action. This difference of emphasis between the two types of case reflects our readiness to think of passion as something that is always liable to 'run away with us' and that the brake is far more often to be employed than the accelerator. This, in turn, I think, reflects a puritanical streak in our moral outlook. For Aristotle there is no such disparity. His Doctrine of the Mean rests on the assumption that the passions are, on the whole, morally neutral, but that we can feel them, and act on them, too little as well as too much. Passionate behaviour is not on the whole deplorable, as it tends to be according to our own standards of good behaviour. The Greek ideal of character which Aristotle reflects, the Kalokagathos, was required to be not only appropriately reserved but also appropriately passionate.

Even Aristotle, however, was compelled to acknowledge that many of the 'vices' which would consist in indulging too little passion are insufficiently notable to have names, while those which do have names tend to describe action which is too passionate rather than too little passionate. This is connected with the topic of Positive and Negative morality, which we shall discuss in Chapter XI. In the meantime, it is enough to note that morality tends to require abstention from action more prominently than it requires action; passions issue in action more frequently than in inaction; and hence we should expect that those qualities of character which gain moral approval, and are called virtues, should be found more prominently to involve the brake than the accelerator.

CHAPTER VIII

# CONSCIENCE AND AUTHORITY (i)

## 1. *'Conscience' and the Para-Political Myth*

The way in which the idea of Conscience presents itself to us is nowhere better illustrated than in the second of Butler's *Sermons Upon Human Nature*:

> There is a superior principle of reflection or conscience in every man, which distinguishes between the internal principles of his heart, as well as his external actions: which passes judgment upon himself and them; pronounces determinately some actions to be in themselves just, right, good; others to be in themselves evil, wrong, unjust: which, without being consulted, without being advised with, magisterially exerts itself, and approves or condemns him, the doer of them, accordingly: and which, if not forcibly stopped, naturally and always of course goes on to anticipate a higher and more effectual sentence, which shall hereafter second and affirm its own.

This is a sustained politico-legal metaphor. All the key words in it belong to the language in which we describe the functioning of a political structure, especially the operations of the legislature and judicature. Conscience is a magistrate, who passes judgment on defendants brought before him, in the light of the laws he has to administer. There is also a Supreme Court to which his decisions may be referred; for the voice of Conscience is the voice of God.

So far I have been rather critical of political metaphors in talk about morality. I suggested in the last chapter that the whole of our ordinary discourse about the facts of moral conflict or perplexity is riddled with metaphors from political, and to a lesser extent mechanical, language; that such metaphors enshrine ancient philosophies purporting to explain such facts;

that these ancient theories should be made explicit, criticised and if necessary discarded; and that a language which is not theory-laden should be adopted instead. It is now time to examine the virtues rather than the defects of the political analogy. It seems that the idea of Conscience cannot be elucidated without the use of a politico-legal explanatory model. Its characteristic features are so closely similar to corresponding features in a politico-legal system that our use in everyday discourse of analogies from that system is not altogether a philosophical perversion. The proposal put forward in Chapter VII, to supersede the language of the 'para-political myth' and talk instead of character-dispositions, is insufficient to deal with what we want to say about conscience; for conscience cannot be reduced to conscientiousness or to any other disposition or collection of dispositions.

The characteristic feature of conscience, on which all the others depend, is (as Butler recognised) its authoritativeness. The meaning of 'authoritativeness' and 'authority' depends, in turn, on the family of politico-legal concepts associated with the idea of an *organisation*. It is these concepts, and in particular the concept of an organisation, that we shall be exploring in order to elucidate the idea of conscience.

## 2. *Butler and his 'Constitution'*

Butler himself begins his exposition of the nature of conscience in much the same way, except that, instead of the relatively precise notion of *organisation*, he takes the more general notion of *system*. His exposition is accordingly more confused than it need be, since there are different kinds of system which he tends to lump together, relying in effect on a number of different analogies rather than a single one.

> Whoever thinks it worth while to consider this matter thoroughly should begin with stating to himself exactly the idea of a system, economy or constitution of any particular nature, or particular anything; and he will, I suppose, find that it is a one or a whole made up of several parts; but yet, that the several parts even considered as a whole do not complete the idea, unless in the notion

of a whole you include the relations and respects which those parts have to each other.

'Every work both of nature and art is a system,' he adds; and his examples show that he is thinking of at least three kinds of system, yielding three different analogies. His first example is a watch; of which, he says, you have no adequate idea by considering the components, but only by considering them as conducive in their various ways to the single purpose of telling the time. A watch is a machine; the system it exemplifies is a mechanical system; the analogy it suggests for human nature is a mechanical analogy; and the philosophy of human nature, to which it tends to lead, is a para-mechanical theory, even though the designer of the watch plays a special part in the analogy and has to be accommodated in the myth.

His second example is taken from St. Paul:

> For as we have many members in one body, and all members have not the same office; so we, being many, are one body in Christ, and every one members one of another.[1]

This is Butler's text for his First Sermon. He adds that, 'since the Apostle speaks of the several members as having distinct offices, which implies the mind, it cannot be thought an unallowable liberty, instead of the *body* and *its members*, to substitute the *whole nature of man*, and *all the variety of internal principles which belong to it*.' This substitution, the legitimacy of which seems so obvious that no argument is thought necessary, depends on a theory which likens the functioning of the mind to the functioning of the body. Now the body is a system; but it is an organic system, not a mechanical one. The analogy it suggests for the moral nature of man is a biological analogy, and it points to a philosophy of human nature which we may christen, in conformity with the others, a para-biological theory.

Butler's third example is not at first stated explicitly. It is the example of an organised society such as a political state with legislative, administrative and judiciary functions. This is what I call an organisation and what, I shall suggest, provides a

[1] *Romans*, XII, 4, 5.

proper analogy for the idea of conscience. Butler oddly allows this type of system to be merely suggested by the other two, instead of bringing it out explicitly. The example of the watch, he says 'is merely by way of explanation, what an economy, system, or constitution is'. And in the second example, the relation between the parts of the body 'is here compared to the relation which each particular person in society has to other particular persons and to the whole society; and the latter is intended to be illustrated by the former'. St. Paul's dictum does indeed exemplify a way of talking (the 'body politic' is another example) which suggests that social and political relations have to be described in terms of analogies with the physiological body. The facts which provide analogies for the moral life have themselves to be explained by another set of analogies. The para-political myth itself rests on the para-biological myth.

Butler's mistake, no doubt, lies in his eagerness to prove that man's moral nature must resemble a 'constitution' because *everything* resembles a constitution. This led him to a search for a still broader concept, under which bodies and watches fall, and to minimise those special features of organisations which distinguish them from other 'systems'. But it can only be in a vacuous sense that everything resembles anything. Not everything resembles a political constitution; but man's moral nature does in some important respects, and these resemblances we must explore.

### 3. *Kant and his 'Kingdom'*

The para-political theory of the moral life is also at the centre of Kant's moral philosophy. According to Kant, morality makes sense only if we suppose that there is a kingdom governed by the moral law and similar in structure to actual earthly kingdoms governed by political law; in this moral kingdom there is both sovereign legislator and subject citizens. But the sovereign is also subject, and every subject is also sovereign; for whatever law the sovereign issues, as legislator, is one to which he is bound to conform, as subject; and whatever law the citizen obeys, in his capacity as subject, is one which he wills to apply to his own and other people's actions, that is, one which he enacts as legislator. In such terms Kant seeks to explain both the universality of moral judgments, and the belief in moral freedom. Kant's concept of 'sovereignty' corresponds to Butler's 'authority', and his 'kingdom' to Butler's 'constitution'. Both wish to assert that, and to explain how, a man can be (in the words of St. Paul) 'a law unto himself'.

## 4. *What is an Organisation?*

What is an organisation? Obviously we cannot begin to answer this question by examining a particular organisation, least of all the political organisation which we call a state, which is the most complex of all organisations. For the sake of clarity we shall have to make some artificial simplifications. I shall try to state what I take to be the minimum necessary conditions for the existence of something that can be called an organisation; and further, a criterion for identifying a particular organisation. Both these will be found to involve the concept of authority.

We can begin with the truism that an organisation exists in relation to a set of activities on the part of individuals. An industrial company has to do with such operations as mining, quarrying, or manufacturing. The M.C.C. has to do with the operations we call playing cricket. The Church of England has to do with religious worship and prayer. The State has to do with all the activities with which it has to do. (There is no general answer, except this tautology, to the question, 'What activities does the State control?') All these activities are, in the end, activities of individual human beings, miners, factory-workers, cricketers, worshippers and — citizens.

But the relation between an organisation, and the activities with which it has to do, is in practice extremely complex. In order to be able to state a necessary condition for the existence of an organisation, we must single out of this complexity one essential factor without which the organisation could not exist as such. Everything else will depend on various practical considerations. For instance, we must avoid specifying that the activities in question must be actually going on. An organisation does not cease to exist when the activity of its members ceases. This is obvious enough in such cases as the continued existence of an industrial firm in spite of total interruption through strikes (not to mention off-duty hours and holidays for the entire staff). We must also allow for more extreme examples such as the formation of a company for a project which is never undertaken. Practical interests apart, an organisation can exist without any operations whatever.

We may next try the suggestion that the relation between organisation and activity is one of purpose; that we do not understand a particular organisation unless we know what it is for, or what interests it is designed to promote. Organisations always exist in order to achieve some specific purpose. And purposes can exist, it may be said, even in the absence of purposive activity, since we can posit a certain end without saying anything about means. But this too is wrong. It is true that in almost all actual cases we can no doubt assign some specific purpose as the purpose of a given organisation. But having a purpose is not a necessary condition of the existence of an organisation. Readers of Kafka and Warner may already be convinced of this, not to mention critics of the Food Ministry towards the end of its career. Again (though this is more relevant to the question of identifying a particular organisation) different organisations may yet have the same purpose. The purpose of a railway undertaking is to run trains, yet a nationalised system is a different organisation from a privately-owned one. Of course this can always be denied by insisting that the purpose of a private undertaking is to benefit shareholders while the purpose of a nationalised one is to benefit the citizens. But this is irrelevant to the question of the nature of an organisation; at most it might be relevant to a discussion of the practical considerations determining the form a particular organisation might take.

### 5. *Organisation and Command: A Two-Storey Model*

In order to see what is the essential condition which an organisation must satisfy, the characteristic relation between organisation and activity, we must consider the simplest possible system that could be called an organisation at all. This will consist of certain people whose activities are subject to control. In simple cases their activities will be subject to control by other people. And the simplest possible case will be a pair of individuals, A and B, such that B's activities are controlled by A.

Now how does A control B's activities? We may exclude the method of physical force (which is comparatively rare, and which, when it does occur, is not really controlling, but overpowering.) We may also exclude 'stick and carrot' methods such as threats and bribes, methods depending on the provision of an immediate motive for B's doing what A wants. ('Forcing' in the usual sense is a case of this sort; when we say 'He was forced at gun-point to hand over the cash' we really mean, not that he was overpowered, but that he responded to a threat of death.) We exclude these methods because they do not depend on any pre-existing relation between A and B.

In order for A to control B's activities in the proper sense, what is necessary is that A should convey to B certain commands, and that B should comply with at least some of these commands. But why should B take any notice of A's commands? It is necessary to add that A should be *in a position to* issue certain sorts of command, and that B should be prepared to obey A's commands because they are A's commands and because A is in a position to issue them. In other words. A must have authority, and B must recognise A's authority. The simplest kind of organisation consists of a person or persons who issue commands in virtue of their authority, and a person or persons who obey them in virtue of their recognition of such authority.

### 6. *The Logic of Commanding*

The choice of the word 'command' is important. It might be objected that it is too strong: we do not speak of a headmaster issuing commands to his staff, or even of a foreman commanding his gang, although these are good examples of organisations. 'Command' has too much of a military flavour; would it not be better to use some vaguer and more general word, such as 'order', 'direct', or 'instruct'? The answer is that these terms are too wide for our purpose. I may order the greengrocer to deliver vegetables, or instruct a builder to repair my house, and this certainly does not mean that we belong to a common organisation. What is missing is the concept of authority: my order to the greengrocer, my instructions to the builder, are not authoritative. To put it another way, there are very many functions of imperative language besides its function in organisations; and these differences are obscured by the common verbal form of 'Report for guard duty', 'Deliver a sack of potatoes' and 'Replace defective tiles'. Not only are there very many different ways of getting other people to act in ways in which we wish them to act; there are also many different ways of employing imperative language for the purpose. My ordering the greengroceries takes place in virtue of a contractual relation, which is quite different from the relation between A and B in our model organisation. The word 'command' expresses exactly the relation required, even if it has overtones which render it colloquially unsuitable in non-military contexts.

It is worth noting that this narrow and proper use of the word 'command' has been overlooked by those who have said that moral judgments are commands, or have the force of commands.[1] Moral judgments do indeed have an imperative function (as I held in II, 6), that is, they are a mode of expression which can be used in order to get someone to act in a certain way. Yet it certainly does not follow that they are commands. To show this it is only necessary to establish that there is no necessary connection whatever between a command and an imperative form of words.

Even the simple and familiar 'Shut the door' is hardly ever a command. It is usually a request. On the other hand, the formally similar 'Slope arms!' is a genuine command. Both are imperatives, but only one is a command. Conversely, a command need not be expressed in an imperative form of words. 'Would you please see that this letter goes by registered post?' might well express a command, and so might even an indicative: 'Your route is via Winchester', though neither of these is imperative in form. As an illustration of the versatility which makes it

[1] E.g. Ayer, *Language, Truth and Logic*, p. 108.

impossible to classify linguistic functions according to linguistic forms, consider the following conversation:

A. (Commanding officer): How are you getting on with the telephone line to Divisional H.Q.?
B. (Junior officer): I think it will be through by tonight, sir.
A. (sternly and emphatically): It *will* be through by tonight!
B. (hastily): Yes, sir, it will be through by tonight.

The same (indicative) sentence occurs firstly as a predictive statement, secondly as a command, and thirdly as a promise.

Now there is a simple device for making it clear whether any given expression is a command or not. First we reduce it, if necessary, to a simple imperative of the form 'Do X'. We then prefix the expression 'I command you to. . . .', and if the resulting expression merely repeats the original, with greater emphasis, then of course it *is* a command. 'Deliver the potatoes' and 'Shut the door' cannot be treated thus (in ordinary contexts) without producing an obvious incongruity; while 'Send this letter by registered post' can, and so can 'Proceed via Winchester' (if spoken, say, by an officer of the Military Police, but not if spoken by an Automobile Association patrolman). Needless to say, the display of naked power in the prefix 'I command. . . .' is seldom called for even in military contexts, and rarely indeed in the secretary's office, but the formula is tacitly acknowledged nevertheless.

'I command' is like 'I promise' in being a performatory use of a verb: that is, in saying 'I command you to do X' I am not *stating* that I command, I *am* commanding you to do X. If, on the other hand, I had said 'I wish you would do X' I might well have been stating that I had a certain wish. I can wish without *saying* 'I wish', and indeed without saying anything at all; and I can also state that I have a wish. But I cannot command without saying 'I command' (or something which tacitly presupposes the formula); for to command *is* to say something. Similarly, in saying 'I promise you to do X' I am not stating that I promise, I *am* promising; I cannot promise without saying 'I promise' (or something which tacitly presupposes the formula); to promise *is* to say something. In both cases (commanding and promising) I need not actually use the performatory verb, so long as the context shows that I presuppose it; I shall actually use it only if it is necessary to emphasise that a future indicative expression, which I am about to utter, is not to be taken as a statement of intention, or as a prediction, but as a promise; or that an imperative expression, which I am about to utter, is not a request or a proposal, but a command.

But there is a difference between promising and commanding. In saying 'I promise', I am drawing attention to a special relation between promisor and promisee which I actually create in the act of promising, in using that formula, just as in saying 'I now pronounce you man and wife' I draw attention to a special relation, the relation of marriage, which (for religious, not civil, purposes) I actually create in the ceremonial act, in uttering that very formula itself. But in saying 'I command' I am not similarly creating a relation of a special type; I am drawing attention to one which already exists. (Of course I am creating *some* relation, namely the relation between myself as commanding X and yourself as being obliged to do X, just as in promising I am creating not only the general relation of promisor to promisee, but also a specific relation between A who has promised to do X and B who has a right to expect X. But this is a trivial qualification.) In commanding, as we have seen, there is not only A who issues commands to B, but also A's being in a position to issue commands and B's being subject to them; and this relation between A and B is not created by a particular act of commanding, but is presupposed by it. Another way of putting it is to say that, as far as logic is concerned, I can promise anything or anyone; but it is not anyone or anything that I can command. I can command only those whom I am authorised to command, and I can demand of them only the sort of actions which I am authorised to command. The first of these points[1] is clearly brought out in military jargon: commands can only be issued by those '*in* command' to those '*under* command'. And this is a logical point concerning the meaning of 'command' and

[1] The second is discussed on p. 158.

'authorise'. For a 'command' addressed to someone with whom I was not already related in the appropriate relation, whom I was not authorised to command, would not *be* a command. This explains an earlier point[1] about the special incongruity of 'I command' prefixed to imperatives which in ordinary contexts suggest the wrong relation. But there is no such incongruity about 'I promise' prefixed to a future indicative in any context whatever.

### 7. *Authority and Justification*

The function of the term 'authority' is to make explicit the existence of this special relation between those who command and those who are commanded. In order for an action to count as obedience to a command, it is not enough for A to utter an imperative and for B to act accordingly, because A's imperative may have been a request and not a command. It is not enough, either, even if A's imperative is a command, that B's action should be one which matches the command; for this might have happened by chance, or by B's anticipating the order. It is not enough even that B deliberately perform the action because he knows that A desires it; for knowledge of A's desires is quite irrelevant. Commands are not expressions of desire. Moreover, it is not even necessary that B should act deliberately. What is necessary, however, is that he should act with good reason; if he does not do it with deliberate intention, he must at least be able to justify his doing it. And the good and only relevant reason is, that A commanded it. If, to the question 'Why did you do X?' a sufficient answer is 'Because A commanded it', the explanation or justification is one which appeals to the relation between A and B, namely the relation of authority. A has authority over B if, and only if, the fact that A has commanded an action X is a sufficient reason for B's doing X. 'Sufficient reason' means that we ask no further question: the appeal to authority either satisfies or frustrates the question 'Why?'.

One way, then, in which we can have a good reason for doing something is that we recognise someone's authority to command

[1] P. 150.

that action. And an explanation in terms of authority is always, as far as it goes, a final explanation. It is final in the sense that no further questions of the same type remain to be asked. It is in this sense that moral justifications in terms of '*prima facie* duty'[1] are final. For example, one may ask, 'Why did B do X?' and be told 'Because X was the fulfilment of a promise.' This a final answer in the sense that no further question of the same type remains to be asked. One can only ask whether X was in fact the fulfilment of a promise, and whether it is a duty to fulfil promises; given that these are so, one cannot give any further reasons why B did X. Similarly, if one is told 'Because A commanded X', one can go on to ask if X was in fact what A commanded, and whether A's command was really a command, whether (for instance) A had the requisite authority. Given that these are so, one cannot give any further reasons why B did X. In both cases, of course, giving a final justification is not the same as giving an absolute justification. There may be countervailing reasons against doing a *prima facie* duty, if for instance one promise conflicts with another; and so there may be countervailing reasons against obeying a recognised authority, if for instance a man is faced with conflicting demands by different organisations of which he is a member.

The explanatory and justificatory function of the term 'authority' is also seen if we consider its use in contexts where we are not doing, but believing. We often quote as good reasons for our beliefs the fact that certain other people have said so. This is called the evidence of testimony. Some things we believe because we have seen that they are so, others because we have been told that they are so. And the limits of our knowledge would be extremely narrow if we had to confine it to what we could verify for ourselves, ignoring the beliefs which we acquire from the body of publicly ascertained facts. Direct verification and public testimony are very different kinds of evidence, but each in its own way is equally final. It is sometimes suggested that belief in testimony rests on a precarious inference of an inductive type; that one's belief in the witness' statement depends on

[1] W. D. Ross, *The Right and the Good*, Ch. II.

certain general propositions about the truthfulness of this man's utterances, or those of human beings in general; and that such general propositions, to the extent that they are verifiable at all, are verifiable by one's own observations of other people's behaviour. There might be some truth in this, if all public information came from sources as unreliable as the witness-box. But in fact we distinguish between reliable and unreliable sources, and apply tests to the latter which we omit for the former. This is not because our inductions turn out to be highly successful in one of the cases. Rather, in such a case the whole notion of inference is out of place; we rely on certain sources without asking why. And we distinguish these sources by calling them our authorities. Aristotle, the Bible, the writings of Lenin, and 'science', are examples of sources which people regard, or have regarded, as authoritative sources of belief. Just as it may be a sufficient reason for B's doing something, that A commanded it, so it may be a sufficient reason for B's believing something, that A asserted it.

### 8. *Organisation and Authority: a Multi-Storey Model*

So far we have considered the functioning of authority in a situation limited *ex hypothesi* to the very simple two-level organisation consisting of those who command and those who obey. This limitation has the advantage of making as clear as possible the relation between authority and command; but it has the drawback that it ignores other aspects of authority and of organisations. It is doubtful if any actual organisation consists of just the two-tier structure. For one thing, this structure leaves unexplained the fact that A has authority over B but not over C. Why should A be 'in a position to' issue commands, and why should B, but not C, be subject to them? Authority is not simply found and recognised; it has to be created. We cannot hope to give a complete explanation why some human beings have and acquire authority over others, even with the aid of political theory and anthropology. For the question 'Why do people obey orders?' is too vacuous to receive an informative answer. It is like the question 'Why do people believe the truth?' All the same, we can say something about the creation of authority by extending our simple two-tier model into a multi-storey block.

The simplest way of doing this would be, of course, to add on extra storeys of the same type. We begin by noting that the foundation-work consists of actual operations by individuals. Let us use the last letter of the alphabet Z for the person (or persons) who actually perform the operations in relation to which the organisation exists. Then, as we have seen, the characteristic feature of an organisation is introduced as soon as we specify a second person (or persons) Y, who is in a position to issue commands to Z. Can we proceed to someone else, X, who issues commands to Y, W who issues commands to X and so on? We can obviously build a multi-tier structure in this way; but without further specifications it will no longer suffice to constitute an organisation.

The commands at the various levels must be related to each other. For consider what is the consequence if they are not. The correlate of a command is an action (including an abstention from action). Suppose that at any given level (say Y) the actions in compliance with commands from X, and the commands issued by Y to Z, are quite unrelated to each other. We shall then have not one organisation but two. Suppose Y is ordered by a magistrate to maintain his deserted wife, and that, as an officer in the army, he orders a soldier to mount guard. These transactions belong to different organisations. Indeed this follows from our original stipulation about an organisation and its activities. There is no common activity involved in maintaining a deserted wife and mounting guard.

Next suppose that the actions taken at level Y, in response to commands from level X, are themselves the issuing of further commands to level Z. Each level commands the next lower level to issue commands to the next lower level, and so on. This will secure a connection between the various levels. But there are still different possibilities. The simplest case is where the lowest-level command (from Y to Z) is an order to perform operation O, and is of the form 'Do O'; the next (from X to Y) is 'Order Z to do O', the next (from W to X) is 'Order Y to order Z to do O', and so on. This will clearly generate a hierarchy of sorts. There will be obvious practical objections about redundancy, but circumstances are conceivable in which an actual organisation might, at least temporarily, approximate to such a system. The chief of the organisation would be prepared to specify every operation in sufficient detail for it to be executed without further instructions, and without the assistance of subordinates except as mere mouthpieces. There is a 'chain of command', if only in an all-too-literal sense.

The approximation holds for these special circumstances only because this situation is the extreme or limiting case of another possibility, namely where the commands issued by A to B, B to C . . . and X to Y do not mention O, and do not take the form 'Order X to order Y to order Z. . . .' Instead they take the same form, but of course a different content, as the lowest-level command 'Do O'. This means that only in the case of Z will compliance with a command take the form of an actual operation. In the other cases compliance will be a complex performance, including the issuing of other commands not identical with, and not specified by, the command received. Conversely, only in the case of Y will a command take the form of a simple imperative to action. In all the other cases it will take the form of indicating what is to be *achieved* without specifying what is to be *done*. It prescribes an objective, of which lower-level commands prescribe sub-objectives. The connection between the Supreme Commander's order 'Destroy the enemy forces' and the platoon-sergeant's 'Fire!' is of this sort.

The chief features of this kind of organisation are the following. At each level commands can be issued to those at the next lowest level, but there is a change at the lowest level of all. There it is a case of compliance with an order which does not itself involve the issuing of any further orders. At every other stage compliance with a command may include, or may wholly be, the issuing of further commands, related to the original in a way which allows the recipient of the command a certain discretion, but not an unlimited discretion, in the choice of his own commands. (This is necessary if the organisation is to have the much-quoted virtues of flexibility, adaptability and efficiency.)

9. *Delegation of Responsibility and Delegation of Authority*

This chain of links between successive levels of a hierarchy can be described in two different ways, depending, roughly, on whether we are looking at it from the top or the bottom. One way is to speak of the delegation of responsibility; the other is to speak of the delegation of authority. Roughly, we speak of the delegation of responsibility when we are interested in the positive functioning of the different levels of the hierarchy in achieving a definite object. In practice we are concerned to achieve that object, to assign blame somewhere if it is not achieved, and to assign it in the right quarter and at the right level. Now the simple command relation provides a simple way of allotting responsibility. If Z is commanded to perform O, and O is not performed, then Z is responsible (barring accidents and other excuses) for not doing O. But at higher levels the word 'command', being less appropriate for a general objective than for a particular operation, tends to be replaced by others ('instructions', 'directives'), and ordinary second-person imperatives tend to be replaced by third-person imperatives and by non-imperative forms. One of these non-imperative forms is specially interesting, as pointing to the close connection between responsibility and command: it is 'W will be responsible for P'. When the Commanding Officer makes it known that 'O.C. 3 Company will be responsible for providing transport to the station', this does not mean 'Captain Smith, you are to find Driver Brown, truck number 123456, etc.'; no doubt Captain Smith will tell the sergeant-major 'Find a driver. . . .', the sergeant-major will tell Driver Brown 'Drive the truck. . . .' and Driver Brown, who alone in this anecdote is not in a position to issue any commands, will drive the truck. But all that the original order conveyed was that, if some such truck is not driven to such a place at such a time, then O.C.3 Company will be blamed. The Commanding Officer may have been required by the Brigadier to move troops to certain positions; he is responsible for the movement, but the effect of his order is to make the company commander responsible for part of the task, by providing transport. He has delegated a responsibility. Similarly the company commander may make the sergeant-major responsible for having certain drivers and vehicles ready; this is a further delegation of responsibility. The notion of delegating responsibility is a way of looking at an organisational chain from the point of view of assigning credit and blame for success or failure of the aim, or part of the aim, of the organisation as a whole.

On the other hand, we speak of the delegation of authority when we are interested, not in the achievement of some objective, but in the explanation, excuse or justification of some particular action, which may itself be the issuing of a command. In the case of actual operations, we have already seen that to quote a command is to give such explanation or justification. But it may be questioned whether the command was a legitimate or authorised command, or (what is in fact the same thing) whether it was a *command*. For instance, if a soldier is asked why he is digging an officer's garden, the answer that he was ordered to do so may not be accepted: it may be disputed whether the officer was authorised to issue such a command. If a magistrate orders an offender to pay a fine of £100, it may be objected that such a fine can only be imposed by a higher court; the magistrate acted *ultra vires*, his order was not one he was authorised to issue. At all levels of an organisation, what may be commanded at one level is limited by commands at a higher level. The twin notions of responsibility and authority between them describe the situation in which, at each level, what *must* be done is somehow specified, while what *may* be done is also specified; but one specification is a positive prescription, the other is a restriction or limitation. Responsibility is assigned; authority is allowed. To make someone responsible for something is a way of getting him to do it; to authorise someone to do something is to remove a possible restriction on his doing it. What is important about a man's responsibilities is that there are certain tasks he must perform; what is important about his authority is that in the pursuance of these or other tasks, there are steps he may, and others he may not, take.

There is another respect in which our model is still too simple. We have spoken as if an organisation controls the activities of its members through the medium of commands (including high-level directives). Our discussion of responsibility did not introduce anything substantially new, since assigning responsibility for something is closely similar to commanding. But the discussion of authorisation does introduce a new factor, since to authorise someone to do something is different from commanding him to do it, as 'you may' is different from 'you must'. To assign responsibility is to give assurance that, if something is *not* done, blame will be forthcoming. To assign authority is to give assurance that, if something *is* done, blame will *not* be forthcoming. Part of the force of 'I authorise you to. . . .' is 'If anyone gets the blame, it will be me and not you.'[1]

10. *Commands and Rules*

But commands and authorisations are not the only instruments of control. An organisation which relied on them exclusively would be extremely inefficient, if not impossible. The company commander in our earlier example does not have to be *told* to look after the welfare and efficiency of his men, nor does he need to be forbidden to issue orders to a civilian. He knows that the one is his responsibility, and that the other exceeds his authority, not because any commands or authorisations have been addressed to him, but because there are certain general rules, positive and negative, and not necessarily listed in a manual, to the observation of which he is committed by holding a certain office. This is true of all organisations. Control exists, at any level, not only, or even mainly, through the medium of explicit commands, but through the existence and observance of general rules prescribing what shall, and forbidding what shall not, be done at that particular level. There is no theoretical limit to the degree of control that can be exercised through rules. There is only the practical difficulty of formulating rules to

[1] Compare T. D. Weldon, *Vocabulary of Politics*, p. 53.

determine action appropriate to all possible circumstances. It is a common complaint of military commanders in the field that battles could be fought as well, or better, without any General Staff. But they could be fought without any officers at all, if rules could be worked out (and remembered) such that an individual soldier, in observing the rules, would always do what was most conducive to victory in all possible circumstances.

This difference between two types of control is an example of a general difference between two types of imperative language, or the difference between what I will call an *ad hoc* directive and a standing rule. All rules are standing rules, except those that are just being set up (just as all laws are in force, except those which are in the process of becoming law); hence we may simplify the contrast to directives and rules. Examples of directives are commands, prohibitions and explicit permissions; examples of rules are laws, licences, traditions, principles, moral codes, professional codes, codes of etiquette, standing orders, conventions, customs, and the rules of games. Directives require speakers; rules do not. The language of directives is, as we have seen, performatory: to speak in a certain way *is* to command, and to command *is* to speak in a certain way. But the language of rules is not performatory; to mention a rule is not to create one, and rules can come into force without the use of any special form of language (for example, customs).[1] The distinction between the two types is illustrated by the story told of an anonymous American University in which a notice appeared embodying the formula: 'This tradition will take effect from the beginning of next term.'

11. *The Authority of Rules*

Rules, as well as commands, must be authoritative. For it is often a sufficient reason, for a man's acting in a certain way, that there is a rule (such as law, or moral principle) prescribing such an action. We have seen something of the way in which a person gets his authority to command. But rules do not require

[1] Rules cannot come into force without expression in *some* form of language, however. See VI, 6.

speakers and cannot be invested with authority as persons can be. Where, then, do they get their authority from? We may suspect that the authority of persons and the authority of rules are not independent of each other. But do rules get their authority because they are (sometimes) promulgated by certain persons, or do persons get their authority because of certain rules?

Suppose I recognise as a rule in force (that is, as authoritative) the law to the effect that a vehicle must not be driven over 30 m.p.h. in a built-up area. Suppose that I am stopped by a policeman and told 'You were exceeding 30 m.p.h. in that built-up stretch. Don't do it again.' If I recognise the authoritativeness of this command, it is not only because I recognise the authority of the law. For if the command had been issued by anyone who was not a member of the police force, I should not recognise it as a command. Furthermore, if the command had been 'Hand over your wallet', I should not recognise this as a command even if I was satisfied that the speaker was a police officer. What is required is both that I recognise the existence in force of some relevant rule, and also that I recognise the authority of some individual to apply that rule in the form of a command. But in other cases, such as a military order, I need not recognise any general rule of which the order is an application, though I must still recognise the authority of the individual to command me. The most we can say is that commands derive their authority from the status of the speaker, but we have still to enquire how that is determined.

The answer is in terms of delegation and limitation. The authority of someone who issues a particular command to someone else is the authority of the entire organisation of which they are both members. The authority of the lance-corporal is that of the whole military organisation; the authority of the policeman over the motorist is the authority of the State. But the authority is delegated authority. And this means that, while its force remains the same, its scope is limited. Our respect for the authority of the police, our readiness to accept their imperatives as commands, is no less and no greater than our respect for the authority of the State. But, for any given official, there are commands which he may issue but which his subordinates may not, others which he may not issue but which his superiors may, and still others which neither he nor his superiors may issue, commands which are altogether *ultra vires*. Rules and commands may have the same authoritative force, but the authority of a command may be called in question at a point where the authority of a rule cannot: for a given imperative, even though logically deducible from a given rule, may yet be void as a command through being delivered on the wrong level, or by the wrong person. The remark 'Stop at the red traffic light' is an imperative which certainly follows strictly (in a suitable situation) from the law that all vehicles must stop at a red traffic light; as a remark from one motorist to another, it may be sound advice; but it cannot be a command, even though I recognise the law and intend to act on it. An imperative deducible from a given rule is not necessarily a command. Or, to bring in again the notion of responsibility; it may be everyone's responsibility to enforce a rule with the powers at their disposal; but the powers which are at one's disposal, and consequently the range of commands which may be used to implement the rule, are always limited, and differ for different people.

12. *Persons and Office-Holders*

An important consequence of this is that authority never attaches to persons as such, but only to persons as having a certain status within an organisation. Actual commands must of course be uttered by speakers, just as actual statements must; but the authority — or authenticity — of their commands depends not on their characteristics as speakers, or as persons, but solely on their capacity as functionaries or officials. An organisation is not, strictly, a system of persons, but a system of office-holders. One person may happen to hold more than one office in the same organisation; several persons may hold the same office. We have already noted that an organisation can exist without undertaking any activities. We can now add that it may exist without being staffed. It may exist 'on paper'. What matters is that there should be offices which can be filled; not that they be actually occupied. Organisations exist in virtue of the hierarchically related positions or offices which persons may hold; these offices exist in virtue of the successive limitations of their powers of command and areas of responsibility; and this limitation is effected by standing rules. The answer to the question: Which is prior, the authority of persons or of rules? is thus answered. Persons have authority only as office-holders; and this authority is determined by rules.

13. *Disobedience and Authority*

A final observation about the nature of authority is concerned with disobedience. What happens when a rule is broken or a command is disobeyed? Part of what happens is extremely simple. Just as a statement is either true or false (excluding ambiguous or vague statements) so a command is either complied with or not complied with. Compliance and non-compliance are to commands what truth and falsity are to statements. The Law of Excluded Middle holds for both. Now the usual purpose of making a statement is to convey true information, and for this purpose what is required is to make the statement conform to the facts. The usual purpose of issuing a command is to make something happen; instead of making the language fit the facts, we want to make the facts fit the language. But while a false statement is just as much a statement as a true one is, though it happens to have the wrong relation to the facts, it is not true that a command which is disobeyed is just a command, to which the facts happen to be wrongly related. A false statement has no special character; it may be amusing, silly, deplorable or of no consequence whatever. But a disobeyed command does have a special character. And so does a broken rule. To compare rules or general imperatives with general statements: breaking a rule is quite different from producing a contrary instance to a generalisation. It has often been pointed out, concerning the use of the term 'law' in science, that a major difference between a natural law and a prescriptive law is that the former is demolished by an exception, but the latter is not. What happens is something quite different.

To disobey a command is to flout authority. To break a rule is, on the face of it, to commit an offence, and this also is a flouting of authority. But rules are not always broken deliberately. They may be broken accidentally, or by an act of negligence which is neither deliberate nor accidental. These differences are important, because on them depends the answer to the question, whether an offence has been committed, whether authority has been flouted. Another difference on which this also depends is the difference between the 'letter' and the 'spirit' of the law. To offend against the letter of the law, but not the spirit, is often called a 'technical' offence, by which is meant that it is not an offence in the sense of a rejection of authority.

All rules, to be operative, must be authoritative. We have seen[1] that the point of a rule is to make people's behaviour different from what it would be if it were unregulated; if people always naturally acted in a certain way there would be no room for a rule to the effect that they *should* act in that way. Such a rule could not even be formulated until someone conceives the possibility of acting otherwise. But until someone does act otherwise, there will be no possible application for the rule. On the other hand, if a Utopian politician were to devise a set of laws for an Ideal State, there being no question of applying them to existing behaviour, such 'rules' could not be genuine rules either. The existence of a rule requires both that people tend of their own accord to behave otherwise, and that nevertheless they are prepared to act as the rule requires, that is, they respect the authority of the rule. Nor is this peculiar to the political rules we call laws. Even the rules of a game have some authoritative force. Whoever breaks them does not merely perform a move which other people would not perform. He commits an offence by 'not playing the game'.

[1] P. 97.

CHAPTER IX

# CONSCIENCE AND AUTHORITY (ii)

## 1. *Is There a Moral Organisation?*

We can now begin to apply this long discussion of the nature of authority to the special case of morality. Moral authority is distinguished from political, military and other kinds of authority (such as are exemplified in organisations) by the apparent absence of a moral organisation. Indeed we think that our duties as members of organisations are ultimately limited by our moral convictions, which come to us as free moral agents and not as members of any super-organisations. But Kant has argued that moral freedom is not incompatible with, and in fact entails, membership of a moral 'kingdom', just as political freedom is not lawlessness but entails membership of some kind of political state. No doubt the moral kingdom is not an earthly one, but it is not necessarily a celestial one either. It has just those features which I have described as essential to a normal organisation. Of course it lacks others, and these others may be more prominent for practical affairs, but their absence may be logically irrelevant. For instance, the moral kingdom is not staffed by officials; but this, as we have seen, is not an essential feature.

## 2. *Self-Commands*

In the cases we have considered so far, it is natural to regard the authority which someone recognises in the persons who command him, or in the rules which apply to him, as something external to himself. The private soldier, who has to obey his company commander's orders, did not himself issue them, nor did he have any hand in the framing of 'Standing Orders for Sentries'. But we have seen that the nature of authority does not depend on its being wielded by specific persons. It follows that the exercise of authority in a particular matter, and the deference to authority in that matter, are not necessarily functions of different persons. They may be combined in one person. A man may deliver commands to himself with the same authority as those he delivers to his subordinates. The company commander who makes a standing order that all ranks will wear polished boots not only authorises subordinate officers to issue the appropriate commands to the rank and file, but he is also in a position to order himself to wear polished boots. He may issue this command, if he is whimsically inclined; but normally it will be 'as if' he has done so, just as the manager's instructions to his secretary operate 'as if' they had been explicit commands. There is nothing in the least peculiar or puzzling about self-commands. In particular there should be no temptation whatever to fabricate stories about one 'part' of the man issuing commands to another 'part'. For even when one man commands another, it is not, strictly, one person issuing commands to another person, but rather one office-holder to another. The company commander is able to issue commands to himself because he holds different offices in the same organisation. He is commander of the company, but he is also a member of it. If his order had stated 'All *other* ranks. . . .' there would be no self-command.

3. *Autonomy and Equality*

Moral rules and moral self-control seem, at first, to resist assimilation to this simple pattern. Unlike military orders, they do not operate within the framework of an actual organisation; but I shall suggest that there are moral offices, even if there are no moral officers. A further objection is that St. Paul's expression about a man being 'a law unto himself' seems to have a real force, in ethics, which is lacking, or at least trivial, in the military example. And thirdly, it seems that in moral matters the notion of command is altogether out of place, since a man is never in a position to issue moral commands to others. We have already criticised the 'neat' Imperative Theory of moral judgments and commands.[1] Surely it is involved in the very meaning

[1] P. 149.

of 'moral' that a decision to do X, because A commanded X, is not a moral decision? Of course nothing prevents a man from commanding another to do X, if he holds (non-moral) authority to command X, and X happens to be a morally right or obligatory act; but the decision to do X is a moral decision only if B decides to do it because it is right or obligatory, not if he decides to do it only because A commanded it. So if a man is never in a position to issue moral commands to others, can he issue them to himself either?

These objections only serve to strengthen the case for a 'moral organisation' on Kantian lines. The fact that A may not issue commands to C does not entail that he may not issue them to B; and the fact that he may not issue them to B does not mean that he may not issue them to A. If A and B are motorists, A may not command B to stop at the red light, even though B respects the rule and has every intention of stopping; C, however, who is a policeman, may command B to do so. For B and C belong to appropriate levels of a common organisation, while A and B do not. What A offers B can only be advice. In ethics, where the rule in question is not an ordinary law but a moral principle, A cannot command anyone else, nor can anyone else command A. A can command only himself.

This might seem to be suggesting that there is no common organisation to which anyone belongs besides A himself; everyone belongs to his own organisation. But Kant certainly wished to say that other people must be regarded as members of the same moral kingdom as the agent himself. How can this be so, if no one is in a position to issue any commands except to himself? The answer is that other people do indeed belong to the same organisation. But they are all on the same level; they all hold offices of the same degree — or, rather, degrees. One moral agent cannot issue commands to another, any more than one officer can issue commands to another of equal rank and appointment. Only so can the autonomy of moral principles be reconciled with the universality of moral judgments. All moral beings are of equal status. Ourselves we can command; but others we can only advise.

The authority of a moral rule, then, appears in the agent's readiness to obey a command, derived from the rule, and issued by himself to himself. In our general discussion of the nature of authority we saw that part of the meaning of the term is given by saying that a person recognises the authority of another person A, or of a rule R, if he is prepared to obey A, or to comply with R, without asking further questions; or to quote A's order, or the existence of R, as justifying what he did, without expecting further questions. Now this readiness to act without asking further questions, and this readiness to accept a reason for someone else's action, again without asking further questions, is a commonplace in ethics. We can ask why some action was done, but having agreed that it was right, or in accordance with a moral principle which we accept, no further question can be asked about reasons for doing it. We can ask why we should do something, but having agreed that it is what we ought to do, no further question remains why we should do it.

4. *The Ultimacy of Moral Authority*

Of course, it is not only in ethics that a man may deliver imperatives to himself, act on them, and justify his action by referring to a rule from which the imperative follows. On the contrary, this can happen with all rules whatever. The rule governing the rook's move, in chess, is commonly applied by someone saying to himself 'I mustn't move the rook to such-and-such a square', by his moving it to an appropriate square, or by defending his move by referring to the relevant rule. He may also have occasion, if he happens to be teaching someone else how to play chess, to issue an imperative 'Don't move the rook diagonally', and this may amount to a command from instructor to novice.

The rules of chess, and the chess-instructor's advice or commands are, of course, externally authorised. But it is not peculiar to ethics that rules and commands should be internally authorised. A man may not only issue self-commands according to the rules of a game like chess, which he has to learn and accept; he may make up the rules himself. One may invent a private game in which one observes certain rules, even though no one else knows what the rules are. One may also devise rules of conduct for oneself; and though these will not be moral rules unless they are also used in assessing the conduct of others, nevertheless their relation to one's own behaviour, *via* self-addressed imperatives internally authorised, may be the same.

What is peculiar about moral authority is not that it is internal but that it is, in an important sense, unchallengeable. All other sources of authority can be challenged. Any given rule can be broken, not only accidentally or negligently, but deliberately. One can, by suitable acts of defiance, reject the authority of the State, the Church, the M.C.C. or any other organisation; and also the authority of systems of rules, such as the rules of chess, hopscotch or a private game, which have not been codified by actual organisations. One can even decide to repudiate all authorities whatsoever and be a universal (not merely political) anarchist. But in practice one usually rejects a certain authority for what one regards as good reasons; and the repudiation takes the form of a preference for some other authority. One may reject the authority of one's schoolmistress who forbids make-up in favour of one's parent who permits it; one may reject the authority of the state which orders training in the arts of warfare in favour of the authority of one's pacifist convictions. Since, then (short of anarchism) every rejection of authority depends on the recognition of some other authority as superior, there are two possibilities. Either all our various sources of authority are recognised only provisionally, that is, we regard none of them as beyond challenge; or else there must be some one source of authority which we recognise as unchallengeable, and by reference to which all other authorities can be challenged.

This second possibility must be the case if there really are moral principles, as distinct from other kinds of principle. We regard a man as a moral agent, only so long as we regard him as having the right to set himself against all external authorities whatever, and to make up his own mind what he ought to do, irrespective of what he may be commanded to do. It is convenient, then, to think of the authorities which are subject to challenge as the external ones, and to think of the authority which alone cannot be challenged as an internal authority. This is imprecise, however, because an 'internal authority' need not be unchallengeable. Certainly it must not mislead us into thinking that there exists any special internal Faculty with mysterious powers. All that is meant is that a man may give orders to himself by reference to some system of principles which he adopts in preference to those which may be adopted by others.

### 5. *Self-Commands and Conscience*

The advantage of speaking in terms of self-directed commands is that it provides a solution to our original problem, 'How are principles translated into action?' or 'How does one's acceptance of a principle make a difference to one's conduct?' It has been tempting to assume that there must be some gap between the intellectual recognition of a principle and the practical performance of the action enjoined by the principle; and that the gap must have a bridge built over it, if ethics — and moral psychology — is to make sense. But no one feels the need to bridge any gap between the chess-player's mastery of chess rules and his commands to the novice not to move the rook diagonally, or between the Latin master's Latinity and his instructions to the schoolboy about the moods of conditional sentences. Why should a gap suddenly appear when the rules are to be applied not to the controlling of other people's actions, but to the controlling of one's own?

The answer is, no doubt, that self-directed commands have been decked out in pseudo-psychological garb which transforms them from the simple unexciting things they are. It is the old story of the Parts of the Soul. A self-directed command must be a command issued by the body's Executive, called the Will; and the chain of authority is completed by attributing cognisance of the relevant rule or principle to another faculty, called Reason or the Intellect. In specifically moral contexts, a third faculty is invoked to play a dual role and is identified with Conscience:

sometimes it plays the intellectual part, grasping or intuiting the appropriate moral principles or standards ('My conscience tells me that. . . .'), sometimes it plays the practical part of issuing commands in accordance with those principles ('My conscience tells me to. . . .'). This dual role is well fitted for the job of bridging the gap, for that is just what it was designed to do. But the gap is fictitious, and the invention of a special moral faculty called Conscience, whose function is to bridge the gap, is unnecessary.

'Conscience' is not the name of any faculty or psychical component. Its function is to figure in expressions which refer to the issuing of self-directed commands in accordance with moral rules which we adopt as authoritative. So far I have suggested that the authority of conscience is ultimate and unchallengeable. For one can challenge an authority only by appeal to some other authority, so that one must rest somewhere with a decision to accept some ruling as final; and this decision will be a moral decision and conscience the final and ultimate authority. But is conscience really beyond challenge? Doubt may arise if we remember that to break a rule is, at least on the face of it, to challenge or repudiate the authority of that rule. And it is notorious that we can act wrongly, that is, we can break moral rules. It is further agreed (except by Socrates) that one can do wrong knowingly, that is, one can break a moral rule which one still accepts. Does not this constitute a challenge to my moral authority?

The answer must be that it does not. If, for example, I sin through weakness or temptation, being unable to bring myself to do what I know I ought to do, or to keep myself from doing what I know I ought not to do, then clearly I do not call in question the moral rule; my respect for its authority is unimpaired. The same is true if I try to comply with the rule but fail through incompetence or oversight, through failure to judge correctly what action is called for, under the rule, in a particular situation. Even if I reject the rule itself, although it is true that I no longer regard it as authoritative, yet provided that I reject it in favour of some other rule, as is usually the case, the authority of conscience remains intact. (One final objection to the unchallengeability of conscience will be dealt with in Sec. 7.)

6. *Kinds of Moral Failure: A Three-Storey Model*

Let us consider in how many different ways one may go wrong in the process of applying moral rules to conduct. Going wrong is easier to investigate than going right, and the positive term can be dealt with by implication. There are three such ways of going wrong, which have close analogies in our organisation model. We consider, this time, a three-storey model[1] in which the commands issued on the second level are derived from, and authorised by, rules or principles originating on the top level. Let us call the three levels the Legislature, the Administration, and the Executive. The Legislature adopts or enacts laws, principles or universal imperatives; the Administration applies these principles to particular situations and issues appropriate commands; the Executive obeys those commands. The same person, we remember, may hold all these positions. Now in how many ways can the operation of this simple organisation go wrong? There are at least five ways, but two of these can be ruled out as inapplicable to the case of morality; the other three, however, have strict parallels.

Two obvious ways of going wrong are the following. (1) The Executive defies the Administration and refuses to obey its commands. (2) The Administration defies the Legislature and applies principles of its own choice. (1) corresponds to insurrection, (2) to usurpation, and each constitutes a rejection of authority. I have already suggested that one cannot reject the authority of conscience. The reason why these cases have no parallels in the operation of conscience is that one cannot reject one's own command, because this would be equivalent to issuing and revoking it at the same time; nor can one repudiate a principle one adopts, for this would be both to assent to and to dissent from it. Neither can occur, because each would involve a contradiction.

But there remain three further ways in which things can go

[1] Not to be confused with the three-tier model of I, 6.

wrong for the organisation. (3) The Executive may fail to obey the Administration, not through deliberate disobedience, but through inability, weakness or negligence. It tries to do what it is told, but fails. Consequently things go wrong, unless by accident they happen to come right. (4) The Administration may fail to apply the right principles to the given situation and so fail to issue the right commands, not because it rejects the principles but because of incompetence. It tries to issue the right orders, but fails. Consequently, however scrupulously the Executive carries out its orders, things will go wrong, unless by accident. (5) Finally, the Legislature may enact or adopt the wrong principles, through wickedness, or foolishness, or lack of foresight. Either it tries to issue the right rules and fails, or it does not even try. Consequently, however scrupulously and accurately the Administration applies the rules and issues its commands, and however scrupulously the Executive carries out those commands, things will go wrong, unless by accident.

The same possibilities exist in individual ethics. In the first place (corresponding to (3)), a man may rightly accept a moral rule, conscientiously decide to follow it, but be thwarted by temptation or weakness, and consequently what he does is morally wrong. (If it happens to 'come right' by accident — if the consequences of his lapse happen to be unexpectedly good — this reflects no moral credit on him.) Secondly (corresponding to (4)) a man may rightly accept a set of moral rules, but may fail in his appreciation of a situation or in his selection of the relevant rule. Consequently, however earnestly he desires to do his duty ('He means well') and however successfully he wards off temptation, yet he fails to do his duty, because he complies with the wrong self-command. Thirdly (corresponding to (5)) a man may deliberately and conscientiously adopt a wrong moral principle. Such a man cannot act rightly, however correctly he applies his principles to a situation, and however strong-willed and resistant to temptation he may be.

Straightforward examples of thoroughgoing moral perversity of this last kind are rather hard to come by, and they impose severe strains on the language used to describe them. The reason for this is that we are forced to speak at one and the same time of a man adopting a moral principle (and, as far as he is concerned, whatever principles he chooses to adopt *are* the right ones) and yet of that principle being a wrong one. We are close to self-contradiction, just because we are dealing with the peculiar situation in which there is a duality of standards and consequently, a conflict of verdicts. A theoretical example is that of a man who rejects the moral code of his society;[1] but we hardly feel the force of the contradiction here, since we need not identify ourselves either with the man or with the society. Examples in which we take sides ourselves do bring home the contradiction. Consider, for instance, Milton's Satan who says 'Evil be thou my good': or Shakespeare's Aaron (in *Titus Andronicus*):

> If one good deed in all my life I did,
> I do repent it from my very soul.

Now evil cannot be good, nor can what is good be repented. The contradiction is only avoided by distinguishing two standards, only one of which we accept; what is good according to this one is *good*, but what is good according to the other is only so-called 'good' and may therefore be abjured or, if done, repented.

These three ways of going wrong morally yield three different kinds of moral defect in a person, and three corresponding kinds of moral goodness. It is an interesting exercise, which I shall not pursue here, to set out the various combinations of one kind of defect or virtue with others, so as to obtain complex part-defects and part-virtues. What are we to say, for example, of the man who combines adherence to an evil moral principle with a weakness or disability in executing it? Can two defects add up to a virtue? Is the conscientiously obedient Nazi soldier, who intends to machine-gun some prisoners but is prevented by fear of reprisals or the like, a better or a worse man than one who is not so deterred? Can two wrongs make a right? Such questions cannot be answered here, since they begin to involve actual moral judgments rather than the analysis of conscience.

[1] See above, p. 40.

7. *Conscience and 'Conscience'*

There remains one objection that can be made against the view that the authority of conscience is unchallengeable. It can be rebutted, but its discussion leads to an important distinction between two senses of 'conscience', and brings in the question of the genesis of conscience. Consider the following conversation:

A. I can't do that. It would be against my conscience.

B. Conscience! Don't let that prevent you. Your conscience is only a conditioned response, produced by your childhood training. When you think your conscience tells you not to do something, this is only a reflection of the occasions when you were told not to do something by your parents, or punished for doing it. That succession of prohibitions and punishments naturally built up in you a certain resistance against acting in the way I propose. But you must see that your reluctance is quite irrational. You have everything to gain, etc. . . .

This sort of argument may well lead A to act in the way B proposes, and he may dispose of his 'conscience' by saying 'I see that I have been misguided in always relying on my conscience. B was quite right about conditioning. From now on I shall ignore my conscience and act as I really think best.'

This is certainly a rejection of the authority of 'conscience'. But it is not a rejection of the authority of *conscience*. We must distinguish between 'conscience' and *conscience*.[1] What A and B in the above conversation meant by 'conscience' was, whatever gave authority to a certain set of rules which A at one time adopted. But 'conscience' in the proper sense gives authority to whatever set of rules one does in fact adopt; and if one chooses to adopt a different set of rules, as A might, one does not reject conscience, but only certain rules. A still has a conscience, after his conversion by B, provided that he has any moral rules at all.

Of course there is something about this particular type of conversion which makes it plausible to speak of rejecting 'con-

[1] Compare the distinction between 'good' and good, p. 174, and Mr. Hare's account of the 'inverted-commas use' of ethical terms, *Language of Morals*, p. 124.

science'. Partly it is that one may reject not one rule in favour of another, but a whole set of rules *en bloc*; partly it is a genuine difference in the *modus operandi* of 'conscience' and *conscience*, suggested by the psychological theorising of B, with its distinction between unreflective response and rational conduct. Conscience involves some degree of reflection; 'conscience' does not. This leads us to consider the question, how 'conscience' originates and how it gets promoted to conscience.

This question also will be answered in terms of authority, and has already been touched on at the end of Chapter IV. Briefly, the answer is that 'conscience' represents an external authority, conscience an internal one, and that the transition between the two is the process which we may call the internalisation of authority. The process begins when we start to question (if we ever do) the finality of the commands issued to us by parents and others responsible for our moral guidance in our years of immaturity. We will suppose that at an earlier stage we accept their commands and prohibitions without question, and take them as sufficient justification for our conduct. This is exactly what I have defined as the recognition of authority in others. We will further suppose that at this early stage, or perhaps a little later, we also become aware of some general principles in the light of which our moral tutors issue their commands and prohibitions. Some of these may be rehearsed explicitly ('One must always. . . .'; 'Good little girls never. . . .'); others we learn indirectly. These general principles, too, we accept as authoritative. We do what Father says, not only because Father says so, but because Father is always right.

Moral maturity is the achievement of moral autonomy. Instead of being guided by other people's commands and principles, we are guided by our own. We no longer do things because Father says so, and his principles are not necessarily right. We learn to submit them to the test of reason and reflection and to take our own decisions about them.

Of course, though Father's principles are not necessarily right, we may decide that they are right, all the same. If so, the hand-over of authority from Father to oneself, the internalisation of authority, proceeds smoothly. There will be no conflict or heart-searching. And we shall have achieved another step in the transmission of a morality from generation to generation.

But what happens if we decide that Father's principles are not right? There will be a break of transmission, and the hand-over of authority will proceed less smoothly. We do not only reject Father's authority to implement the rules, we reject the rules themselves. We have to deal with two sets of rules which are incompatible. Actions prohibited by the one set are permitted or prescribed by the other.

### 8. *Assenting to Rules and Acquiring Dispositions*

Difficulties arise in practice because accepting and rejecting rules of conduct is not simply a matter of saying Yes and No. To practise conformity to a given rule may be to have a disposition or tendency of character towards acting in the way required by the rule. Yet we have seen that there would be no place for a rule, if we *always* acted in the way which such a rule would prescribe. In practice the matter of observing rules falls midway between two extremes. We do not attend to the rule every time we act on it. The chess-player does not think about the rules of chess every time he makes a move; and the moralist does not 'consult his conscience' every time he decides to act or to criticise. On the other hand we do sometimes attend to the rule; if we never did, there would not *be* a rule. The chess-player has to think about the rules of chess if the legitimacy of a move is challenged, or if he is instructing a novice. Similarly the moralist has to consult his repertory of moral principles if another moralist challenges his decision, or — the case which concerns us directly here — if he is teaching a morality. Or — still more to the point — if he is learning one.

The disposition to conform to a rule comes as a result of practising conformity, as Aristotle emphasises in his theory of moral training. When we are learning a rule, we must attend to it regularly; when we have learnt it, we need attend less often. But we must attend to it sometimes, if it is to be a rule at all.

(As I suggested in VI, 5, attending to a principle is part of what actually makes it a principle.) Now our amateur psychologist in the conversation above touched on an important truth — though he misdescribed it — when he spoke of conscience (that is, 'conscience') as a conditioned response, produced by training in youth. Dispositions to act in certain ways are certainly produced in us by our trainers and educators. Dispositions to act in accordance with certain rules can indeed be built up by a system of rewards and punishments, or by any other way in which the observance of rules can be encouraged. But the nature of a disposition is such that it cannot have either a determinate beginning or a determinate ending. Both its genesis and its elimination are essentially gradual. Abstemiousness and sportsmanship are not acquired in a day, nor can irritability or cowardice be shed in a single session with either psychiatrist or preacher. (Stories of people who became 'different persons' as a result of a crisis or encounter testify to the rarity of such apparent changes.)

It follows that the disposition to obey certain rules cannot always or often disappear simultaneously with a decision to adopt different rules. It also follows that such a decision to adopt different rules does not at once generate a disposition to act accordingly. The building-up of the one disposition, and the breaking-down of the other, must overlap to a greater or less extent. Where the overlap is considerable, or where the rule is a particularly important one, moral crises are apt to occur such as that which sets the context of our conversation above. Such a crisis is on us when we say 'I feel that I ought to do X, but I know that really I ought to do Y.' 'Feeling' is a thoroughly misleading word here and has nothing to do with inclination or the conflict between 'Reason' and 'Passion'. Rather the 'conflict' is between two dispositions, an unreflective tendency towards or against X resulting, say, from parental training, and a reflective attitude to a new moral rule about X. Or, preferably, since dispositions cannot literally conflict, we are in a quandary because we are acquiring a disposition towards X before we have lost another kind of disposition against it.

9. *An Illustration*

This conflict between 'conscience' and *conscience* can be illustrated from our earlier example, *Brief Encounter* (VII, 3). We may ask ourselves what Laura really ought to do, and we may decide that she ought to go with Alec and leave her husband. Clearly if we can decide thus, so can she. But even if she does, even if she decides that it really is her moral duty to go with Alec, yet (being the person she is supposed to be) she will certainly have feelings of remorse, if she acts accordingly. But why, if she is doing what she sincerely believes to be her duty, do these remorseful feelings persist? The answer is: because of the time-lag between the reflective decision and the dispositional re-orientation required for 'whole-hearted' conduct. The old authority persists, even though explicitly repudiated. 'Conscience' can still cause remorse and misgivings, even though these are not reasonable. It is still an internal authority, though it may be a mere shadow of an external one. And in this borderland of overlapping dispositions, one can indeed challenge conscience — but only if we write it as 'conscience'. One cannot challenge *conscience*, because this would involve the contradiction of both recognising and also repudiating an authority.

10. *Summary*

We may sum up this whole discussion of conscience and authority by returning to Butler. The mistake of Butler and others who speak of the authority of conscience is not that they make use of a bad analogy or model or set of theory-ridden metaphors. On the contrary, the analogy of an organisation is a sound one, in fact the best there is. The essential features of a moral agent's experience and behaviour cannot be brought out without it.

The mistake is to extract from the model more than is needed. Conscience is not, after all, a magistrate, and in listening to the voice of conscience I am not my inferior, earthly or animal nature or part of myself listening to the voice of my superior, godlike or rational nature or part. No such agencies need be presupposed or invented. The essence of an organisation is not that it should be staffed: it is that provision should exist for the authorisation of commands. The notion of a command, and the inseparable notion of authority, are all that need be extracted from the analogy. And they are all that are needed to explain the relation between moral principles and moral actions.

# *PART III*

# TOWARDS A NEW HUMANISM

*The moral law, we may say, has to be expressed in the form, 'be this', not in the form, 'do this'. . . . Christianity gave prominence to the doctrine that the true moral law says 'hate not', instead of 'kill not'.*

LESLIE STEPHEN

CHAPTER X

# MORAL PRINCIPLES AND MORAL MAN

## 1. *Theory and Fact*

Ethical theories seem to fall into types with much more radical differences between them than any other philosophical theories. Indeed one may even be in doubt whether two so-called moral philosophers — Plato and Kant, say — are discussing a common topic at all. And in fact, I shall suggest, they are not. Different ethical theories are not usually different discussions of the same things; they are often about different things. One reason for this is the enormous complexity of the data for ethics. Consider, for instance, the great variety of things to which the word 'moral' can be applied. One can speak of moral qualities, attitudes, feelings, judgments, rules, decisions, scruples, character, education, etc. And if the fundamental question in moral philosophy is 'What is the meaning of "moral"?' or 'What makes a moral X different from a non-moral X?', it is not surprising that philosophers have been either unable, or unwilling, even to look for an answer which would apply to all these uses of the term. Their procedure has been something like this: let us concentrate on one of these Xs — qualities, say. We say that certain things are good or bad, others red or blue. What is the difference between the kinds of thing we are saying in each case? Or again, 'Let us concentrate on another of the Xs: rules, say. There are rules of games, and the rules we call laws of the land: there are also the moral rules which we call moral principles. What is the difference between moral and non-moral rules?' And so on.

Now it is perfectly proper to confine oneself to a limited enquiry of this sort, provided one does not go on to extend one's findings uncritically to the other ethical topics. But moral philosophy cannot rest there. It must needs claim to have something to say — at least by implication — about the moral life, and not merely one aspect of it. And it may well be that different approaches to this task — approaches, that is, *via* a different selection of Xs — will be of very different value in the general conclusions they afford about the moral life as it is actually lived. Consequently there is room for criticism of an ethical theory not only for its particular conclusions, but also for what I might call its presuppositions — for being a theory of a certain type, based on a certain selection of the facts, committed in advance, as it were, to a certain one-sidedness in its review of the moral life. The type of theory which I have been so far promoting in this book does not escape this criticism. It makes its own selection of the Xs of the moral life — and it chooses rules, or moral principles. In what follows I shall be pointing to certain defects of this kind of theory, resulting from this particular selection. But I want to make it quite clear that the defects are only the inevitable result of the need to make a selection. And the selection which does the most justice — or, rather, the least injustice — to the moral life as a whole, is just this one — the ethics of moral principles. So before coming to the defects of this kind of theory, I will recall its principal virtue.

2. *On Describing Man*

A theory which shall not be false to the facts of the moral life must not, *a fortiori*, falsify the nature of man who lives it. Ethical theories are never independent of other branches of philosophy; this was implicit in my discussion of philosophy as the mapping of bridges and barriers; ethical theories both influence, and are influenced by, other ways of thinking and, in particular, the way in which philosophers of a particular school or generation tend to think about human beings — their way of answering the old-fashioned but perennial question 'What is the nature of man and what is man's place in the Universe?' (Such questions need not be, and seldom are nowadays, put point-blank, and by 'answers' I do not mean necessarily explicit answers, but assumptions and presuppositions about the nature of human beings and the proper way of describing them, which may be implicit in the kind of answers given to other questions, including ethical ones.) For instance, is a man an assemblage of psychological mechanisms? Is he a machine, with or without a ghostly engineer? Is he a creature actuated by pleasure and pain? Is he a temporary product of the evolutionary process? Is he a temporary union of the earthly and the divine? And so on. Affirmative answers to these and similar questions carry with them characteristic ethical theories; those of Hobbes, Bentham, Huxley and theological ethics can be correlated with the above list.

One view about the nature of man, which has already come in for incidental criticism, is what I may call the Parts-of-the-Soul doctrine. This is a family of doctrines which has in common the belief in a real distinction between Body and Soul, or Body and Mind; they differ about further distinctions between parts or faculties of the Soul or Mind: Reason and Passion, Intellect and Will, Cognitive Conative and Affective, and so on. The moral life seems to lend itself particularly well to such (mis)description. We have already seen how Conscience is plausibly, but wrongly, thought of as a sort of horse-and-rider combination of Intellect and Will. And the Will, in turn, seems to be necessary because a moral decision is an act of mind, yet its execution is an act of body; and how can these be linked (our original question: 'How can assenting to a moral judgment make a difference to our actions?') unless we postulate some mind-body linkage which we call the Will?

### 3. *The Dynamic Function of Principles*

The great virtue of an ethics in terms of moral principles is that it makes this problem superfluous. Of course the mere introduction of the term 'principle' is not enough: Kant's is a pure theory of principles, but he finds the notion of Will indispensable. We can still say that the decision to accept, or to act on, a moral principle, is an act of mind, and this gets us no nearer the execution of the decision, since we can still ask, 'How can the acceptance of the principle make any difference to conduct?'

But if we start from the notion of a principle, rather than from the preconceived idea of a mind-body synthesis, the problem becomes less intractable. There is, of course, a germ of truth in the old view. It is true that a moral principle is a *principle*, that is, something we can formulate in words, something we can understand in thought, something from which we can derive arguments, something for or against which we can produce reasons, and so on. Moral principles, then, do have an intellectual aspect; they are something we assent to (or dissent from) in much the same way as we assent to (or dissent from) statements which we think are true (or false). But on the other hand, moral principles have a practical aspect. They are *moral* principles: they have to do with conduct. They are not *merely* something we assent to or dissent from: what matters about a moral principle is that whether we assent to it or dissent from it makes a difference, and may make an enormous difference, to our actions. The conscientious objector is not just one who enunciates certain moral principles; he is one whose actions tend to conform to those principles, and are quite different from what they would be if he held other principles. One who preaches, without also practising what he preaches, is rightly condemned for insincerity, and indeed inconsistency: he only pays lip-service to morality. In other words, there is not only something intellectual about moral principles: there is also something practical and dynamic. This dynamic feature is what makes it congenial to some people to talk about moral Values: a Value just is something that we both understand and pursue. And this dynamic feature is what the traditional mind-body metaphysics can only explain on the hypothesis of the Will: the Will just is something which both assents to a moral principle and executes the movements required for the appropriate action.

### 4. *Intellectualists and Anti-Intellectualists*

Now any satisfactory ethical theory must give some account

of this dynamic feature — of the relation between moral understanding and moral action. It follows that there are two ways in which a moral theory can go wrong. It can go wrong by attending to the intellectual aspect of morality and ignoring or belittling the practical aspect; we shall then get a moral theory couched in terms of judgments, reasons and conclusions. Or it can go wrong by attending to the practical aspect and ignoring or belittling the intellectual aspect; we shall then get a moral theory in terms of actions and feelings. In both cases the word 'principle' will tend to be avoided because it draws attention to a relation which the theory is not equipped to deal with. The first of these two mistaken theories could be called intellectualistic, the other anti-intellectualistic. They could also receive the labels 'Objectivist' and 'Subjectivist', because I wish to associate each of them with a type of theory we have already discussed and criticised: Objectivism in Chapter V and Subjectivism in Chapter IV.

Objectivism attends to the intellectual features of morality and especially to the subject-predicate form of sentence in which some moral judgments are couched. There are, it is held, ethical characteristics, such as goodness, which can be predicated of subjects. But how can such a theory account for the dynamic aspect of morality? Only, it seems, in a highly artificial way. Ethical characteristics are peculiar, not only in being 'non-natural', but also in possessing, it seems, a unique capacity for moving people to action. Now there is nothing peculiar in things or qualities moving people to action, that is, being attractive or repulsive. What is peculiar is that ethical qualities must *necessarily* attract or repel. The attractiveness of certain foods, for instance, their power of moving people to take steps to obtain and taste them, has nothing necessary about it; some people dislike what others like; to what extent such goods are liked is a matter for empirical investigation, and even if no one could be found who disliked, say, strawberries, this would still be an empirical fact. But the attractiveness of the good cannot be a mere empirical fact; it must be a necessity.

This introduction into the world of mysterious necessities is enough to condemn the theory as too tailor-made. They are just put in, it seems, to explain the dynamic feature of morality in the only way that is open to a theory already committed to the existence of ethical qualities. And it was committed to this, in the first place, by the initial assumption that words like good and bad, right and wrong, are like other simple adjectives in referring to qualities and relations. The mistake of the Objectivists was to think that expressions such as 'Torturing is wrong' are like expressions such as 'Rice pudding is nutritious': not merely grammatically, but also logically alike: they are both statements. This is the typical mistake of a theory which concentrates on moral judgments and not on moral principles. It starts by insisting on what we have already seen to be an unreasonable demand: that moral judgments should be true or false; and it then has to deal with the dynamic feature of morality in a highly artificial way.

The extreme anti-intellectualistic view, by contrast, is the type we have already considered in the discussion of the Emotive Theory in Chapter IV. It is enough to recall that there is no room in this theory for moral principles, as there defined. For a moral principle is a *principle*, that is, some rule which applies to my actions generally, which I can consider apart from the occasions of acting, and which I can formulate in words. None of this is true of feelings. This was the first dimension of universality; and the second was, that a *moral* principle is a rule which applies to other people as well as to myself; and this again has nothing to do with feelings.

A theory in terms of moral principles, then, may be expected to avoid the mistakes both of the intellectualist and of the anti-intellectualist type of theory. It will not claim that moral judgments are statements of a peculiar kind of fact, nor yet that they are expressions of a peculiar kind of emotion. But even if this is so, it is not enough. So far, it does not do justice to the germ of truth that is in both mistaken theories. We must be able to show that it can answer the double question: How can morality have an intellectual aspect? and, How can morality have a practical, dynamic aspect? Can we answer these questions without falling back on to the kind of answer which the intellectualist and anti-intellectualist theories are waiting to give us — the one suggesting that moral principles must after all be apprehended by something, and what can this be but the Intellect? while they must make a difference to conduct, and how can this be except through the intervention of the Will? — the other theory demanding to know, on the contrary, how anything can move us to action except a motive, and how moral principles can actuate us except by arousing desires or aversions?

### 5. *Moral Imperatives*

The answer is most clearly stated by reverting to the logic of moral discourse. It is notable that both Kant and Mr. Hare — to take two examples of moral-principle philosophers — find it necessary to talk much of *imperatives*. The term 'imperative' already suggests the answer: for an imperative is both something in words which points to the intellectual aspect, and something whose function is to alter conduct, which is the practical aspect. But this is not enough. Putting something into words is not enough to make it an exercise of the intellect, as the Emotive theorists were well aware. Simple second-person imperatives will not do. But moral principles are not singular second-person imperatives. They are universal third-person imperatives. Their force is not 'Do this here and now', but 'Everybody is always to do this on such-and-such occasions'. (Third-person imperatives have no grammatical existence in English; there is only the periphrastic 'Let everyone. . . .'; but other languages have them.) The rule according to which it is wrong to tell lies is, 'Let no one ever tell a falsehood'. This is doubly universal: it applies to all occasions ('always' or 'never'), and it applies to all people ('everyone' or 'no one'). These are precisely the two dimensions of universality we have already ascribed to moral principles.

Why should a universal third-person imperative qualify as an exercise of intellect? The short answer is that any universal locution whatever is such an exercise. The ability to generalise, whether in description or prescription, to speak of all members of a certain class, is a characteristic intellectual ability. The ability to relate such generalisations to each other, to create structures of scientific theory or legal code, to establish relations of deducibility or inconsistency, to deduce predictions from universal statements, and injunctions or verdicts from universal imperatives — all this is, even less disputably, a set of intellectual capacities. This is the short answer. A fuller one is given in the chapters on 'Reason in Ethics' and 'Truth in Ethics'.

So much for the intellectual aspect of moral principles. But what of the dynamic aspect? Again, it is not quite enough to say that an imperative is just the sort of utterance whose function is to have an effect on conduct. For this suggests that morality is a matter of issuing and responding to commands, and this will not do even if we stipulate, as we must, that such commands shall be singular imperatives derived from universal third-personal imperatives or moral principles. Morality is not telling people to do things, not even telling them in accordance with a rule.

An imperative is not necessarily a form of speech by which A gets B to do something which he, A, *wishes* B to do. This is not even true of commands; and those who asserted that ethical judgments 'have the force of commands'[1] were not entitled to infer that their function is therefore to *stimulate* people to act. Imperatives are used in many other ways: for instance, in giving advice. We often ask for advice; the form of our question is 'What shall I do?' and the form of the answer is 'Do so and so'. But when B asks A for advice, and A gives it, A is certainly not trying to make B do what he, A, *wants* B to do; on the contrary, he is encouraging B to do what B himself would have wished to do, if he had not needed the advice. A (singular) imperative is not necessarily a command. It is just anything which gives an answer to the question 'What shall I do?'

Of course, I can address my question to a second person, and he can tell me what to do. If my tap drips I can ask a plumber 'What shall I do?' and he replies 'Fit a new washer'. Morality is not like that. As we saw in our discussion of Conscience, it is part of the meaning of morality that a man has not taken a genuinely moral decision if he has merely done what somebody

[1] p. 149. Also criticised by R. M. Hare, *The Language of Morals*, I, 7.

else told him to do. A moral imperative must always be self-addressed. This does not mean that I cannot consult others about my moral problems. It only means that my decision to accept their advice is itself a moral decision; there is still a self-addressed 'What shall I do?' question, even if the question is 'Shall I accept A's advice or not?' And the function of a moral principle is to supply an answer to such a self-addressed question. Even in the case of consulting another, a moral principle must be involved in the decision to accept (or reject) his advice: for example 'A's advice is always sound' means 'A's advice ought always to be (adopted, pondered, preferred to B's, etc.)'.

This function of moral principles is by no means peculiar to *moral* principles. The rules of chess, or the principles of Latin grammar, can also serve to answer self-addressed deliberative questions: 'What shall I do with my queen?'; 'What shall I write for the accusative of *rex*?'

But if we think of the advisory function of moral judgments, we are less likely to be puzzled about the dynamic aspect of moral principles. We do not first think out and establish our moral principles, as an intellectual exercise, and then turn to the entirely different problem of putting them into practice. Such a two-stage process would be absurd. Rather, we only formulate our moral principles in order to be able to tell ourselves what to do in certain difficult or perplexing situations. Morality is not something we come up against in the world outside us; neither is it the product of feelings and emotions within us. Morality is something that satisfies a need of our human predicament. We cannot live except by principles.

This is perhaps the truth in Kant's curious doctrine of the Holy Will.[1] A being whose inclinations were always in accordance with his duty, who always wanted to do what, as it happened, it was also his duty to do, would not be a supremely moral being, he would not be a moral being at all. Exempt from temptation and weakness, he would have no knowledge of moral problems and moral perplexity, and the words right, wrong, and duty would have no meaning for him.

[1] *Groundwork* (ed. Paton), p. 81.

### 6. *Moral Concepts and Legal Concepts*

We must next begin to consider some objections to the philosophy of moral principles. In what ways is it inadequate or misleading as a characterisation of moral man and the moral life? It is often alleged in criticism of Kant's ethical theory that it is 'too formal' (and, of his successors, that theirs are 'too logical' — which comes to the same thing). Formality means attending only to certain features of a subject, to the exclusion of others. As a term of disparagement, it suggests that these others ought not to be excluded. What is wrong with the moral-principle philosophers, then, is that they regard human beings as obeying or disobeying rules, and that morality is more than that.

The most familiar and typical examples of rules, which seem to provide the closest analogy with moral principles, are the sort of rules we call laws. The philosophy of moral principles maps the bridges between morality and law; more, it borrows its methods and concepts from the philosophy of law. The concept of a rule already has its own logic, and this infects the philosophy of moral principles. Kant's whole ethical theory, for instance, is framed in legal and legislative language: not only does he speak of the moral *law*, he constantly brings in the relation between legislator and subject, and frames new concepts in political terms, such as the 'kingdom of ends'. It is not enough to say that he overdoes the analogy, or is really quite well aware of the differences between law and morality, or that his successors have played down the political metaphors. The point is that by speaking of rules and principles at all, we are already in the field of legal theory.

Now from the point of view of legal theory, an individual human being is considered only in his capacity as a legal subject; the law is not concerned, for instance, with his thoughts and feelings, but only with his actions, and only with a small selection of those, namely, those which are the subject of actual or proposed legislation. The individual's relation to the state (even in totalitarian regimes) is not his whole being. As far as the law is concerned, he is merely a litigant, or a defendant, or a person having certain legal rights and obligations.

Now the ethics of moral principles, with its emphasis on universality, assimilates the moral agent to the citizen. Morality is not concerned with individual human beings as such, or the totality of their characteristics; it may or may not be concerned with thoughts and feelings as well as actions (we will allow that it is, and that there are beliefs one ought not to entertain, emotions one ought not to feel); but it is still concerned only with a selection of these, namely those which are the subject of moral principles. The moral agent is not the whole man; he is a moral critic, a moral defaulter, or a person having certain moral rights and moral duties. Of course there are differences as well — moral principles are not enacted by persons or institutions, or limited by national frontiers, and so forth — but we are concerned now with the supposed resemblance.

7. *Existentialists and Kantians*

The objection of 'formality' attacks this assimilation of the moral agent to the moral citizen. The general objection seems to be that, while the citizen is admittedly not the whole man, the moral man is. A moral agent who acted merely in accordance with principles would be in the position of one who merely came to certain decisions, irrespective (to a considerable extent) both of what he happened to be feeling at the time, and of what the particular features of the situation happened to be. All he does is to recognise the situation as having *certain* features and belonging, accordingly, to a certain type of situation which, under a certain rule, requires action of a certain sort. This is held to be an inadequate account, if not a grotesque caricature, of the nature of moral decision. It falsifies both the moral agent and the character of moral experience. The moral agent is not just someone who adopts a rule, recognises a situation as coming under that rule, and decides to act accordingly; he is a unique individual with a particular history, character and emotional state, none of which can be ignored; further, the situation in which he finds himself is itself a unique situation, involving other unique individuals different from himself and each other, and in fact an infinite assemblage of individualising factors. A genuine moral decision, it is argued, must be a response to the uniqueness of the total situation, and not an application of a rule which takes account of only a limited number of general features. Indeed the rule itself, it may be suggested, comes to be formulated only by a sort of inductive procedure; as a result of a series of decisions, each in a unique situation, when certain resemblances among the situations, and among the ensuing actions, have been noted; and even then it serves only as a rough guide for future unique decisions, never as a substitute. We may conveniently use Kantianism and Existentialism as labels for the two sides in this controversy: the extreme Kantians maintaining that generalisation is always, and uniqueness never, relevant to moral decision, the extreme Existentialists maintaining precisely the opposite.

I believe that the Existentialist or counter-Kantian thesis I have just sketched is completely false. I have already stated a counter-Existentialist view in my earlier book *The Logic of Personality*, in which I argue that personal relations are never moral relations. But since I there attempted to combine a counter-Existentialist theory of morality with a near-Existentialist theory of personality, it is not surprising that I have been accused of sinning both with the Existentialists and with the Kantians. It will not, I hope, be out of place to restate my original position in so far as it is relevant to the present discussion.

I return, then, to the assertion of the 'Existentialist' that every situation in which a person has to come to a moral decision is a unique situation involving unique persons. This is perfectly true: what is not true is that this has any bearing on the moral decision. But first some explanation is required of the use of the terms 'unique' and 'person'.

8. *Uniqueness and Generality*

There are two ways of knowing people, and indeed of knowing any kind of object in the ordinary world. These have received the names 'knowledge by acquaintance' and 'knowledge by description'; elsewhere[1] I have criticised the uses to which

[1] *The Logic of Personality*, Ch. III.

these terms have been put by philosophers. I use the terms in the ordinary sense in which they correspond to the distinction between *connaître* and *savoir*, *kennen* and *wissen*, *novisse* and *scire*, and in English (which is peculiar in not having different verb stems) between knowing somebody or knowing something (being acquainted or familiar with it) and knowing *of* somebody or something, or knowing *that* something is the case, or knowing *about* something or somebody. The fundamental distinction between them is that the second kind of knowledge cannot occur without the use of language. This does not mean merely (what is obvious) that we cannot *formulate* such knowledge unless we have the appropriate words in our language. It means that we could not have such knowledge. If our language happened to have no word for *red*, we not only could not formulate our knowledge that a particular flower was red: we could not know that it *was* red. We might know that it was not green (if we had the words 'green' and 'not') but nothing could count as knowing the flower to be red. Of course, we might notice something about the flower which suggested the need to have a word describing what that flower had in common with other flowers which resembled it in that respect. But this would not be noticing that the flower was *red*. It could only be after the word became current in the language that we could say *ex post facto* that somebody noticed that the flower was red. And the same is true of all the features of things which we notice or know. We can only notice or know what we have words to describe, or what at any rate we are prepared to find words to describe.

Knowledge by acquaintance, on the other hand, has nothing whatever to do with language. It is indeed only possible for organisms possessing a minimum sensory apparatus, but it is certainly not confined to language-users, that is, to human beings. But human beings, though language-using is the pride of their species, have also inarticulate and inarticulable experiences. The experience of personal relations is one of these. Acquaintance is the minimal element of what I call the personal relation, which is a unique relation between unique persons (or between a person and a thing).

It might be said that this is not very illuminating because all relations are unique since the objects they relate are unique: everything is, in the last resort, different from everything else. This is true but not a valid criticism. The point is that the uniqueness of things is precisely what is ignored or omitted in our dealings with them, except in the case of personal relations, where it just is the uniqueness that matters, that makes the relation a personal one. When I speak of the relation between myself and my wife as a marital relation, I classify it with the similar relation existing between other husbands and wives; and so I do if I call it romantic, or incompatibility of temperament, or anything else whatever. Yet what I classify in this way is, after all, not exactly like that with which it is classified, in every respect; and that of which this is true, is what I call the personal relation. To call this unique is merely to say that, however, exhaustively its features are listed, such a list cannot be completely exhaustive. This does not mean that there is a peculiarly unlistable quality called uniqueness. It merely points to the difference between an actual concrete situation, and the possibilities of describing that situation in language, or between knowing that situation by participating in it, and knowing it by being able to describe it.

## 9. *Personal Relations and Morality*

Now such a personal relation cannot be a moral one any more than it can be a legal one, simply because to attend to it as a relation of a certain type is to cease to treat it as a personal relation at all. Nor can a moral decision be one based on attention to the uniqueness of the situation or of the persons involved in it. For if a moral decision is to be a reflective decision — meaning not necessarily the outcome of deliberation, but at least capable of reflective justification (and if it is not even that, it cannot be a moral decision at all) — then it must indeed involve 'attention' to certain features of the situation. But the 'Existentialist' was mistaken in suggesting that such 'attention' could include attention to uniquenesses, or individualising factors. For what can be attended to is necessarily a feature or characteristic;

a characteristic is what is named by a universal word or phrase; a universal word is any that is capable of functioning as a predicate; a predicate is necessarily capable of being attached to any subject; therefore what it names cannot be unique. 'Unique feature' is a self-contradiction. Hence what is 'attended to' in moral (or any other) deliberation or reflection cannot be any kind of uniqueness. Uniqueness can be experienced but it cannot be described.

An example may show how the Existentialist's claim, that moral decisions must take into account particularities, is plausible but false. Suppose my friend has done something illegal and I am wondering whether I ought to report the matter to the police. Here the duty of citizenship is, we may suppose, clear enough, and is obviously capable of being formulated and applied in general terms. But what of the personal claims of friendship? Certainly the relation is a unique one; my relation to my friend is not at all like my relation to the state and the law, and not *just* like my relation to any other friend. But if a moral question arises for me at all, I must necessarily ignore the uniqueness of my friend and of my relationship with him. I must consider my friendship as creating for me certain greater or lesser obligations, comparable with those created by my relations with other people, and in particular with those obligations I accept towards the state. There is no alternative, if I am to act or think morally at all. Of course I may not act or think morally. I may remain fully engaged in the concrete situation, acting unreflectively. My action may be a spontaneous demonstration of friendship (or citizenship). But then it will not be a moral action.

Persons and their predicaments may, then, as the Existentialists claim, be 'unutterably particular'; but this does not refute the Kantian universalistic ethics, indeed it serves to sharpen it. But there is a final objection to be considered. The wide distinction I have drawn between personal relations and moral relations might be held to suggest an unwelcome morality of its own. It might seem to condone moral laxity in personal relationships: to say, in effect: 'Moral principles only apply to your dealings with other people so long as you choose to regard them as moral agents. A sufficient degree of intimacy, however, absolves you from moral considerations.' This would indeed be a dangerous and frankly immoral doctrine; which very point shows that something has gone wrong, since it follows from Hume's principle (No moral conclusion can be drawn from non-moral premisses) that an analysis of morality cannot itself have moral consequences, and cannot therefore have immoral ones either. The mistake is to confuse 'personal relations' in my sense with 'personal relations' in the sense in which personal relations may be said to be of a certain type: for example, romantic, strained, or intimate. What I call a personal relation cannot be described at all, and therefore cannot be the object of moral judgment; what can be described as being a relation of a certain type *is* a relation of that type — 'behaving romantically with', 'not getting on well together', 'intimacy' and so on.

Similarly one cannot object that there must be some connection between personal relations and morality because it is the purpose of morality to control personal relations. What it is the purpose of morality to control is, doubtless, the relations between people, but so is the purpose of law, social etiquette, and so on. Personal relations cannot be controlled by morality because they cannot be controlled at all; not because they are peculiarly recalcitrant or unamenable to regulation, but because they are not the sort of thing of which it makes sense to speak of making them different. They exist or occur; they are lived, experienced, and they change; but they are not controlled. They cannot be controlled for the same reason that they cannot be described.

The difference between moral and personal relations can be illustrated by a felicitous remark of a novelist on the difference between loving and liking: 'We like someone *because* . . . we love someone *although*. . . .'[1] 'Because' introduces a clause mentioning a reason for whatever is asserted in the main clause; 'although' introduces a reason against what is asserted in the main clause: a reason, however, which must, to avoid a contradiction, be inadequate or inconclusive. 'I like Smith because he has a sense

[1] Henri de Montherlant, *Pitié pour les Femmes*, p. 40.

of humour' depends for its force on an assumption that anyone with a sense of humour is likely (other things being more or less equal) to be the object of a favourable attitude on my part; liking is such an attitude; moral approval is another. The force of 'I love Jones although he is unkind' is that anyone having the characteristic of unkindness is unlikely to be favoured by me, yet that this reason must be inadequate, since the implied conclusion ('I dislike or disapprove of Jones') is untrue. But the point of the epigram is more subtle. For it may be that the implied conclusion *is* true. I may indeed disapprove of Jones for his unkindness, yet love him all the same. Love is a personal relation which has nothing to do with reasons. Morality has everything to do with reasons.

CHAPTER XI

# NEGATIVE AND POSITIVE MORALITY

## 1. *Duty and Virtue*

It has been said that the whole of Western philosophy is a set of footnotes to Plato. This is a pardonable half-truth for, say, metaphysics, but it is very far from true of moral philosophy. The philosophy of moral principles, which is characteristic of Kant and the post-Kantian era, is something of which hardly a trace exists in Plato. Plato speaks at great length of goodness and the good; we also speak of the word 'good' as a moral word, but, as we saw in Chapter II, it is an evaluative and not an imperative word, and is less at home in the context of moral principles than are such words as 'right' and 'wrong'. These words, on the other hand, do not occur in Platonic ethics. Plato says nothing about rules or principles or laws, except when he is talking politics. Instead he talks about virtues and vices, and about certain types of human character. The key word in Platonic ethics is Virtue; the key word in Kantian ethics is Duty. And modern ethics is a set of footnotes, not to Plato, but to Kant, and, more remotely, to the Old Testament and Roman Law.

We shall now consider a family of objections to the philosophy of moral principles, some of which point to genuine shortcomings of that philosophy. I consider them all under the heading of 'Positive and Negative Morality' because their general trend is to suggest that Duty and its related concepts (obligation, principle, and so on) refer only to the negative aspect of morality; that there is a positive aspect; and that the concept of virtue, unjustly neglected recently, may point to the missing positive factor.

## 2. *Seven Negative Features of Duty*

There are a large number of different reasons for saying that Duty represents a negative aspect of morality. I shall mention seven; the first three I disallow.

(1) The first reason, which I reject, is the point already discussed in the latter half of the last chapter. It concerns the neglect of the uniqueness of the moral agent and his situation. The rules which determine what one ought to do can only mention a selection of general features of situations, and one who acts according to rules must leave all other features out of account. This I regard as no objection since, if it were valid, it would amount to a denial that moral judgments could be supported by reasons or could properly be based on judgments of what is morally relevant in a situation. It would also count equally against any reflective process whatever. All reasoning involves abstraction.

(2) A second objection in terms of negativity might be that a moral principle cannot originate any moral action; it can only be used to test whether a given action is right or wrong. We have to wait until something is actually done, or actually proposed, before we can bring our moral principles to bear. This may be true of moral verdicts on other people's actions, but surely our own moral decisions are not just a matter of waiting until some possible course of action occurs to us and then seeing if our principles forbid it or not?

The answer to this objection is that morality, like all rational activities, is a matter of applying criteria, of which moral principles are one sort. Applying criteria to an activity is itself an activity of a very different kind, and has nothing to do with the origination or continuance of the first activity. (We distinguished these activities with the aid of our three-tier model in I, 6). Moral principles no more help to originate moral actions than geometrical principles stimulate the development of a theorem. The function of geometrical principles is to enable the geometer to criticise or correct what he writes down or what comes into his head. They have nothing to do with the processes by which certain marks appear on his rough paper, or as a result of which certain propositions come to his lips. These processes may be of interest to the psychologist, or neurologist, but they are of no interest to the philosopher of mathematics. Nor is the moral philosopher interested in the causal processes whose upshot is the deed or its contemplation. What he is interested in are the criteria by which the deed, whether actual or contemplated, will be judged. The origination of actions, in the causal sense, belongs to psychology and sociology, not to ethics. And if this is the positive feature which the ethics of principles is supposed to lack, then all ethics will lack it, and so, moreover, will all reasoned activities.

(3) Next after the objection that a philosophy of moral principles can give no account of the springs of moral action, is the objection that it can give no account of the origin of the principles themselves. If all moral judgments and decisions must be related to a set of moral principles, then surely these principles must be treated as pre-existing; yet surely there is such a thing as creative morality, or 'moral pioneering'. The answer is that there certainly is, and we have treated of it already in Chapters II and VI; further, we did so in terms of moral principles. There is no more difficulty for moral theory in accounting for moral creativity than there is for legal theory in accounting, not only for litigation, but for legislation. Someone makes a moral decision; if it is a moral decision, he makes it in accordance with a moral principle; but the principle need not be one that he already holds. He may decide there and then to adopt it, perhaps in preference to some other which he thereby rejects. The legal parallel is not so much with new legislation (which, generally speaking, is not enacted with a view to dealing with a specific situation) but rather with the doctrine of judicial precedent, where a ruling by one magistrate in a particular case is taken as setting up a principle to be followed in similar cases by other magistrates.

So far we have considered (only to reject them) three objections to the concept of obligation as too negative to serve as the basis of a moral theory. We now come to a set of objections which have greater weight.

3. *Kant and the Utilitarians*

(4) The fourth way in which moral principles tend to be negative in force can be brought out if we consider again the stock objection to Kant's ethical theory that it is 'too formal', in contrast, say, with the Utilitarian theory which seems to give a 'material' consideration in the maximisation of general happiness. (We shall see in a moment that this antithesis is not as sharp as it looks.) According to the present objection, when Kant formulates his Universalisation Principle and says 'Act only on that maxim which you can will to be a universal law', the 'only' is significant. The principle does not tell one what to do, but only gives a necessary (not a sufficient) condition of something being one's duty. It tells one not what to do, but what not to do; not what is right, but what is wrong. His examples bear this out; one must not tell a lying promise, must not commit suicide, must not waste one's talents, and so on. However it might be thought that this is merely due to Kant's mismanagement, and that he could have found other examples illustrating principles which were positive in force, which told us what to do rather than what not to do. Utilitarians are supposed to do this, and this brings me to the fifth point.

(5) It does look at first sight as if the Utilitarian criterion of general happiness offers us some positive guidance. Not only is an action which diminishes the sum of happiness a wrong action; also, an action which increases it is positively a right and good action. Here we may recall some of the stock objections to Utilitarians: that happiness is an extremely vague concept, referring to something which is difficult to assess and compare even when only an individual is concerned, difficulties which are vastly increased when we have to deal with a whole community. On the other hand the concept of unhappiness is not so vague; we know a good deal about the sources of unhappiness, what sort of things make people unhappy: overwork, poverty, disease, injustice and so on; in other words, we may not know what happiness is, but we do know what sort of things tend to diminish or cancel it. The upshot of this is that the practical Utilitarian

is much more likely to condemn actions which detract from the general happiness than to praise actions which increase it. Utilitarianism, in spite of its theoretical promise to supply the positive aspect missing from Kantian ethics, tends to fall short of this in its practical applications. But the practice is important.

The founders of the utilitarian movement were not only, or even primarily, moral philosophers. They were practical men, interested in legislation and political reform. Now anyone interested in the fundamental questions of legislation is concerned with the general function of law in society. Consequently their moral philosophy was likely to reflect the philosophy of law. And this brings me to my sixth aspect of negativity in rules and principles: the negative function of law.

4. *Prohibitive Laws*

(6) With certain apparent exceptions, which I shall consider later, the function of a law is to prohibit something. This is not perhaps obvious. The function of a rule in general, of course, is to get people either to do something or to refrain from doing something; and, one may add, it must be something which they would not be likely to do, or to refrain from doing, without the rule — if they just followed their inclinations. Now the function of laws, I suggest, is not to get people to *do* what they would not do if left to themselves, but to stop them from doing what they *would* do if left to themselves. There are certain possible actions, on the part of individual members of a society, which it is in the interest of the members of the society as a whole to prevent them doing. The examples quoted by Glaucon, in Plato's *Republic*, are typical.[1] (They are murder, theft, housebreaking and rape.) This version of the Social Contract theory, like all the others, has this element of truth in it. It is indeed more important to stop people from doing things than to get them to do things; prevention is more necessary than prescription. It is no accident that practically any list of laws, rules or moral precepts is sure to contain far more prohibitions than positive injunctions. Even the Decalogue, where social utility is somewhat hidden beneath

[1] *Republic*, 360.

a layer of theocracy, is no exception. The primary function of law is to prevent. It may have a secondary function — to punish — but this too is negative, for all advocates of punishment, except Retributionists, argue that the aim of punishment is to prevent crime.

But what about the positive laws? Surely, it may be objected, not all rules prohibit. What about the Commandments to honour thy mother and father, or to keep the Sabbath day holy; or the law that motor accidents must be reported to the police, or that live births must be registered? These certainly look positive at first sight, though some of them look less so at second sight. For instance, perhaps we should find it easier to explain what the fifth Commandment really means if we said that one should not act dishonourably towards one's parent, and went on to say what sort of actions count as dishonourable — neglect, abuse and so on. The marks of dishonour are easier to read than those of honour. But this would be a negative statement, or rather a negative injunction.

However one cannot, of course, deal in this way with the law about motor accidents, or about births. What one can do is something which looks entirely trivial and pointless: one can translate 'Always report a motor accident' into 'Never fail to report a motor accident'. This looks entirely trivial, because it looks like purely verbal manipulation; like translating 'All men are mortal' into 'No men are immortal'. And if one is allowed to do this, one might just as well translate 'Never do X' into 'Always do something other than X', and at this rate it will be entirely arbitrary whether *any* rule or law is positive or negative. But I think that in the case of rules and laws this is *not* trivial; and this is just one of the differences between the logic of statements and the logic of rules. The negative formulation of the rule does express more of its force than the positive formulation does. Which brings me to my seventh, and most radical, way in which rules are negative; for this applies even to rules which are ostensibly positive, like the rule always to report accidents, which certainly *appears* to enjoin something and not merely to prohibit.

5. *The Prohibitive Function of All Laws*

(7) So far I have suggested that most laws are negative, because their function is to prohibit something; while admitting that other laws may be positive, because they prescribe something. I am now suggesting that this is only one sense in which a law may be negative: and that there is a second and more fundamental sense, such that laws which are negative in the first sense are also negative in the second sense, and — this is the crucial point — even laws which are positive in the first sense are negative in the second. This connects with objection (2) above — that rules have nothing to do with originating actions, but only with testing them. Now what are the possible results of such a test? The verdict must be either 'right' or 'wrong' (excluding 'neutral' or 'indifferent', which would merely mean that the rule does not apply, or perhaps that no rule does). If the verdict is 'right', we say that the rule has been observed, and if the verdict is 'wrong', we say that the rule has been broken. But what do we mean by saying that the rule has been observed?

I suggest that we merely mean that it has not been broken. What else could we mean? We can't mean that the person *observed* the rule in a literal sense, that he watched it; or even in a nearly literal sense, that he was carefully thinking about it, attending to it, because of course he need not have been thinking about it at all; he may have acted from force of habit, or in compliance with orders, or accidentally, or according to some other rule which prescribed the same action, or he may even have intended to break the rule, and made a mistake which happened to put things right. There is no end to the possibilities, and there is nothing in the situation which we can point to and say '*That* is observance'. But when the rule is broken there is something quite obvious that we can point to; for there just is the glaring discrepancy between what has been done on the one hand — the corpse, the broken window, the forged banknote — and the law on the other. It does not matter what the other features are: whether, for example, the killing was accidental or in self-defence; facts such as these may make a difference to subsequent proceedings — they may count as an excuse or a plea for mitigation of sentence — but they have nothing to do with the bare fact that the law has been broken. In other words, a discordance between fact and rule is all the evidence we need that a rule has been broken: whereas an accordance between fact and rule is no evidence that a rule has been observed in any other sense than that it has not been broken. There is a *corpus delicti* but no *corpus observati*.

This negative feature of rules — that we can only point to breaches and not to observances — is not due to the fact that rules prohibit, because it also applies to rules which prescribe. It is due to the way in which rules work, both in prescription and in prohibition. Consider the case of someone who duly reports a motor accident to the police. The law has been observed, but we have no means of telling, from the bare facts of the case, whether the motorist even knew that there was such a law, let alone whether he was thinking about it. He might quite well have acted as he did, even if there had not been such a law; and we can only find out by interrogating him about his beliefs and intentions. If, on the other hand, he fails to report the accident, the law has been broken, and interrogations of the sort I have just mentioned will be irrelevant.

Now the intention of the legislators in this case, as it happens, was not to stop people from doing something, but to get them to do something, namely to report accidents. They might conceivably have tried to get people to do what they wanted them to do by different methods: by propaganda, say, or by writing letters to everybody, or to all motorists. But what they actually did was to legislate; and the characteristic way in which legislation makes people do things is by defining certain actions as obligatory by law; the effect of this is not on people who would have done these actions anyway, but on people who would not or might not have done so; and the effect on such people is to confront them with two alternative courses of action: either they alter their conduct, or they take the consequences of acting in a way which will henceforth count as lawbreaking. The effect, I repeat, is on the people who would not act in the way required. And that is why the translation of 'Always report motor accidents' into 'Never fail to report motor accidents' is not trivial. What matters about a rule is what counts as breaking it.

### 6. *From Law to Morality*

I will now illustrate this point with two examples, one from law and one from morals. The legal example is this. On the morning when the newspapers reported certain proposals for new legislation affecting motorists, the *Manchester Guardian* carried the headline NEW ROAD OFFENCES PROPOSED. News editors have a flair for going straight to the heart of the matter, and this one evidently takes for granted the point that legislation means the creation of *offences*. More generally, making a rule means deciding what actions are henceforth to count as breaking the rule.

By way of introducing my example from ethics, I will refer to Mr. Hare. It is to be noted that when Mr. Hare sets out to give us the logic of the moral word 'ought',[1] he suggests a translation on the following lines: 'You ought to do X' means 'If you do *not* do X, you will be *breaking* a principle to which I hereby subscribe.' The original is grammatically affirmative, but the logical translation is doubly negative. The actual illustration I take from a novel, *Sons and Lovers* by D. H. Lawrence:

> Paul went home and busied himself supplying the guests with drinks. His father sat in the kitchen with Mrs. Morel's relatives, 'superior' people, and wept, and said what a good lass she'd been, and how he'd tried to do everything he could for her — everything. He had striven all his life to do what he could for her, and he'd nothing to reproach himself with. She was gone, but he'd done his best for her. He wiped his eyes with his white handkerchief. He'd nothing to reproach himself for, he repeated. All his life he'd done his best for her.
>
> And that was how he tried to dismiss her. He never thought of her personally. Everything deep in him he denied.

'Doing his best for' Mrs. Morel means, for Mr. Morel, doing just those things, the failure to do which would have been an

[1] *The Language of Morals*, 12. 5. Admittedly Hare's 'ought' is an 'artificial word', but it is claimed as an adequate substitute for the 'natural word' in its prescriptive uses.

occasion for self-reproach. Mr. Hare's analysis fits the case exactly. Morel is in the position of one who, if he had not done X, would have broken a principle, but who has not broken a principle. Such is the ethics of duty. Notice Lawrence's comment on the man who tries to persuade himself that the morality of duty is the whole of morality: the best that such a man can say is that he has *nothing to reproach himself with*: 'everything deep in him he denied'.

7. *Doing and Being*

Attention to the novelists can be a welcome correction to a tendency of philosophical ethics of the last generation or two to lose contact with the ordinary life of man which is just what the novelists, in their own way, are concerned with. Of course there are writers who can be called in to illustrate problems about Duty (Graham Greene is a good example). But there are more who perhaps never mention the words duty, obligation or principle. Yet they are all concerned — Jane Austen, for instance, entirely and absolutely — with the moral qualities or defects of their heroes and heroines and other characters. This points to a radical one-sidedness in the philosophers' account of morality in terms of principles: it takes little or no account of qualities, of what people *are*. It is just here that the old-fashioned word Virtue used to have a place; and it is just here that the work of Plato and Aristotle can be instructive. Justice, for Plato, though it is closely connected with acting according to law, does not *mean* acting according to law: it is a quality of character, and a just action is one such as a just man would do. Telling the truth, for Aristotle, is not, as it was for Kant, fulfilling an obligation; again it is a quality of character, or, rather, a whole range of qualities of character, some of which may actually be defects, such as tactlessness, boastfulness, and so on — a point which can be brought out, in terms of principles, only with the greatest complexity and artificiality, but quite simply and naturally in terms of character.

If we wish to enquire about Aristotle's moral views, it is no use looking for a set of principles. Of course we can find *some* principles to which he must have subscribed — for instance, that one ought not to commit adultery. But what we find much more prominently is a set of character-traits, a list of certain types of person — the courageous man, the niggardly man, the boaster, the lavish spender and so on. The basic moral question, for Aristotle, is not, What shall I do? but, What shall I be?

These contrasts between doing and being, negative and positive, and modern as against Greek morality were noted by John Stuart Mill; I quote from the *Essay on Liberty*:

> Christian morality (so-called) has all the characters of a reaction; it is, in great part, a protest against Paganism. Its ideal is negative rather than positive; passive rather than active; Innocence rather than Nobleness; Abstinence from Evil, rather than energetic Pursuit of the Good; in its precepts (as has been well said) 'Thou shalt not' predominates unduly over 'Thou shalt'. . . . Whatever exists of magnanimity, highmindedness, personal dignity, even the sense of honour, is derived from the purely human, not the religious part of our education, and never could have grown out of a standard of ethics in which the only worth, professedly recognised, is that of obedience.

Of course, there are connections between being and doing. It is obvious that a man cannot just *be*; he can only be what he is by doing what he does; his moral qualities are ascribed to him because of his actions, which are said to manifest those qualities. But the point is that an ethics of Being must include this obvious fact, that Being involves Doing; whereas an ethics of Doing, such as I have been examining, may easily overlook it. As I have suggested, a morality of principles is concerned only with what people do or fail to do, since that is what rules are for. And as far as this sort of ethics goes, people might well have no moral qualities at all except the possession of principles and the will (and capacity) to act accordingly.

## 8. *Principles and Ideals*

When we speak of a moral quality such as courage, and say that a certain action was courageous, we are not merely saying something about the action. We are referring, not so much to what is done, as to the kind of person by whom we take it to have been done. We connect, by means of imputed motives and intentions, with the character of the agent as courageous. This explains, incidentally, why both Kantians and Utilitarians encounter, in their different ways, such difficulties in dealing with motives, which their principles, on the face of it, have no room for. A Utilitarian, for example, can only praise a courageous action in some such way as this: the action is of a sort such as a person of courage is likely to perform, and courage is a quality of character the cultivation of which is likely to increase rather than diminish the sum total of human happiness. But Aristotelians have no need of such circumlocution. For them a courageous action just is one which proceeds from and manifests a certain type of character, and is praised because such a character-trait is good, or better than others, or is a virtue. An evaluative criterion is sufficient: there is no need to look for an imperative criterion as well, or rather instead, according to which it is not the character which is good, but the cultivation of the character which is right.

Dispositions of the special sort applicable to human beings are, as we saw in VII, 12, in an important sense 'elastic'; that is, from the information that someone is timid we cannot rigorously deduce that he will be frightened on a given occasion, as we can rigorously deduce from the solubility of sugar that it will dissolve when immersed in water. Timid people sometimes act courageously, that is, as courageous people behave; in general, people can act 'out of character'. Acting out of character is interestingly different from breaking a principle. There are no degrees about rule-breaking: the rule is either kept or broken. In terms of rules, all we are entitled to consider is the relation between an action (the subject of judgment) and a rule (the criterion of judgment), and the verdict is either Right or Wrong. But in considering action by an agent, we have to take into account as well a whole range of other actions by the agent, on the basis of which we form a judgment of character. Actions are 'in character' or 'out of character' in varying degrees, and, further, we can never state precisely what a person's character is. Instead of the extreme simplicity of the moral judgment based on a moral principle and an instance of conduct which either does or does not conform to that principle, we have a double complexity. Corresponding to the moral principle (which represents the conduct of an ideally righteous man) we have, instead, the idea of a virtue (which represents the conduct and conduct-tendency of an ideally good man). But whereas a man's action can be compared directly with the principle and only two possible verdicts result (or three, if we include 'indifferent'), it cannot be compared in this way with the standard of virtue. For we cannot say exactly either how far the action is 'in character' for the man, nor how far the character of the man matches or fails to match the ideal. It is not surprising that moral principles, with their superior logical manageability, have proved more attractive than moral ideals as material for ethical theory.

No doubt the fundamental moral question is just 'What ought I to do?' And according to the philosophy of moral principles, the answer (which must be an imperative 'Do this') must be derived from a conjunction of premisses consisting (in the simplest case) firstly of a rule, or universal imperative, enjoining (or forbidding) all actions of a certain type in situations of a certain type, and, secondly, a statement to the effect that this is a situation of that type, falling under that rule. In practice the emphasis may be on supplying only one of these premisses, the other being assumed or taken for granted: one may answer the question 'What ought I to do?' either by quoting a rule which I am to adopt, or by showing that my case is legislated for by a rule which I do adopt. To take a previous example of moral perplexity,[1] if I am in doubt whether to tell the truth about his condition to a dying man, my doubt may be resolved by showing that the case comes under a rule about the avoidance of unnecessary suffering, which I am assumed to accept. But if the case is without precedent in my moral career, my problem may be soluble only by adopting a new principle about what I am to do now and in the future about cases of this kind.

This second possibility offers a connection with moral ideals.

[1] IV, 3.

Suppose my perplexity is not merely an unprecedented situation which I could cope with by adopting a new rule. Suppose the new rule is thoroughly inconsistent with my existing moral code. This may happen, for instance, if the moral code is one to which I only pay lip-service; if (in the language of IX, 7) its authority is not yet internalised, or if it has ceased to be so; it is ready for rejection, but its final rejection awaits a moral crisis such as we are assuming to occur. What I now need is not a rule for deciding how to act in this situation and others of its kind. I need a whole set of rules, a complete morality, new principles to live by.

Now according to the philosophy of moral character, there is another way of answering the fundamental question 'What ought I to do?' Instead of quoting a rule, we quote a quality of character, a virtue: we say 'Be brave', or 'Be patient' or 'Be lenient'. We may even say 'Be a man': if I am in doubt, say, whether to take a risk, and someone says 'Be a man', meaning a morally sound man, in this case a man of sufficient courage. (Compare the very different ideal invoked in 'Be a gentleman'. I shall not discuss whether this is a *moral* ideal.) Here, too, we have the extreme cases, where a man's moral perplexity extends not merely to a particular situation but to his whole way of living. And now the question 'What ought I to do?' turns into the question 'What ought I to be?' — as, indeed, it was treated in the first place. ('Be brave.') It is answered, not by quoting a rule or a set of rules, but by describing a quality of character or a type of person. And here the ethics of character gains a practical simplicity which offsets the greater logical simplicity of the ethics of principles. We do not have to give a list of characteristics or virtues, as we might list a set of principles. We can give a unity to our answer.

Of course we can in theory give a unity to our principles: this is implied by speaking of a *set* of principles. But if such a set is to be a system and not a mere aggregate, the unity we are looking for is a logical one, namely the possibility that some principles are deducible from others, and ultimately from one. But the attempt to construct a deductive moral system is notoriously difficult, and in any case ill-founded. Why should we expect that all rules of conduct should be ultimately reducible to a few?

### 9. *Saints and Heroes*

But when we are asked 'What shall I be?' we can readily give a unity to our answer, though not a logical unity. It is the unity of character. A person's character is not merely a list of dispositions; it has the organic unity of something that is more than the sum of its parts. And we can say, in answer to our morally perplexed questioner, not only 'Be this' and 'Be that', but also 'Be like So-and-So' — where So-and-So is either an ideal type of character, or else an actual person taken as representative of the ideal, an exemplar. Examples of the first are Plato's 'just man' in the Republic; Aristotle's man of practical wisdom, in the Nicomachean Ethics; Augustine's citizen of the City of God; the good Communist; the American way of life (which is a collective expression for a type of character). Examples of the second kind, the exemplar, are Socrates, Christ, Buddha, St. Francis, the heroes of epic writers and of novelists. Indeed the idea of the Hero, as well as the idea of the Saint, are very much the expression of this attitude to morality. Heroes and saints are not merely people who did things. They are people whom we are expected, and expect ourselves, to imitate. And imitating them means not merely doing what they did; it means being like them. Their status is not in the least like that of legislators whose laws we admire; for the character of a legislator is irrelevant to our judgment about his legislation. The heroes and saints did not merely give us principles to live by (though some of them did that as well): they gave us examples to follow.

Kant, as we should expect, emphatically rejects this attitude as 'fatal to morality' (*Groundwork*, p. 76). According to him, examples serve only to render *visible* an instance of the moral principle, and thereby to demonstrate its practical feasibility. But every exemplar, such as Christ himself, must be judged by the independent criterion of the moral law, before we are entitled to recognize him as worthy of imitation. I am not suggesting that the subordination of exemplars to principles is incorrect, but that it is one-sided and fails to do justice to a large area of moral experience.

Imitation can be more or less successful. And this suggests another defect of the ethics of principles. It has no room for ideals, except the ideal of a perfect set of principles (which, as a matter of fact, is intelligible only in terms of an ideal character or way of life), and the ideal of perfect conscientiousness (which is itself a character-trait). This results, of course, from the 'black-or-white' nature of moral verdicts based on rules. There are no degrees of rule-keeping and rule-breaking. But there certainly are degrees by which we approach or recede from the attainment of a certain quality or virtue; if there were not, the word 'ideal' would have no meaning. Heroes and saints are not people whom we try to be *just* like, since we know that is impossible. It is precisely because it is impossible for ordinary human beings to achieve the same qualities as the saints, and in the same degree, that we do set them apart from the rest of humanity. It is enough if we try to be a little like them.

## 10. *The Plurality of Moral Standards*

Now there is a term which includes both principles of conduct and qualities of character: namely the term 'standard'. In Chapter II we spoke of 'right' and 'wrong' (the typical words of principle-verdicts) as belonging to imperative language, and of 'good' and 'bad' (the typical words of character-appraisal) as belonging to evaluative language. Some philosophers have failed to emphasise the differences between the two, while others have over-stressed them. Mr. Lamont, for example, in *The Value Judgment*, claims that evaluative words do not belong to morality at all, and are more at home in economics. It is better, I think, to retain 'good' and 'bad' within moral theory, and quite indispensable if we are to apply the terms to character-traits, that is, to speak of virtues at all. Economics is concerned with what we choose to have; the ethics of principles is concerned with what we choose to do; and the ethics of character is concerned with what we choose to be. It is true that the second involves no evaluation (being an 'all-or-none' choice); but the third involves evaluation and scales of preferences, just as much as the first. We can arrange house, car, TV set, and so on, in order of preference; and so we can arrange in order or preference the characters of moral heroes and villains.

The point that different ethical theories each attend to a limited segment of the moral life, and overlook the rest, is well brought out in an interesting recent article[1] in which the author distinguishes between three different kinds of moral standard. These are, firstly, the 'Self-Respect' standard, so-called because it is the standard below which we cannot fall without loss of self-respect; it expresses the minimum required of us as moral beings; and it is one in which we are blamed for failure but not praised for success. Notice how all these are negative features. This is the standard that corresponds with my discussion of rules and principles, where it is breaches or infringements that matter; what is right is only what is not against the rules; one is blamed for neglecting one's duty but not praised for doing it. Secondly there is the 'Aspirational' standard, and this is not what one seeks merely to maintain, but what one seeks to achieve; not a minimum requirement, but a positive goal; and failure is no longer blameworthy, while success deserves praise. This is not a standard of principles, unless the 'principles' are so difficult to live up to that we praise a man 'of high principles', but this is really an allusion to character. Then there is a third standard, which corresponds to my Saints and Heroes: it is the 'Inspirational' standard, the moral ideal or standard of perfection, which is not what we seek to maintain, nor yet to achieve, since it is unachievable. It is in the light of the example set by the finest men that we set our own moral targets.

11. *Law and Education*

Earlier I suggested that the ethics of principles is a philosophy which takes a certain model or paradigm, namely law, and develops its ethical theory in parallel with legal theory. We have now to ask what sort of model or theory might be expected to lie behind a moral philosophy which would emphasise virtue and

[1] H. J. N. Horsburgh, 'The Plurality of Moral Standards', *Philosophy*, xxxix, p. 332.

character instead of rules and principles. The answer will be, I think, the theory of education. Education stands to the ethics of character as the Law stands to the ethics of principles. But what are we to understand by education? It is no longer customary with us, as it was with the Greeks, to think of education simply as the process of character-formation. In our modern society there is a greatly increased emphasis on achievement, and this means the production of capacities rather than the production of qualities. There is even, perhaps, an increased emphasis on rules, since educational establishments are large and complex organisations requiring systems of discipline. Thus we tend to get a concentration on non-moral standards in education (namely achievement) and on negative moral standards (namely rules) to the exclusion of the standard of virtue or moral character. I am not, of course, saying that this factor has gone, but that it has gone into the background. There are, indeed, very many other factors which could be considered, but such a consideration would involve a sociological survey and analysis. I will mention only a few.

First we have the current disuse and degradation of the key-words 'virtue' and 'vice', as already noted;[1] but this is probably a symptom rather than a cause. Then there is the suggestion that the Greek ideal of character was not, after all, a universal human ideal, but only the ideal of a small group, namely the leisured aristocracy. An ethics which ascribes a supreme value to *theoria* or contemplation, as Aristotle's does, cannot possibly represent the views of the ordinary man. Each class or section of a community has its own ideal type (the worker, the business-man, the civil servant, the professional, the gentleman, and so on) and so long as each of these sections has its own educational system there will be no difficulty in relating education to character-formation; but once we have universal education there ceases to be any agreed and significant expression of a desirable type of character. One could add that we do not share the happy confidence of the Greeks in the right of the state (or of anyone) to impose moral standards for the training of its citi-

[1] P. 127.

zens; or, worse, we are not at all confident about even our own standards of character. This uncertainty is perhaps reflected in our half-hearted and half-embarrassed attitude to the heroes and saints of old. We are a bit bashful about advising people, or telling ourselves, to be more like St. Francis. The same uncertainty is reflected in the very unsatisfactory state of educational theory today, as admitted by educationalists themselves. In its extreme form, it is represented by Froebel theory and the emphasis on 'free activity' and the 'flowering of personality'.

All this tends to drive us back to the minimum 'self-respect' standard. One could also recall Mill's comment on the negative morality of the Church with its emphasis on Sin; and its link with a common idea of Conscience, which most characteristically manifests itself as conscientious refusal, or a sense of guilt or remorse. All these are suggestive of the legal aspect of morality and the legal model of moral philosophy. We have only to add the immense influence of Kant's principle-philosophy, couched in terms of law, and the explicit preoccupation of the other great school of moral philosophers, the Utilitarians, with legislation, to understand how Law, rather than Education, has tended to provide the background of so much moral theory.

Finally, there is the enormous advantage in logical simplicity which moral principles seem to offer. One can handle rules, applications or rules, reasoned verdicts, and so on, in terms of a very simple and powerful logic. One can also (though with limited success) try to build up systems of principles having the logical properties of deducibility and inter-consistency. Even Aristotle's typical Greek preoccupation with virtue and character did not prevent him from developing his doctrine of the 'Practical Syllogism', which is a pioneer work in imperative logic.

But virtues and vices do not lend themselves to this kind of logical handling. They do indeed unite, but not according to logical principles. The way they hang together is by way of belonging to a particular person or kind of person. But that is a much more difficult matter for philosophy than imperative logic is.

CHAPTER XII

# CONCERNING MORAL FREEDOM

## 1. *Ought Implies Can*

It is customary in books about morality to deal with the time-honoured question of moral freedom. Indeed it may well be felt that the whole of the foregoing discussion is vitiated by a persistent avoidance of this topic; for if those who argue against moral freedom are right, then what I have been saying about morality will be at best superficial and at worst senseless.

The term 'freedom' has no positive content but gets its meaning from what it excludes: to assert that one is free in any respect is to deny that a particular sort of restriction or compulsion exists. For example, I am free to grow my own potatoes, but not to turn them into alcohol; the only difference being the presence of a specific restriction (namely a law) in the case where I am not free, and the absence of any such restriction in the case where I am free. Accordingly, the task of the moralist here is a negative one; not to prove that morality involves an extra factor which he has so far failed to establish; not even to prove that no restrictions exist, of the sort alleged by his opponent; but merely to remove any alleged reasons for thinking that such restrictions may exist.

What sort of restrictions? We can eliminate one class of restrictions at once. We do sometimes use the expression 'morally free' when we are debating whether our doing something may conflict with a moral obligation. For instance, if I had promised to meet someone in town, I should not be free to cultivate my potatoes at that time. Indeed, even keeping my promise might be something I am not morally free to do; if my wife were suddenly taken very ill I might consider myself unable to keep my appointment, even though this would be something that, in other circumstances, I ought to do. But this type of restriction is involved in the very nature of morality and cannot be what is meant by those who intend the denial of moral freedom to strike at the basis of morality.

The real challenge comes from determinism. Tough-minded protagonists of science often claim that the scientist, proceeding on the abundantly well grounded belief that all events are caused by other events, must in consistency adopt the same attitude to human conduct and regard our actions as just such a set of events, caused by and causing other such sets of events. And the claim that all our actions are caused by events which are all in principle open to scientific observation is supposed to mean that, whenever I am said to be debating what to do, what I shall in fact do is already settled and could be foretold by anyone who knew enough about the antecedent facts; so that all talk about what I 'ought' to do is strictly irrelevant. Moreover there will be no room left for the common-sense belief that we are responsible for at least some of our actions; for there is nothing corresponding to 'I' in the determinist's account, but only physical events. Therefore, it seems, either these common-sense beliefs are false, and morality a delusion, or else human action must be mysteriously proof against scientific investigation.

Both these alternatives are unwelcome, and the great bulk of philosophical literature on the subject consists of arguments which either work out some kind of compromise, or else end in agnosticism. Kant's solution, in terms of a distinction between causal determination of the self as phenomenal object, and moral freedom of the self as intelligent will,[1] is an example of the first kind; Sir David Ross[2] is an example of the second.

Let us first examine the common-sense belief embodied in the Kantian formula 'Ought Implies Can'. It is hardly an over-simplification to say that this formula embodies the whole of the moralist's case for the freedom of the will. The ethical argument is so simple that little space is devoted to it as a rule; most of the arguing is about the scientific counter-claims. Which explains,

[1] *Groundwork*, ed. Paton, p. 125.
[2] *Foundations of Ethics*, end of ch. X.

perhaps, why this chapter, ostensibly about morality, will be largely about science.

It is certainly true that ought implies can. If we know that a person literally cannot do what might otherwise be expected of him — if, say, he has broken his leg, or is in prison, when the time comes for fulfilling a promise to meet us at Piccadilly Circus — then it is not merely ineffective to say that he ought to keep his appointment, it is meaningless to say so: the word 'ought' has no place in such a context. And it is perfectly true that when a person 'can't help' doing something, then it makes no sense to say that he ought not to do it, and it would be wrong to blame or punish him for doing it. The crucial question is, whether what is said on the scientist's behalf about the determination of human action really amounts to saying that *all* actions, and not merely those which are literally forced on us, are such that we 'can't help' doing them.

The answer is, up to a point, already a commonplace. It consists in drawing attention to a distinction between the logical function of the term 'determine' in scientific contexts, and certain irrelevant associations of the word and its etymology. These associations are those which the word 'determine' shares with words like 'compel' and 'force'. When one event determines another, in the sense of causing it to happen, it is certainly not a case of compelling. All that is meant is, that from the occurrence of the first event we can predict the occurrence of the second. No event, as Hume pointed out, even implies the occurrence of any other, much less forces it to occur. Implication is a relation between propositions, not events, and it is in virtue of this relation that we are able to make predictions. In a genuine 'can't help it' situation, such as superior force or incarceration, we can certainly predict the outcome; but the converse is not true. Events which we can predict are not necessarily, and in fact are very seldom, the results of 'can't help it' situations. Consequently, the imputation of moral unfreedom is unfounded.

Predictability, so far from casting doubt on the authenticity of moral conduct, is in fact a prerequisite of it. To suggest that a person's conduct is unpredictable might easily amount to a moral aspersion. The epithets dependable, reliable, trustworthy, which we employ in praise of someone's moral character, point directly to predictability. Really unpredictable (as opposed to imperfectly predictable) behaviour would not be human behaviour at all. As we saw in VII. 13. the ability to acquire and preserve dispositional characteristics of certain sorts is part of our being human beings.

However, it may be objected, we noted in the same context that there was something peculiarly 'elastic' about human dispositions, as compared with those which can be studied in, say, chemical substances; something which made it impossible to obtain definite and specific predictions, but only approximate and more or less tentative ones; that human behaviour is after all, as suggested in the last paragraph, only imperfectly predictable; and that it is only this imperfection which gives colour to the notion that we are morally free. Complete predictability, by contrast, really would impugn freedom; and this is what our protagonist of science has in mind. He is, moreover, unimpressed by my distinction between 'can't help it' situations and predictability; he wishes to insist that complete predictability does amount to a 'can't help it' situation, and thence to a denial of moral freedom and responsibility. As things are, I can indeed predict that someone will do what I think he ought not to do, and I am, admittedly, entitled to go on saying that he ought not to do it, even though I predict that in fact he will. But this, it will be said, is only because I use 'predict' in a loose sense; if I can predict the behaviour in some stricter sense which science is supposed to sanction, then I shall no longer be entitled to say that he ought not to do what I predict that he will in fact do, because, as I should then see the situation, there would be nothing else that he possibly could do. 'Can't help' would then exclude 'ought', according to the formula.

If we ask what is this stricter sense of 'predict' which is here appealed to, I think there are two possibilities. In the first place, we may mean a *complete* prediction, as opposed to a partial one: the account of what is going to happen would be complete to the last detail; nothing would be overlooked. This possibility of a strict sense of 'prediction' will concern us in Section 4. The other possibility, which I shall examine first, is that a prediction might be *infallible*. An infallible prediction about someone's behaviour would indeed seem to be incompatible with any significant sense of 'choice'. For it would follow by tautology that a person must necessarily do whatever it was infallibly predicted that he would do. But it remains to show that the idea of an infallible prediction is completely extraneous to science.

It will be easily admitted that no human being is able to predict future event without possibility of error. But this may mean either of two things. It may mean that the whole character of scientific prediction involves an essential uncertainty, marked by qualifications of the 'more or less' or 'other things being equal' kind, which are quite indispensable. Or it may mean that infallibility is an ideal which actual predictions are not in fact capable of attaining, but which is not logically unattainable. I adopt the first of these alternatives and reject the second. I shall proceed by considering the Principle of Determinism, which is capable of two corresponding interpretations.

## 2. *Metaphysical Assertions and Methodological Principles*

Corresponding to the second sense of 'predictability' (in which infallible prediction is logically possible) is that formulation of the Principle of Determinism which states that 'Every event has a cause', or 'The state of the whole universe at any instant is the consequence of its state at the previous instant'.[1] Such statements, taken at their face value, must be regarded as *statements*, that is, as assertions about the world. But they are not scientific statements. For they are not testable either by observation or by the deduction of observable consequences, as scientific statements are. They are not testable by observation, because, as Hume devastatingly showed, causal connections and 'consequences' cannot be observed 'in the objects' at all. And they are not testable by the deduction of observable consequences either. For, even if we waive the foregoing objection about the unobservability of the causal relation; yet, when I

[1] J. S. Mill, *System of Logic*, III. iii. 7.

deduce that *this* event must have a cause, 'only, as far as I can see, it hasn't one!' I shall still not allow this ostensible counter-instance to falsify the 'hypothesis' that every event *has* a cause: I shall take refuge in the 'as far as I can see *at present*' qualification — and go on looking. Consequently, the statement is not testable because it is not falsifiable: nothing counts as a counter-instance. And consequently the statement is not a scientific statement. If it is a statement at all, it must be a metaphysical one.

Such a metaphysical assertion would have as its content the existence of real connections among objects and events; determinism in this sense involves an actual assertion about what the world is like, and how it would be even if there were no scientific investigators. The universe is a causal nexus. And the sense of 'prediction' corresponding to this is the sense in which a prediction will be either more or less in accordance with the nexus; together with the suggestion that the ideal of a perfect accordance between prediction and nexus is practically but not logically unattainable.

A second interpretation of the Principle of Determinism involves no metaphysical assertions at all and is completely agnostic as to what the world is 'really like'. This interpretation starts from the sort of situation just described, where the investigator, faced by an apparently uncaused event, does not give up and acknowledge its lack of cause, but persists in looking for a hidden cause. The principle 'Every event has a cause' is not now taken as a metaphysical assertion, but as a methodological maxim or statement of policy: a recommendation to 'go on looking', supplemented with a definition of what it is that is to be looked for, whether cause, sufficient conditions, statistical correlation, or natural law. What all these have in common is predictability: the investigator is looking for some formula according to which, given certain data, the phenomenon in question can be inferred independently of its actual occurrence. This is what prediction is. And it is entirely in accordance with Hume's maxim that there is 'no necessity in objects'.

There is no room for me to dwell on the characteristics of scientific formulae. I only want to emphasise three things out of many: first, that the grounds for accepting such a formula are (apart from its consistency with other formulae already accepted) its conformity to actual observable phenomena, whether by direct comparison or, more usually, by deduction of observable consequences; secondly, that nothing is added by saying that the formula is a true account of the world, beyond our resolution to accept it on just these grounds; and thirdly, that its acceptance is always subject to revision and correction. Consequently, any prediction made on the basis of the formula is provisional and approximate by its very nature, and not by reason of a merely human incapacity to come to grips with the real order of things.

### 3. *Mechanism and Teleology*

So far we have considered the question of the determination of action in terms of simple causal transactions as exemplified in mechanical phenomena. Here the determination of an event is by an antecedent cause; or by a set of sufficient conditions not necessarily involving precedence in time; or, finally, by a set of laws which, in conjunction with a statement of initial conditions, imply as consequence an event of the type in question. But it is at least questionable whether this type of determination applies outside the fields of mechanics, physics and chemistry and allied disciplines. For instance, it may prove a less useful concept in the field of biological phenomena (to which human action incidentally belongs), and still less profitable in the field of psychology (to which human action specifically belongs). We cannot here go into the hotly debated question whether biology is ultimately reducible to physico-chemical laws, whether, that is, explanations and predictions of the mechanical type will eventually be found to work as successfully in the field of biology as they now do in physics. What we can do is to draw attention to the sort of differences between the two fields of phenomena which make such a reduction unplausible.

Two such differences are worth mentioning, both concerned with the fundamental biological concept of organism and organic behaviour. The first does not concern us directly, but only as an introduction to the second. It is the concept of 'function' as contrasted with 'structure' in an antithesis which is familiar to biological scientists. The structure of an organ or of an organism can be described in spatio-temporal terms, in common with descriptions of mechanical systems: this is called morphology. But such an account is held to be inadequate. There is required, in addition, the physiologist's account in terms of the *function* of the organ in relation to the whole organism. And this is very different from a causal account in the mechanistic sense. To say that the *effect* of the heart's beating is to cause blood to circulate is oddly insufficient. What is required is to say that its *function* is to do this.

It has been suggested that this difference is merely one of relative proficiency in the two departments of science, physical and biological; that the physicist is very often in a position to specify sufficient conditions for the occurrence of a phenomenon, while the biologist is seldom in a position to specify anything but necessary conditions. It is true that the physiologist can very seldom specify sufficient conditions: he is much better able to say what sort of operations on the heart will result in its *ceasing* to perform its characteristic 'function', than what actually causes it to perform as it does. And whatever is removed or interfered with by those operations would be a necessary condition of the blood's circulating. But this does not mean that he is only concerned with necessary conditions. Certainly the heartbeats are necessary for the circulation of the blood, the latter for the conveyance of nutrients to the tissues, and so on up to the level of the continued existence of the living organism; but the biological fact is not so much the necessity of such conditions for the final state, as the constant actual achievement of the final state itself. It is the final state that is appealed to in functional explanation — the maintenance of biological equilibrium in the complete organism. And in this sense the behaviour of the part seems to be 'determined' by the whole. But the determination is not of the type 'this, so consequently that' which characterises mechanistic causation; rather it is of the type 'that, in order to this'. And this is the teleological concept of causation.

The second difference between mechanical and biological behaviour is associated with the concept of purposive behaviour. The concept of an organism as a self-maintaining system is enlarged by the consideration of 'goal-seeking' processes which tend towards other ends than that of mere equilibrium. Examples of such goal-seeking processes are growth, reproduction, nest-building habits, and of course the consciously purposive activity of human beings whether in the technical or in the moral field. We shall not need to enquire into the problematic distinction between conscious and unconscious purposes, since the problems raised for determinism by conscious choice on the part of human beings are also raised by the goal-seeking activities on the part of other organisms. Once again a teleological explanation seems an inevitable complement, if not a substitute, for the mechanical type.

It might be suggested that determinism need not, after all, be restricted to mechanical causation, and that we should perhaps recognise a teleological as well as a mechanical determinism. Perhaps we should rehabilitate an older slogan than 'Every event has a cause': namely, 'Nature does nothing in vain'. And after all, if we are prepared to argue that the present is determined by the past, why should we not be prepared to accept that the present might be determined by the future? Indeed, this can be argued even with respect to mechanical causation. The distance of the moon from the earth a century hence can be inferred from their present state plus the laws of motion; but it could be just as easily inferred from the state of the bodies a thousand years hence. The laws of motion are neutral as to time; it is only our ignorance of the future which generates the prejudice that mechanical determinism has a one-way time-dimension.

If a teleological determinism were accepted as a metaphysical thesis, not only a heuristic principle, then we should have, in effect, a return to Aristotle. Such a 'science' would be so far from impugning the concept of moral freedom, that the fact of moral choice would be the very paradigm of a self-explanatory phenomenon. I do not suggest that the concept of moral freedom should be safeguarded by such an outrageous *volte-face* in science. I merely mention the possibility in order to emphasise that the threat to moral freedom comes not from 'science' but from a principle which, even if interpreted (as I have argued it should not be) as a metaphysical assertion, is not necessarily involved outside the physico-chemical field.

### 4. *The Logic of Prediction*

I shall next contend that, even if we were to regard teleology as a mere impostor, waiting to be ousted by the inexorable advance of mechanism on all fronts, including the biological and psychological, yet there are still certain characteristic limitations of prediction, even mechanical prediction, which would ensure that ample room was still left for moral freedom in human action.

There is a logical distinction between what is predicted and what actually happens. What is predicted is (to begin with the obvious) an event; but what actually occurs, when a moral agent makes a choice, is a unique configuration of events. Nor is this a peculiar feature of moral choice or human action. Rather it is a quite general limitation on the possibilities of prediction. What can be predicted is an event of a certain type, never a unique event. Consider a simple case such as predicting a peal of thunder after seeing a flash of lightning. What actually occurs, to verify the prediction, is not merely thunder, but thunder at a certain place, audible to certain people at a certain time, having a unique sequence of sound-waves, and so on. But what is predicted is not that *this* unique event will occur, but only some member of the class of events described by the general term 'thunder'.

Now it might be thought that this kind of limitation arises only from the departmentalisation of the sciences. Physicists predict physical phenomena, chemists chemical phenomena, and so on. But is there any reason why there should not be, in principle, the possibility of a conjunction of scientific disciplines issuing in a comprehensive prediction about a future event and embracing all possible aspects of it? The reply to this is that the limitation of prediction is not principally a matter of scientific departmentalisation. It is a matter of language. We can, in principle, make our specification of the predicted event as detailed as we please; but the addition of further characteristics will never arrive at the goal of a complete specification. For the term 'complete specification' involves a logical impossibility. An event can be specified in as much detail as we please; but it cannot be *completely* specified. However detailed the description of the predicted event, it always remains possible that any one of an indefinitely large number of different events could satisfy that description, and hence verify the prediction.

This is quite a general point about description, which is relevant because predictability involves describability. What is predictable is not, after all, an event, strictly speaking, but certain describable characteristics of an event which is not uniquely determined by those characteristics. No more is a man uniquely identified as Ebenezer Wilcox by a description of his features: it always remains possible for someone else to have those features. What is predictable is only what is describable. Only what is describable in human action is, therefore, predictable.

There is, indeed, a further reason, peculiar to human action, for asserting that it must always contain an indescribable element. Consider the case of a man who sets himself to record in a diary every detail of his day's activities. In the first place, no such record will be complete, for reasons which we have just examined. It is always possible to add more and more details about what happened, say between midday and one o'clock; and however many are added, it always remains possible that those actions took place on some other day, or even that they were performed by some other person. But in the second place, no such record can be complete because it cannot include a record of the act of recording. Or, if it does (for instance, 'I have just written the foregoing') then it cannot record the act of recording the act of recording. Or if it does. . . . And so on. There must always be, so to speak, a vanguard of unrecorded activity. On both counts, then, human action is in principle not completely describable and therefore not completely predictable.

If anyone wishes to insist that human behaviour is nevertheless determined, even if it is not completely predictable, this assertion cannot amount to anything more than an unverifiable postulate, receiving no support from the procedures of science on which it relied in the first place. Nor is it relevant to object that the unpredictability in question has had to be relegated to a mere residue of undescribed — even if undescribable — aspects of behaviour, since on our own admission this residue can in principle be reduced to as small a compass as we please, even though it cannot be entirely eliminated; and that this is too small a concession to satisfy the moralist, like claiming to find free-will in the unpredictability of electron-jumps. This objection is not relevant, because the size of the field is not a measure of its importance. What is important is that the existence of this uneliminable residue throws doubt on the legitimacy of a whole conceptual system.

There is, however, a further and more formidable objection which concerns the first of the two types of indescribability in human action. It is an objection of the *tu quoque* form. Agreed that the scientist is not concerned with unique events but only with certain types of event: yet has it not been abundantly argued (notably in X. 8) that the moralist is not concerned with unique events either? Certainly we have argued that in coming to a moral decision it is necessary for the moral agent, if he is to act morally at all, to attend only to certain features of the total situation and so try to bring it under a moral principle which takes no account of individualising factors. It was on this issue that we took sides in the quarrel between Kantians and Existentialists.

Part of the answer is that moral abstraction and scientific abstraction work in quite different directions. The scientist might consider, say, a smash-and-grab raid in such terms as 'a brittle substance shatters on impact' or — at the other extreme — 'manifestation of destructive and acquisitive obsession'. But the moralist will consider it in such terms as 'damage and theft of property'. The abstractions represented by the moralist's terms are quite different from those represented by the scientist's.

For whereas the latter's terms are entirely 'naturalistic' or descriptive, those of the moralist always involve an evaluative element. To *damage* is to change the configuration of some material in a way in which it *ought not* to be changed; *theft* is taking what you *ought not* to take; *property* is what someone has a *right* to keep.

The rest of the answer is that the concept of uniqueness was introduced as a stumbling-block to the determinist, while it is no obstacle at all to the moralist. The fact that an event cannot be completely described is one of the reasons why only certain characteristics can be predicted of it; to alter one's description is to alter the content of one's prediction. But to alter one's description of an action is not necessarily to alter what one makes a moral judgment about. The fact that the smash-and-grab raid occurred in Hammersmith rather than in Knightsbridge makes no difference. The moralist merely dismisses as irrelevant such particularising features of a situation. But the determinist is prevented by his own principles from dismissing such particularities. For either they will make some difference to the result, in which case he admits the essential and unlimited modifiability of any prediction; or else they will not, in which case determinism is not universal.

5. *Conclusion*

To sum up. I have contended that determinism is not a threat to moral freedom for three distinct reasons. (1) It is not a metaphysical assertion, but a methodological principle (Section 2); (2) its universality is not agreed by all scientists (Section 3); (3) even if its universality were granted, yet the logic of prediction is such as to exclude the notion of complete predictability.

It may still be asked whether we can give any positive meaning to the concept of moral freedom, or whether we must be content with the merely negative concept of unpredictability. In terms of this antithesis, the question is misleading. Once we have got rid of the imputation that morality as commonly conceived does not make sense, because of certain alleged implications of science, then we are free to say that morality does make sense;

there is nothing 'merely negative' about the refutation of a criticism. On the contrary, we shall, if successful, have marked out a few more of the bridges and barriers between science and morality; and also removed one of the major obstacles in the way of giving a philosophically satisfying account of what it is for a human being to act.

# INDEX

PRINTED IN GREAT BRITAIN BY ROBERT MACLEHOSE AND CO. LTD
THE UNIVERSITY PRESS, GLASGOW